Ruth Montgomery
Writes Again!

Ruth Montgomery Writes Again!

Deceased Author Writes from Beyond the Grave and Launches GoodAgainstEvil.com Book Series

As Revealed to the Macomber Family

Waterside Publishing
CARDIFF-BY-THE-SEA, CALIFORNIA

Although the authors and publisher have made every effort to ensure the accuracy and completeness of information contained in this book, we assume no responsibility for errors, inaccuracies, omissions, or any inconsistency herein. Any slighting of people, places, or organizations is unintentional. And if you spot any flaws in this book, we would appreciate you pointing them out by e-mailing us at: improvements@goodagainstevil.com.

First printing 2008

ISBN 978-0-9766801-9-2
LCCN 2007926457

ATTENTION RESELLERS, CORPORATIONS, UNIVERSITIES, COLLEGES, PROFESSIONAL ORGANIZATIONS, AND BOOK CLUBS: Discounts are available on purchases of this book for resale, fundraising, educational, gift purposes, or as premiums for increasing magazine subscriptions or renewals. Special books or book excerpts can also be created to fit specific needs. For information, please contact Waterside Publishing, 2376 Oxford Avenue, Cardiff-by-the-Sea, California 92007, 760-632-9190.

CONTENTS

Part I

The Cast of Characters:
One Remarkable Woman, a Dozen Dead
Writers, and Three "American Mutts"

Part II

The Passing of the Torch

Part III

Heaven Unleashes a Flood…of Information

- "Robert Macomber has chosen to give his life to alcohol and such for one and only one reason—so that he may teach his children the power of love, understanding, and *forgiveness.* It is a very purposeful journey that he is on, and it is not to be taken lightly."   236
- "It is this great union of Marge and Bob that has taken so many years, that is the teacher in this family."   238

Part IV

Heaven's Call to Action...to All of Us

NOTE TO THE READER

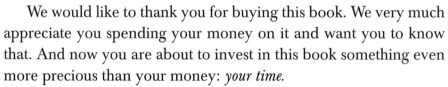

We would like to thank you for buying this book. We very much appreciate you spending your money on it and want you to know that. And now you are about to invest in this book something even more precious than your money: *your time.*

We do not take lightly your decision to spend your precious time reading about how our very ordinary family came to have the extraordinary experience of receiving communications from Ruth Montgomery and her Spirit Guides. To the contrary, we are most grateful for your interest in this unusual story and, from our hearts to yours, send out three wishes:

1. That you have fun reading this book and enjoy discovering what messages Ruth Montgomery and the Spirit Guides asked us to share with others.

2. That, when you get to the end of the story, you will feel good about spending both your money and your time on *Ruth Montgomery Writes Again!*

3. That, long after you've finished reading the messages the spirit world says are so urgent for all of us to understand, you will be able to go forward in your day-to-day life feeling a little less fear and a lot more love.

So, thanks again…and *enjoy!*

–The Macomber Family

PART I

The Cast of Characters:

One Remarkable Woman, a Dozen Dead Writers, and Three "American Mutts"

"Although our names may appear as the authors of this book, we are just messengers for these spirits who so very much want to help humanity. But they can't do it by themselves. Heaven is asking for *your* help."

–The Macombers

"It is fun doing this work from 'The Other Side' [Heaven]. There is so much freedom up here. It is indescribable. The best way to put it is a magnificent sunset feeling all day long that never ends. It's like a timeless sense of joy that returns to you each and every second of the day and night. It is beautiful, and I can't wait for the day when humans on Earth will experience this kind of bliss. It is our intention to let the world know that it is very possible to have peace on Earth."

–Ruth Montgomery

"To give away our many secrets is such a relief..."

–The Spirit Guides

CHAPTER 1

"The Most Amazing Experience of Our Lives"

S ince early 2002, three members of our family–Jane, Paul, and Rob, all siblings–have been involved in the most amazing experience of our lives: receiving communications via "automatic writing transmissions" from the spirit of the late award-winning journalist and noted author of many groundbreaking books on psychic phenomena, Ruth Montgomery. These transmissions occur when the energy of a departed spirit enters the body and moves the pen in the hand across the paper on its own. This is the same method by which Mrs. Montgomery, the one-time "Diane Sawyer of Her Day" turned "First Lady of the Psychic World,"[1] received information from spirits she called her "Guides" from The Other Side, penning numerous titles about the paranormal while she was alive.

Ruth Montgomery's last written words in her final book, *The World to Come,* were "*adios* but not good-bye."[2] This prolific author's sign-off has proven to be more prophetic than she likely ever intended or could have possibly imagined at the time she wrote her final book.

We are from a New England family and never knew Mrs. Montgomery while she was alive; yet we began receiving automatic writing transmissions from her less than a year after she died on June 10, 2001. Ruth explained to us that she was "alive and well" and had joined the Spirit Guides–including her close friend, the famed medium Arthur Ford–in Heaven. She also said that we were to continue the work to help humanity that she had begun while she was on Earth. Ruth and the Guides said that the human race was at a critical juncture and described how they would be providing information to our family–more than one of us–that was to be used to write a series of books that would spell out how humanity can save itself from self-destruction.

A Sneak Preview

This book series is based upon the hundreds of pages of transmissions we have received over the past several years–and continue to receive–from Ruth Montgomery and her spirit companions. Their voluminous messages have consistently stressed the urgency of the human race making some major changes if Earth is to have the bright future they see as possible for the planet and its inhabitants.

Because of how critical Ruth and the Spirit Guides have said it is that humanity recognize what needs to be done in order to turn things around for our world, this first book is a sneak preview of some of the Heaven-sent information that is going to be revealed in this series. Here is what we will be covering in the pages ahead in this series' debut title:

1. A synopsis of Ruth Montgomery's career and her involvement with the Spirit Guides while she was alive. A brief summary of each of the books Mrs. Montgomery wrote will be included.

2. A detailed description of the Macombers as a family and how we came to write the book you are now reading.

3. An overview of a three-part "Action Plan for Planet Earth." It provides solutions to what these spirits say their perspective from Heaven has allowed them to identify as the troubles that pose the greatest danger to the survival of our world. The overview concludes by answering the question, "What's in it for you?" and shows how helping to solve Earth's biggest challenges will benefit you directly.

4. Some sample chapters of the type of information we have been receiving from Mrs. Montgomery and the Spirit Guides. We will describe why 50 percent of the book's profits will be donated to help address what these spirits in Heaven say is the planet's single most pressing problem—and what is the biggest focal point of the Action Plan for Planet Earth: the plight of Third World countries. Included in these chapters will be a significant amount of material detailing our own take on the subjects addressed in each one.

5. Several chapters about major figures on the world stage. These chapters were the result of two things: (1) Initial information transmitted by the Guides saying that certain individuals of note possess the ability to play significant roles in making the Action Plan for Planet Earth a reality and helping save the world; and (2) "Homework," which we did in preparation for writing this book, led us to become aware of the important work of other famed figures from different walks of life. In both cases, we followed up with questions to the spirit realm about these high-profile people as we sought to explain to the world at large how these individuals and their work are viewed by those in Heaven.

6. Sprinkled throughout the book are many references to various individuals, books, Web sites, articles, songs, and other sources

of information that we have found helpful as we have embarked on this journey with the world of spirit.

7. An examination of the forces of good and evil and how they correspond with the primary human emotions of love and fear. Our exploration of this matter was an integral part of our work on this book and is absolutely central to understanding Heaven's advice to the human race about how to save ourselves. It is the core issue that will be the connecting thread for this entire book series.

8. A look ahead at some of the topics that will be written about as this series continues beyond this book. *Ruth Montgomery Writes Again!* is but the beginning of our work to bring Heaven's messages to you and our fellow sisters and brothers around the globe. Because the spirit realm has shared much more information with us than can be contained in this first book, we will explain where this series is headed in its next volume.

NOTE: Much of what you will read in this book has been written in our collective voice as a family, just like the words you are reading right now. But we have also written to you in our individual voices as well throughout the book and identify ourselves along the way when we have done so.

Now, you may be thinking to yourself: *This is pure poppycock. There's no way this type of stuff can be for real.* If so, we don't blame you. We've repeatedly thought the same thing ourselves as we have worked on this book. But while we have sometimes questioned whether what has been going on could possibly be real, the fact that Ruth and her fellow Guides have come through to more than one of us—two of whom live on opposite sides of the country—has kept us from questioning our own sanity. In fact, the Guides have communicated to all three of us: to Jane, a great deal; to Paul, a fair amount; and to Rob, just a little bit. Furthermore, the Guides have been imparting information on a wide variety of subjects about which we had little or no knowledge—or interest—before these communications began.

So, as you read this first book and evaluate its contents, we would respectfully request that you ask yourself just one question: *Even if much of this seems totally impossible, is there even the slightest bit about what I am reading that possesses authenticity, striking a chord somewhere deep within me that says that this is real?*

We are just messengers for these spirits. Although our names may appear as the authors of this book, we are just messengers for these spirits who so very much want to help humanity. But they can't do it by themselves. Heaven is asking for *your* help. Here's a little more of what they've said in their call to action to all of us:

> *"Please get as many people involved as you can. Please put up a pleasant place for humankind, and all will benefit. This mission in life is the most important thing. It can do good things for us all."*
>
> —The Spirit Guides

> *"Action is the key word here. Action of all peoples, [all] parties."*
>
> —The Spirit Guides

> *"We want to see every person available involved in some way, even if it is a small contribution. Small contributions add up to big love. This is the whole reason we are doing this book—and we want everyone who joins in to know that we are grateful for your efforts in advance."*
>
> —The Spirit Guides

> *"We will be working as hard as we can, because we know that this can work. We will be willing to do things from this side as much as possible, as we don't have the challenges that you have on the Earth."*
>
> —The Spirit Guides

"And again, we stress when this thing takes off, it will spread faster than any disease you've seen. It is so simple a plan and so smart—and to execute it will take much faith and belief. But we want to stress the joy—real joy—people will feel when it happens. If misery loves company, then joy revels and spreads like a wildfire out of control. We will want more and more people in the world to put out not only money, but heart and real love."

–The Spirit Guides

"Ruth Montgomery says that she will be guiding anyone and everyone on Earth to get it done. That is her job, [to] guide not so much on pages as in the minds of men, women, and children to read, publish, provoke, look, ask, and, yes, believe."

–Ruth Montgomery and the Spirit Guides

"In the next few decades, much good work will come from this project. And it is truly a project for the entire world. It will be the product of many hands..."

–The Spirit Guides

"We don't want people going out and working so hard that it's counterproductive. We are not saying that a man should go leave his family to fend for [itself] so he can go build villages in Africa. We want people who are in a position to do that to do it—and there are many people in the world today who are not only capable of that, but in need of such a task themselves. Our point is, as we have said before, that everyone has something to offer. What one man can offer, another man cannot. It is up to the individual to decide what he can offer. We can make suggestions....But for most of the world it will be a singular decision. Or a family decision. But it is a decision everyone must make."

–The Spirit Guides

"Fueling the Earth's people will not take a large spark. They are ready for a change and want to be good and want to get going on this. Even people who are dark are getting tired of the permeating darkness. Everyone needs light. And the darkness is smothering that. But the light's starting to burst out at the seams because there is a real desire to get back to doing good."

–The Spirit Guides

Putting this book together really has been an amazing experience for us, one that has provided all of us with great enjoyment along the way. It has also been a journey filled with tremendous emotion, with countless smiles to ourselves and each other throughout the process, as well as numerous instances in which we have just sat quietly with tears streaming down our faces.

If you get even a tiny fraction of the joy from reading this book that we have gotten from writing it, then our efforts will have been worthwhile. Who knows? Perhaps, just as Ruth Montgomery and the Spirit Guides have helped us find our mission in Life, the information they've sent from Heaven will allow you to figure out what your own purpose is here on Earth. And if you're fortunate enough to know in your heart that you've already found your Life's mission, then we would like nothing better than for this book to inspire you to help others find theirs.

CHAPTER 2

So Just Who Was Ruth Montgomery Anyway?

"And what of Ruth's own purpose for this lifetime? As a child, she dreamed of becoming a foreign missionary. Yet life led her through a stunning career, first as a widely respected and accomplished journalist who traveled the world to interview presidents and kings, then as a skeptical reporter of things supernatural. 'I believe that I came into this life with a definite mission, as we all do,' [Ruth] began softly. 'I think mine was to dispel the illusion that there is such a thing as death. I wanted to spread the word that life is eternal, and that there is continuing communication between the living and the so-called dead. When I was a little girl, those subconscious promptings came as suggestions for missionary work, but as I look back over my lifetime, I realize that it was necessary for me first to establish my credentials as a widely syndicated newspaper reporter who wrote truth, before the path could be opened for me to help others accept the still greater truth that we are all one, and as such, we are all a part of God.'"[1]

–Ruth Montgomery with Joanne Garland,
Ruth Montgomery: Herald of the New Age–The Spiritual Odyssey of the World's Leading Psychic Authority

W e believe that Ruth Montgomery was a person who definitely fulfilled her life's mission while she was alive here on
Earth. But exactly who was this woman in whose illustrious footsteps we are now following? And why do we feel so strongly that
she achieved her mission prior to her "dying," joining the Spirit
Guides on The Other Side, and beginning communications from
Heaven with us via automatic writing?

If you have read Mrs. Montgomery's books, then you may already know a good deal about her and her noteworthy achievements
as a journalist and author. On the other hand, if you're like we were
before reading any of her sixteen titles, then you probably have
little, if any, awareness of who she was or what she did before she
passed away at age eighty-eight on June 10, 2001, in Naples, Florida.

Ruth, the Reporter

Ruth Montgomery was born in 1912 in Sumner, Illinois, and was
educated at Baylor and Purdue universities.

It was while she was a student at Baylor that Ruth began her
journalism career by working part-time for the *Waco News-Tribune*.
Following a subsequent stint at Purdue, her reporting career included
stops in Louisville and then Detroit.[2]

In Detroit, the young journalist landed the first interview ever
granted by Doris Duke, the tobacco heiress who was the world's
wealthiest woman at the time. How did Ruth do it? By using the
type of bold initiative that was to become a hallmark of her career:
hiding under a room service table as it was being wheeled into the
wealthy woman's hotel suite.[3]

In 1943, Ruth Montgomery achieved another notable break-
through when she became the first woman to be named a member
of the Washington bureau of the *New York Daily News*. Ruth also
served as Eleanor Roosevelt's White House Press Conferences' final president and, in 1945, was the only woman reporter selected to

attend President Franklin D. Roosevelt's funeral service at the White House.[4]

In 1947, NBC did a radio series called *The Big Story*, based on a 1936 Detroit murder case Ruth had helped solve. She had gone undercover and posed as a member of an extremist hate organization known as "The Black Legion." Ruth's stature as a leader in the field of journalism was confirmed in 1950 when she was elected president of the Women's National Press Club.[5]

Firmly established and highly regarded in the male-dominated field of journalism, Ruth Montgomery continued writing about political and foreign affairs for the following two decades. While she covered the White House, Capitol Hill, and the State Department, her column was syndicated by Hearst Headline Service and UPI to two hundred papers throughout the United States. A veteran of numerous presidential campaigns and political conventions, Ruth enjoyed a reputation on both sides of the aisle as a reporter who was both objective and accurate.[6]

As the 1960s came to a close, Ruth had decided that it was time for her to retire from reporting. Her professional resume included winning a multitude of journalism awards, being a regular guest on *Meet the Press*, and receiving two honorary doctor of law degrees. A stellar career to be certain.[7]

CHAPTER 3

Ruth, the Conventional Author

Long before Ruth Montgomery left her beat as an acclaimed syndicated journalist, she had also established herself as an author of considerable stature. Not only an award-winning reporter possessing an intimate knowledge of the national political scene, but a popular Washington socialite herself as well, Ruth commanded the respect of many of her era's major figures in government. This, in turn, led to her writing four books:

1. *Once There Was a Nun* (1962)–Ruth's first book describes the life of Mary McCarran, the daughter of Nevada Senator Pat McCarran. For more than three decades, Mary McCarran lived as a nun, until her father's passing resulted in her departing the convent to look after her mother. A candid account of Ms. McCarran's experience as a nun, Ruth's initial book provides intriguing insights about life inside a convent.[1]

2. *Mrs. LBJ* (1964)–Shortly after President John F. Kennedy was assassinated on November 22, 1963, Ruth, who had been personal friends with Lyndon B. Johnson and his wife, Lady Bird,

for twenty years, was asked to write the biography of the nation's next First Lady. Written with the close cooperation of both the First Lady and President Johnson, this book introduced Lady Bird Johnson to a grief-stricken nation. Involving in-depth interviews with not only First Lady and President Johnson, but also with many of their closest friends and associates, *Mrs. LBJ* was greeted with glowing reviews when it came out in April of 1964. Quickly climbing up all the national bestseller lists, it established Ruth Montgomery–already an internationally renowned syndicated political journalist–as a prominent book author.[2]

3. *Flowers at the White House* (1967)–At the suggestion of Homer Gruenther, an assistant to Presidents Eisenhower, Kennedy, and Johnson, Ruth wrote this illustrated book about flower arrangements for state dinners at the White House.[3]

4. *Hail to the Chiefs: My Life and Times with Six Presidents* (1970)– This is a personalized account of Ruth Montgomery's life as a prominent Washington journalist during the administration of six U.S. presidents. Ruth narrates the more than a quarter of a century she spent in the nation's capital covering the political scene, detailing both the professional and personal relationships she had had with six different occupants of the Oval Office: Franklin D. Roosevelt, Harry S. Truman, Dwight D. Eisenhower, John F. Kennedy, Lyndon B. Johnson, and Richard M. Nixon.[4] For anyone interested in learning more about Mrs. Montgomery's remarkable career as a political journalist, this is the book to read.

In and of themselves, these Washington-based books would have made for a credible sideline career as an author for Ruth Montgomery. But these four books constitute only a quarter of the sixteen titles she wrote. Indeed, it is the other twelve she authored that make us say Ruth was a human being who achieved her Life Mission during her tenure here on Planet Earth. And in order to understand why we make this statement, we now need to introduce you to the unconventional side of Ruth Montgomery's writing.

CHAPTER 4

Ruth, the Automatic Writer

"Automatic writing happens when the spirit world actually presses us to convey its communication through written messages. One of the more famous psychics known for this type of interface with spirit was the renowned journalist and author Ruth Montgomery. Every morning at nine, she sat at her desk in front of her typewriter waiting for her guides to come through with messages. At first this was a spontaneous occurrence, but as she explains in her books, this automatic writing session became a permanent appointment with spirit. We are lucky to be recipients of the abundance of information she has brought through." [1]

–James Van Praagh–psychic, author, and co-executive producer of the television show *Ghost Whisperer*–from his book, *Heaven and Earth: Making the Psychic Connection*

In the latter half of the 1950s, as a change of pace from her normal routine of covering politics and foreign affairs, Ruth had done some journalistic investigation into psychic phenomena. Although the curious reporter's foray into the realm of the paranormal uncovered evidence of fraud among some spiritual practitioners, she also encountered many examples that appeared to lend credibility to the reality of a world lying beyond the five known senses.

As a result of her inquiries into spiritual matters, Ruth Montgomery began a friendship in 1958 with that era's most famous medium, Arthur Ford. During the next two years, Ruth witnessed multiple examples of her new friend's ability to receive information from The Other Side, some involving many topics about which he could not possibly have had prior knowledge.

In 1960, Arthur Ford told Ruth that the spirit world was saying she possessed the capability to do automatic writing. Although she had previously read about this form of psychic communication and failed in her attempts to do it, the celebrated journalist had developed such a high degree of respect for Arthur's abilities that she decided to give it another try. Here is how Ruth described what happened when she did:

> Always keen for a new adventure, but exceedingly skeptical, I sat daily at the same hour at my desk and, after meditation and a silent prayer for protection, rested a pencil tip lightly on a sheet of paper. For days nothing happened, but on the tenth day the pencil began to write, and when I later opened my eyes, I could read messages from deceased family members. Then one day it drew a lily, wrote the word "Lily" with a flourish, and announced that thereafter he would identify himself in that manner. Beautiful philosophy began to flow from the daily writing, and since then Lily has gathered together a group of discarnates who have dictated most of the material for my...books. After his death Arthur Ford joined the writing group, and I now refer to them collectively as the Guides.[2]

Although Ruth's automatic writing began with a pencil, her communications with the spirit realm soon progressed to the point where she was receiving information from the Guides via the typewriter:

Ruth's fifteen-minute sessions of automatic writing continued each day, growing in strength and speed—as well as illegibility. "I could hardly read some of it," she [admitted]. Then one morning it spelled out, "GO TO YOUR TYPEWRITER!" which I did, feeling a bit foolish, and the automatic writing thereafter became automatic typewriting, with little punctuation or capitalization, but with surprisingly few mistakes." By typewriter, Lily and the other discarnates ...could fill two or three pages a day with lengthy philosophy about life and death, spiritual progression, and the power of unselfish prayer.[3]

Although Ruth was not aware of the words until they began to be typed on the paper, she gradually became more and more inspired by the Guides' messages. Explaining how each individual arrives on Earth with a very specific mission, Lily and friends repeatedly emphasized the importance of love, prayer, and, above all else, helping others in life.[4]

Part of Ruth's own personal mission, the Guides said, was for her to disseminate their teachings around the world by writing books about the automatic writing communications she was receiving from them. So write about her contact with the spirit world she did. But before we examine her pioneering writing in the psychic field, let's take a closer look at the ones who provided most of the core information contained in Ruth Montgomery's many spiritually oriented books: the Guides.[5]

CHAPTER 5

Ruth Montgomery's Spirit Guides

As you've just learned, a fellow who called himself "Lily" became Ruth Montgomery's self-appointed spiritual mentor. Ruth referred to him and the other invisible spirits who made themselves known to her through the automatic writing process as "the Guides" or "Spirit Guides."

Lily Takes Charge

Lily soon established himself as a very serious, take-charge kind of chap who explained that he was the principal spokesperson for a number of disembodied spirits. Almost immediately, he began admonishing Ruth for smoking cigarettes, drinking alcohol, eating chocolate, and wasting time on a failed sideline real estate investment. Lily constantly stressed to Ruth the importance of her curbing activities that would interfere with her physical ability to be the best possible receiver for automatic writing transmissions or distract her by taking time away from working with The Other Side to help others.[1]

But Who Were These Mysterious Guides?

In the first book Ruth wrote "with the Guides," *A Search for the Truth*, she shared what they had told her about their generic identity:

> *We were writers, and that is why we want to work through you....We want you to be the success in life that we were not, by helping others and bringing this message to them through your own writings. As writers we were fantastic successes in the worldly sense, yet what we failed to do was help other people. We were too busy pouring out our torrents of words and enjoying public acclaim. We should not have been so concerned for fleeting earthly fame, but for the survival of the souls of all of us....*

> *We are eager for you to learn by our mistakes in that life; for by aiding you we can progress, just as you will progress by helping others in your own life. The most important thing you will ever learn is this:* ***To live for self alone is to destroy one's self....***

> *We who made names for ourselves in your world—and we did—find them of no value here. That is why we are reluctant even to speak of our earthly identity, because it might seem to be a boastful utterance....*

> *We want you to feel no particular thrill that we were once renowned personalities there, because we actually failed. Had we been truly successes, we would not have to be doing that which we are now attempting—to save thoughtful people through you. Had we lived useful and fruitful lives there, we would have accomplished so many good things that we could have by now moved on to an earth-free existence in a still higher phase of our progression. As it is, we must try to atone for the good works that we left undone while on earth.*[2]

Lily Is Unmasked

In the early 1970s, more than a decade after their automatic writing communications with Ruth began, the Guides finally explained who Lily had been in a past life on Earth:

"'Lily' in the fifteenth century was a writer of note who dwelt in [Florence], Italy and wrote on philosophical subjects...."[3]

Although Ruth wasn't personally familiar with who Savonarola had been in history, the Guides explained that he had been an "Italian Dominican priest" who had penned "fiery writings against the corruption of the Catholic Church and the de Medici court."[4] Going into more detail about this previous incarnation of Lily, they said:

> He was [a mystic,] a sensitive who was aware of others' intentions and secret thoughts, but he was practical in his application of the laws of God to man, desiring freedom and equality for all men and eager to direct them inward to the search for God rather than outward for personal gain. Some considered him a fanatic, and perhaps he was, in his burning zeal to reform state and human kind, but so powerful was his message and his performance that he influenced the course of history and rang a bell for liberty that is still to be heard. A godly man...[whose] ideals...knew no boundaries of nation or creed.[5]

Fascinated by what the Guides were telling her about who Lily had once been, Ruth pressed them for more details. Assenting to her request, her invisible co-authors wrote:

> Savonarola was highly esteemed by his peers and was eager to establish equality among men....He wanted the State to treat all men alike and to establish a rule by law and not by the capricious fancy of men in power. He was ahead of his times....

A good, good man who made rapid advances in his spiritual development, so that he has been much loved on this side of the door called death. He had succored the helpless and given of himself to worthy pursuits, enduring the scorn of his superiors with bravery....Later, in another incarnation, he became a noted writer whose words lifted the hearts of many, as he sought to justify the works of those who would aid the suffering, but we will not tell you about that at this time....

Now as to Lily when he was Savonarola: a fiery intense man ...who believed anything possible if men would pull together for the common good. A fierce intolerance for greed and hatred for the ma-nipulation of people....[6]

Interested in doing some fact-checking to see if the Guides' writings about this purported past life of Lily could be backed up with any historical information, Ruth did a little research on the topic in the *Encyclopædia Britannica*. There she found the following description of Savonarola:

[B]orn to an excellent family in 1452, scorned court life and entered a Dominican order, where he wrote poems of burning in-dignation against the corruption of Church and court. A mystic, he had prophetic visions that came true, and he seemed to read others' thoughts.

...Savonarola became the lawgiver for [Florence]...relieving the suffering of the starving and reducing taxes on the lower classes. He guarded the public weal with extraordinary wisdom....

He left behind an immense number of devotional and moral essays, numerous sermons, some poems, and a political treatise on the government of Florence.[7]

Ruth was nothing short of amazed to get such specific confirmation about the Guides' words, but had to admit that Savonarola's intense personality was quite consistent with that exhibited by her very impatient invisible mentor, Lily. Moreover, her twentieth-century Guide sure did seem to possess the same type of fervent desire to help others that Savonarola had displayed in fifteenth-century Florence.[8]

Arthur Ford: Psychic, Friend, Alcoholic, and Guide

Prior to his death on January 4, 1971, Arthur Ford had been one of the twentieth century's most noted mediums. While "in trance," he was able to make contact with spirits on The Other Side, provide facts about matters of which he had been previously unaware, and even sometimes speak in foreign languages he didn't know.

Like James Van Praagh or John Edward in today's society, Ford's name was known around the world. In his frequent public appearances, numerous lectures, and many guest spots on television shows, Arthur exhibited a deep-rooted desire to explain to others that life did not end with one's physical death.[9]

Encouraged early on in his career to pursue his abilities as a medium by Sir Arthur Conan Doyle, author of the Sherlock Holmes series and a longtime student of the paranormal, Arthur Ford was particularly interested in helping members of the clergy gain a greater understanding of life beyond the five senses. Although he ended up becoming an ordained Christian minister, Ford possessed an open mind about spiritual matters and studied with the Indian mystic, Swami Yogananda, while the latter was touring in the U.S. in the 1920s.[10]

Yogananda made a lasting impression on Arthur Ford, prompting him to state: "From him I learned that truth belongs to neither East nor West, but it is a universal thing, which only seems different when one does not look beneath its varying cultural expressions.

Yogananda was constantly trying to show the interrelatedness of mankind's problems...."[11]

As mentioned previously, it was during her own initial studies of the paranormal that Ruth Montgomery first met Arthur Ford in 1958. Originally quite skeptical about his purported abilities, a series of firsthand experiences with Arthur persuaded her that he was for real.

Initially, Ford provided Ruth with accurate details of a personal nature from her deceased father. After that, she observed him give numerous people he had never met, some of whom were noted public figures of their day, various types of consistently correct information about departed friends and relatives.[12]

Ruth's early interactions with Arthur evolved into a deep and lasting friendship between the two. Not only did Ruth and Arthur go on to give numerous lectures together, but Arthur was also a frequent guest at Ruth and her husband's home. Ruth didn't just like Arthur; she truly respected him as a human being and as a human rights advocate. One thing that had especially impressed her was the fact that, even though he had just had a major heart attack, he participated in Martin Luther King, Jr.'s original march on Washington in 1963.[13]

Although Arthur Ford was a humanitarian who was very much interested in the problems of mankind, he also had his own troubles—especially with alcohol. In the 1930s the talented medium, after having sustained major injuries during a car accident, had become addicted to morphine during his subsequent rehabilitation. Ford successfully kicked the habit, but then found himself in a constant state of stress.

After an acquaintance recommended that he have an occasional drink to take the edge off, Arthur began drinking heavily and developed a chronic problem with the bottle. Thankfully, Alcoholics Anonymous later "came to his rescue. He was everlastingly grateful. Thereafter, his framed and autographed photograph of Bill

Wilson, AA's [co-]founder, went with Arthur Ford wherever he traveled. It was the first item to be packed and was always displayed in a prominent place."[14] Arthur's gratitude toward Wilson was further amplified when the latter, following an inner urge to stop unexpectedly by Ford's apartment, once literally saved the medium's life when he found that the medium had suffered a heart attack and was lying unconscious on the floor.[15]

Apparently, there was a mutual respect between Ford and Wilson. That is evident from an interview the latter gave in the 1940s to a journalist, Jerome Ellison, who himself was a member of Alcoholics Anonymous and was writing a magazine article about the organization. When Ellison commented that he had been doing some research on ESP, Bill Wilson replied by saying, "If you're really interested in this stuff, you should get to know Art Ford....He's one of us, you know...."[16]

We include this description of Arthur Ford's struggles with drugs and alcohol for a very important reason. That is, because we believe, just as he did, that although a person may be blessed with well-developed psychic abilities, it doesn't mean that individual may not wrestle with the same agonies of addiction that confound so many others. It's called being human.

As you shall soon learn, we've had our own personal experiences involving drugs and alcohol. We've seen firsthand the heavy toll that substance abuse takes on people and those around them. Indeed, the Macombers are a family who understand the challenge addictions can pose to navigating successfully the mystic maze called Life.

When Arthur Ford's own life ended in early 1971, his transition to The Other Side involved making almost immediate contact with Lily and the Guides. In fact, on the same day he died, Ruth got word from Lily and the Guides through the automatic writing process that her dear friend Arthur was with them and was fine.

The very next day Arthur himself made a statement in another transmission that really reinforced to us just what a privilege it is for our family to have been allowed to carry on Ruth Montgomery's work: "'This Lily is quite a guy. I sort of sensed his presence sometimes after I knew you in your plane, but he's a brilliant white light of radiant power and a mighty good influence to have on your side, so don't ever neglect him or fail to take advantage of his help.'"[17]

During a subsequent session, Arthur elaborated further about Ruth's principal Guide: "'He will probably not return to another incarnation in the physical plane, although that choice for him remains.

"'He was a writer in his last incarnation, and since there are many writers now, he needs to advance his growth here in work that many others are not able to do, such as counseling those writers who are progressing here and working directly with those in physical body who would write spiritual treatises of a higher order.'"[18]

Arthur ended up joining Lily and the Guides in writing regularly through Ruth from The Other Side. So much so that the Guides' trademark opening in their automatic writing sessions with her went from "Ruth, this is Lily and the group" to "Ruth, this is Lily, Art, and the group."[19] (Lily once told Ruth that there were, including himself and Arthur, twelve Guides in all, though she never asked about the identities of the rest.)[20]

Bonus Information

If you are interested in learning more about Arthur Ford, we would suggest that you consider reading *The Arthur Ford Anthology: Writings by and about America's Sensitive of the Century.* Compiled and edited by Frank C. Tribbe, this book contains fascinating information and insights regarding the famed medium's entire life, including Ruth Montgomery's poignant eulogy to her dear departed friend Arthur.

The Guides Are Trying to Help All of Us

As you have just learned, the Guides are spirits who used to live on Earth but are now simply on a different plane of existence. Call it what you will—Heaven, The Other Side, The Great Beyond, or whatever term you might use—it is a place where, after physical death, one's spirit functions at a faster level of vibrations. At least, based on what the spirit realm has told us, what we have read in various books, and what our own intuition and experience tell us, this is our understanding of where we go when we "die."

This group of spirits called the Guides apparently took on a long-term project, first with Ruth, and now with us, in hopes of waking up humankind about the true reality of Life. They want all of us to realize that there is much more to existence than the three-dimensional world perceived by our five senses and that "There is a reason for everything."

CHAPTER 6

Ruth Montgomery: Psychic Author Extraordinaire

Now that you've gotten a feel for who Ruth Montgomery was and the role played by the Spirit Guides in her work, it's time to take a look at the various books about the psychic world she wrote during her career. As you read through the following summaries, keep in mind the courage it took for Ruth back in the 1960s to begin putting her prestigious reputation as an impeccably credentialed journalist on the line by writing about such a topic and publicly revealing that she was in touch with the spirit world.

A Gift of Prophecy: The Phenomenal Jeane Dixon

Ruth did, however, have plenty of initial reservations about being an author who wrote about receiving messages from disembodied spirits. So much so, in fact, that the first book she wrote in the psychic field did not involve her communications with the Guides. Rather, it was a book about the legendary seer Jeane Dixon. The following provides a brief description of this major event in the book world of that era:

A Gift of Prophecy: The Phenomenal Jeane Dixon (1965)–With more than three million copies in print, Ruth Montgomery's biography of this internationally renowned psychic, the Sylvia Browne of her era, was one of the biggest sellers of the entire decade of the 1960s. After repeated personal requests from fellow Washington socialite Mrs. Dixon, Ruth finally agreed to write the story of the woman who purportedly predicted President Kennedy's assassination right down to the day and place. Although Jeane Dixon's prophecy about John F. Kennedy's assassination and her feelings about the alleged conspiracy behind the killing are recounted in great detail, this book also tells the story of how Mrs. Dixon, a devout Catholic, became a popular figure in the nation's capital and around the globe by making numerous other accurate predictions about a wide variety of momentous happenings throughout the world.[1]

A Search for the Truth

After completing *A Gift of Prophecy*, Ruth Montgomery turned her attention to the insistent pleas of the Guides for her to write a book that would bring to light the material she was receiving through her automatic writing sessions with them. Relenting at last to go public with her contact with the spirit realm, Ruth came out in 1966 with her first book about her communications with Lily and the Guides, *A Search for the Truth*. Her life would never again be the same.[2] Below is a synopsis of this book that changed not only the life of its author, but also that of many of her readers:

A Search for the Truth (1966) chronicles Ruth's decade-long investigation into psychic phenomena, presenting a very objective portrayal of what she had uncovered in her inquiries. Ever the fact-seeking journalist, Mrs. Montgomery dutifully reported a number of instances in which she had encountered apparent fraud, as well as repeated situations that seemed to present evidence of psychic happenings that defied conventional explanation. What made this book especially interesting at the time of its publication was its in-clusion of psychic episodes that numerous famous individuals of that era had experienced and who were alive and could verify at the time of the book's publication.[3]

This book presents a riveting account of Ruth's personal jour-ney into the world of the paranormal. Soon becoming a bestseller, *A Search for the Truth* recounts in great detail how a world-renowned journalist became increasingly persuaded about the reality of an existence beyond the five known senses. Indeed, almost a quarter of a century before the movie *The Sixth Sense* came out, Ruth sug-gested in this book that perhaps there was indeed a "sixth" sense that all people possess to a varying degree and that this latent ability in all of us could be utilized to help humanity.[4]

Several years after the publication of *A Search for the Truth*, here is how Ruth described its impact:

> *Besides writing my columns, I was flying around the country to make speeches and appear on television programs....*
>
> *Boston, Philadelphia, New York, Baltimore, Columbus, Cleve-land, Chicago, and the West Coast. I began to feel like a railway conductor, except that I had to make a series of personal appear-ances, autograph parties, lectures, and television. My family had not wanted me to write **A Search for the Truth**, fearful that those who disbelieved in psychic phenomena might consider me a crack-pot, but the public response to it was more gratifying than anything I had ever before written. Now I was even being invited to speak from the pulpit of Protestant churches throughout the country and on innumerable college campuses, including Notre Dame. Letters poured in from every section of the country, saying such heartwarm-ing things as, "This is the most important book that I have ever read, except the Bible," "This book has changed my entire life for the better," and "Your book, which came into my hands by chance, has saved me from suicide."[5]*

In short, by overcoming the fear of being associated with something so "different," Ruth Montgomery helped open the minds and hearts of countless people across the U.S. and around the globe. For anyone who is interested in learning more about Mrs. Montgomery and her exploration of the psychic realm, *A Search for the Truth* is a must read.

Here and Hereafter

Two years after the resounding effect that *A Search for the Truth* had on Ruth and her readers, she followed it up with another title in the field of the so-called paranormal, *Here and Hereafter*. This one was about reincarnation:

Another pioneering work at the time of its publication, *Here and Hereafter* (1968) is an examination of the concept of reincarnation. In this book, Ruth describes how it helped shape the lives of many prominent Americans, including Benjamin Franklin, Henry Ford, Henry David Thoreau, Ralph Waldo Emerson, and Thomas Edison. *Here and Hereafter* also details multiple accounts of living individuals' personal experiences with reincarnation, a concept that is believed in by the majority of the world's population.[6]

When this book—the second one written with the help of the Guides—first came out in August of 1968, Ruth was interviewed right away on three major talk shows in succession: by Barbara Walters on the *Today* show, by Johnny Carson on *The Tonight Show*, and then on Phil Donahue's program. This type of television exposure represented an unprecedented degree of coverage by the mainstream media for the decidedly nontraditional (for the United States, that is) topic of reincarnation.[7]

Here and Hereafter ended up playing a major role in the United States in helping to popularize the consideration of the possibility of reincarnation. Although others in America had previously written about the subject, never before had a skeptical, world-renowned journalist investigated the phenomenon and reported such a clear and persuasive set of explanations for the theory.[8]

A World Beyond

The next book Ruth wrote with the Guides, 1971's *A World Beyond*, is based on the automatic writing communications she began receiving from Arthur Ford after her friend and colleague died in January of that year. Having now been retired from her journalism career for two years, Ruth was not prepared for the massive and enthusiastic reception that awaited her with *A World Beyond*'s publication. Although she had made plans to do a major publicity tour—including an appearance on Mike Douglas's TV program—when the book first came out, she was overwhelmed with the resulting outpouring of gratitude from its legions of readers.[9]

What was the fuss all about? Well, here's a recap of *A World Beyond* that we hope will inspire you to want to read it in its entirety:

A World Beyond: A Startling Message from the Eminent Psychic Arthur Ford from Beyond the Grave (1971)—Another trailblazing book in the field of reincarnation and life after death, *A World Beyond* provides a virtual blueprint of Heaven and a strikingly detailed framework for our overall existence. Not surprisingly, more than a million copies of the book were sold, for it directly addressed the big questions we all harbor in our hearts: the purpose of life, whether there's a God, and the vastness of the universe.[10]

This book is a remarkable account of the afterlife, resulting from numerous messages she received from her close friend, the renowned medium Arthur Ford, after his passing on January 4, 1971. At the time, Ruth had given up her automatic writing, already having proved to herself that communication with those who had passed into spirit was possible. Then, later in the day of Arthur's death, she felt compelled to sit down at her typewriter. Lily and the group announced that Arthur Ford had arrived safely on The Other Side.[11]

Within a few days of passing over to The Other Side, Arthur made it quite apparent–through the automatic writing process–that Ruth and he were to collaborate on a book together that would explain to the world what life on The Other Side is like and what one finds after dying. Thus, from a series of ongoing communications that took place from January 4, 1971, to May 7, 1971, Ford confirmed that life exists beyond the physical plane and described the afterlife with tremendous specificity.[12]

If you're at all a fan of the world-famous psychic Sylvia Browne and her 2000 classic, *Life on The Other Side: A Psychic's Tour of the Afterlife*, then *A World Beyond* is a book you should read. Containing lots of descriptive details about The Other Side, Ruth's collaboration with Arthur Ford is filled with a powerful sense of hope about what lies beyond our physical lives and takes away the fear of death in a manner that is both uplifting and logical.[13]

Of all of Ruth's books, *A World Beyond* is the one we feel bears the most striking resemblance to the one you are now reading. We say that because it was based on communications from a known person who, after passing over, began communications with the living from The Other Side that resulted in the writing of a book. The big difference, however, is that whereas Ruth Montgomery and Arthur Ford were close friends before she passed away, we never even knew Ruth…at least in "this" life.

Born to Heal

Two years after the resounding success of *A World Beyond*, Ruth wrote another national bestseller, *Born to Heal*. This book tells the story of an amazing healer she called "Mr. A." in order to protect his privacy. Here is a short profile of what it is about:

Born to Heal: The Amazing True Story of Mr. A and the Astounding Art of Healing with Life Energies (1973) describes how Mr. A used the most ancient healing art, the one used in biblical times and in days before and since, "the laying on of hands," to successfully treat a wide variety of apparently incurable cases. It is the true tale of a gifted man whose thousands of grateful patients, noted personalities and ordinary folks alike, were healed of conditions ranging from severe arthritis to almost total paralysis, from cancerous tumors to heart attacks. An eye-opening look at one healer's success at tapping into the life energy that exists in all of us and his ability to use it to help his fellow man, *Born to Heal* offers a truly uplifting story that not only provides hope that miracle cures can happen, but also explains how and why they are possible.[14]

Companions Along the Way

Steaming along in her career as an author of books about a diverse range of spiritual topics, Ruth followed up *Born to Heal* the next year with *Companions Along the Way* (1974), an extraordinary description of Group Karma and of ten incarnations Ruth shared with world-famous medium Arthur Ford, spanning thousands of years. Ruth claims one of her earlier incarnations was as a Palestinian sister of Lazarus during the time of Jesus Christ. Filled with new details about Jesus' life and ministry, this book describes how Ruth's Palestinian incarnation was deeply impacted by the life of her friend Jesus.[15]

Companions Along the Way explains how we return to Earth in successive incarnations and repeatedly reunite with the same core group of souls we have known before in a cyclical phenomenon called Group Karma. In her explanation of this concept, Ruth included intriguing information about noted figures such as Henry Kissinger and King Hussein of Jordan.[16]

An inspiring account of how Group Karma allows all of us to return for repeated lifetimes with those closest to us, *Companions Along the Way* offers an inspiring perspective on the way in which we hone the rough edges of our souls through doing good for others as we march along the path toward perfection and a long-awaited reunion with our Creator.[17]

Ruth's response from Christian readers to *Companions Along the Way* was overwhelming. Many of them wrote to tell her that it made the New Testament more real for them than ever before. Even non-Christians wrote in to say how the book allowed them to understand better why the teachings of Jesus had such a momentous effect on so many followers. Most significant, perhaps, was how so many of Ruth's Christian readers said that *Companions Along the Way* helped them reconcile the concept of reincarnation with their deep belief in Christianity and how the two philosophies no longer seemed mutually exclusive.[18]

The World Before

As Ruth continued her automatic writing communications with the Guides, they kept expanding the scope of the type of knowledge they imparted to her. A great example of this was her next book, *The World Before: A Remarkable Account Dictated from The Other Side by World-Famous Medium Arthur Ford and The Spirit Guides of Creation and Life on the Lost Continents of Mu and Atlantis* (1976), which provides remarkably detailed explanations of many of mankind's greatest mysteries, including not only Creation and the mythical lost continents of Mu (also known as Lemuria) and Atlantis, but also the biblical Great Flood, the Bermuda Triangle, and the Great Pyramids of Egypt. This book also includes information about the past lives of many notable world figures, including Elizabeth Taylor, Richard Burton, Franklin Roosevelt, Mao Tse-tung, Richard Nixon, Anwar Sadat, Gerald Ford, and Winston Churchill.[19]

Examining the history of the world, Ruth's Guides describe how the Earth has shifted on its axis several times and foretold of another such shift that is fast approaching. In recounting these remarkable claims of the Guides, Ruth details how the findings of many scientists and geologists support the notion that the magnetic poles of the Earth have indeed reversed themselves numerous times in the past and that our polar ice caps have previously been located in parts of the Earth other than where they are now. Although the Guides' predictions of such "Earth Changes" involve discussion of the potential for widespread physical destruction, their message in *The World Before* is ultimately uplifting in that by working through such an ordeal, human beings will, out of necessity, finally begin working in harmony with each other, thus ushering in an era of unprecedented peace and fellowship around the globe.[20]

Strangers Among Us

The topic of Earth Changes was one the Guides kept returning to again and again in their messages to Ruth. Not only that, but as her automatic writing interactions with her unseen co-authors evolved, they kept pushing the envelope in terms of tackling the existence of seemingly improbable phenomena. Such was certainly the case with *Strangers Among Us: Enlightened Beings from a World to Come* (1979), which describes how the Guides had explained to her that, because of the approaching shift of the Earth on its axis and the many other pressing problems besetting the world at this critical time in Earth's evolution, helpers have been sent to the planet in the form of beings called "Walk-ins." These are advanced souls who have made enough spiritual progress in previous lifetimes so that they are allowed to incarnate in the bodies of adults, rather than being born as babies and having to wait to begin pitching in to assist mankind's preparation for the imminent Earth Changes.[21]

These Walk-ins come to Earth through a process of "soul transferal" in which they literally switch places with individuals who wish to move over to The Other Side. The initial occupant of the body that the Walk-in moves into may have become tired of life as a result of prolonged depression, have suffered a horrific injury in an accident or battle, have come down with a debilitating illness, or have had a near-death experience. Although the "Walk-outs'" will to live may have diminished, this is not to suggest that the switch is made without the consent of the soul who is leaving the body. To the contrary, a Walk-in only takes residence in another's body with the permission of a soul who wishes to move to The Other Side.[22]

After the soul transferal is completed, Walk-ins are often unaware of what has happened, because they then possess the memory banks of the departed soul. They may or may not eventually realize what has transpired, but the concept does help explain the dramatic transformations of personalities and attitudes of people who have gone through a major trauma, near-death experience, or prolonged depression.[23]

In *Strangers Among Us*, Ruth claims that the Guides had explained that many famous historical figures had been Walk-ins. Among their ranks had purportedly been Benjamin Franklin, Abraham Lincoln, and Gandhi.[24]

Enlightened, yet by no means perfect, servants of the Creator, such Walk-ins supposedly live anonymously among us, trying to help guide humanity in the turbulent times to come. As the Earth Changes draw near, many are attempting to teach others it is crucial that people start caring about one another more, that it is essential to cooperate and work harmoniously with both one's friends and one's "enemies," and that death is not something to be feared, but only another exciting transition in the soul's journey through eternity.[25]

As it turned out, one of Hollywood's major players seemed to think the notion of soul transferal was one worth exploring on film. Around the same time that Ruth brought the Walk-in concept to the attention of her readers, Warren Beatty came out with the movie *Heaven Can Wait*.[26]

Initially deemed by the critics to have a preposterous plot, *Heaven Can Wait* told the fictitious story of a star athlete who dies in a bicycling accident and is allowed to enter another's body whose earthly time was up. Beatty not only played the film's leading role but was also involved in its production, direction, and screenwriting. The movie ended up being a hit with the public and received eight Academy Award nominations. Although Ruth was unaware of *Heaven*

Can Wait prior to *Strangers Among Us* going to print, the parallels between the two and the public's enthusiastic response to both suggested that the Guides' information about Walk-ins was a timely topic and one worthy of consideration.[27]

Threshold to Tomorrow

The public reaction to *Strangers Among Us* was so strong that Ruth and the Guides teamed up for another book about Walk-ins. This time, however, they did so with a great deal more specificity:

> *Threshold to Tomorrow* (1982), a follow-up to *Strangers Among Us*, "named names" and revealed the identities of numerous twentieth-century Walk-ins. Further adding to the credibility of the concept, *Threshold to Tomorrow* also included—with their permission—contact information for some of these souls working on making our world a better place.[28]

The Guides identified a number of public figures whom they stated were Walk-ins, including Watergate figure Chuck Colson, who subsequently turned his life completely around and became a major force in leading huge numbers of prisoners to find Christ. Another Walk-in written about by Ruth in *Threshold to Tomorrow* was a man named Jason Winters, who had been told by his doctors that he was doomed to die from cancer. Inspired by the repeated references to herbs in the Bible, Jason went on a worldwide search to see if he could locate any that would allow him to live.[29]

As a result of his life-seeking trek, Jason Winters developed an herbal tea that not only permitted him to live, but has also since been credited with saving the lives of countless other people. Indeed, in *Threshold to Tomorrow*, Ruth Montgomery wrote, "It is possible that Jason Winters has been an instrument in effecting more remissions from the mysterious malady called cancer than any other single individual living today. Yet he is neither a doctor nor a scientist, and his formal schooling ended at the age of fourteen." That is because he began offering his specially blended herbal tea for sale to others, with the result being that he started a company that now sells the tea and other products all over the world.[30]

We single out Jason Winters's tea not just because it is something that Ruth wrote about, but also due to the fact that it has helped a friend of ours regain her health. Just as Jason Winters was told by his doctors that the end was near, so, too, was a Vermont woman who had been diagnosed with cancer. She was informed by physicians from one of America's leading medical facilities that, even though there was a full range of conventional medical treatments, she should tidy up her affairs and prepare for an imminent end to her life. This lady resigned from her job and began the proverbial business of putting her affairs in order. She also, however, started drinking some Jason Winters's tea that Rob and Phyl had given her and, to her doctors' great surprise, made a remarkable recovery.

Just a coincidence? Who's to say? But we know for sure that there's one New England woman who believes that Jason Winters's tea saved her life. So much so that she now sells what she calls "The Magic Tea" in her spare time and uses the profits to help a sick relative and her family.

Bonus Information

If you would like to learn more about the tea developed by Jason Winters, you can find it on the Internet at the following address:

www.SirJasonWinters.com

And if you are interested in additional information about Walk-ins in general, we would recommend not only that you read both *Strangers Among Us* and *Threshold to Tomorrow,* but also that you visit www.walk-ins.com on the Internet.

As Ruth said in *Threshold to Tomorrow*:

> *Even the often pragmatic medical profession is beginning to rec-*
> *ognize the feasibility of a soul-transference to explain the remarkable*
> *alterations in character and personality that follow many near-*
> *death experiences, and some outstanding psychiatrists are quoted*
> *on the subject in this book. As one of them views it: In this era, when*
> *transplants of kidneys and hearts are becoming commonplace, why*
> *should it be so difficult to believe in body transplants as well?*[31]

Aliens Among Us

Aliens Among Us (1985)–Ruth Montgomery's next book includes
reports of widespread sightings of UFOs by a broad cross-section of
credible individuals, the visitation of Earth by extraterrestrial beings,
people actually being contacted by such aliens, and even the supposed
entering of human bodies by extraterrestrials using the Walk-in process.[32]

Using material collected from multiple eyewitnesses as well as
respected authorities on the topic–people with excellent credentials and high integrity, from varied locations and backgrounds,
possessing widely divergent interests, and all sincerely and seriously
looking for answers–*Aliens Among Us* explains how there are many
extraterrestrials involved in seeking to help mankind foster peace,
decrease pollution, and avoid using nuclear weapons. Apparently
these beings are also very much aware of the impending cataclysmic shift of the Earth's axis and wish to do their part to help our race
prepare for that event.[33]

And why would these aliens be interested in helping us? Because
they see the people of Earth as their sisters and brothers and understand that aliens and humans alike are souls with the same Divine
Parent: God.[34]

Ruth Montgomery: Herald of the New Age

Ruth Montgomery: Herald of the New Age–The Spiritual Odyssey of the World's Leading Psychic Authority (with Joanne Garland, 1986) is an autobiography co-written with Joanne Garland, a woman who had been the first person to introduce Ruth to the concept of Walk-ins. A Walk-in herself, Joanne initially appeared in *Strangers Among Us* under the name of "Laura" in order to shield her true identity.[35]

This is a wonderful account of Ruth's life that makes it a natural choice for anyone who wants to get an overview of who Ruth Montgomery was. This is especially true if you've never read any of her books, as it makes for a great introduction to this multitalented woman and her wondrous life.

The World to Come

Published just two years prior to her death, this was Ruth Montgomery's literary swan song. Because it had been more than a decade since she had released her previous book, she used her final book to update her readers on the Guides' most recent automatic writings on a variety of subjects. Here's a look at how Ruth closed out a writing career that allowed her to fulfill her own Life Mission and, at the same time, opened the minds and touched the hearts of millions of others:

The World to Come: The Guides' Long-Awaited Predictions for the Dawning Age (1999) covers a variety of topics, including Earth Changes, aliens, animals, the Antichrist, the reincarnation of some of Christ's original apostles, and the Millennium.

In *The World to Come*, Ruth describes how the Spirit Guides had explained that the shift of the Earth on its axis was being delayed and would occur no sooner than somewhere in the vicinity of 2010–12. Having previously been predicted by the Guides, as well as numerous noted psychics, to happen right around the turn of the century, the Guides said that the spiritual awakening that was beginning to unfold in the world was helping to forestall the impending shift and to lessen the severity of its eventual impact.[36]

The World to Come not only sheds light on some of the Guides' ongoing messages for all of humanity, but also contains a touching account of how Ruth dealt with the emotional experience of her husband, Bob, passing over on January 31, 1993. Especially fascinating is how, less than two weeks after his death, the Guides informed Ruth that her husband had arrived safe and sound on The Other Side and was with them.[37]

As time went on, Bob himself began directly transmitting messages to his wife during her automatic writing sessions. This was a very significant development, for when he had been alive, Bob had lived a pretty conventional existence. With a background that included a science degree in college and training as an engineer, Ruth's husband had not at all embraced learning about the paranormal the way she had.[38]

Prior to his death, Bob Montgomery had pursued a traditional career as a successful management consultant, once serving as deputy administrator for the Small Business Administration. A practical individual with a very pragmatic approach to life, Bob had initially been concerned when Ruth's automatic writing had begun that it might hurt her in some way. After this early concern, however, he had become a quiet supporter of his wife's exploration of the unusual. At the same time, he was also never the type of staunch advocate for Ruth's books that he became once he died and arrived on The Other Side.[39]

It is somewhat ironic that Ruth's final book included confirmation from Bob of the reality of much of what had been contained in her books about death—and existence in general. In fact, Bob was quite vocal in his writings to his widow that she should write this one last book—and so she did. Indeed, reading about Ruth and Bob's relationship continuing on even after he had died and gone to Heaven gave new significance to the words of the Guides when they had first started communicating with her more than three decades before: "Bob is to play a big part in our project."[40]

Like her first book with the Guides, *A Search for the Truth*, Ruth's final one is a must-read for anyone interested in her work. Not only does *The World to Come* provide her last batch of published information about the Guides' messages for mankind, but it also serves as an excellent reference to put in context the materials contained in this book, *Ruth Montgomery Writes Again!* Indeed, if you want to know where Ruth Montgomery left off before "passing the torch" to us from beyond death's door, then you'll find *The World to Come* to be an invaluable resource.

We Would Enjoy Hearing from You

So that's it. Our brief tour of the landscape of Ruth Montgomery's writings is complete. This remarkable lady obviously wasn't afraid to tackle two of the most controversial topics possible: politics and the spiritual side of life.

If this overview of Ruth's writings has aroused your curiosity about this pioneering author, we would strongly encourage you to follow up and read the actual books themselves. At the very least, you will come away with a lot more information to consider about a wide variety of fascinating issues. Who knows? Perhaps reading a Ruth Montgomery book might end up changing your life.

Finally, for anyone wishing to provide us with feedback of any type—comments, criticisms, or questions—our contact information is:

E-mail: comments@goodagainstevil.com

Mail: Distinctive Publications for the World
          P.O. Box 888
          Hanover, NH 03755

Whether you're a longtime fan of Ruth Montgomery or have never even heard of her before picking up this book, we would sincerely enjoy hearing from you. So, let us know what topics you would most like to see addressed in future books or what questions you have for the Spirit Guides about pressing issues in today's world.

CHAPTER 7

And Who, Pray Tell, Are the Macombers?

There are three Macomber siblings who are the primary participants in the writing of this book–Jane, Paul, and Rob. We have three other siblings, Laura, Sarah, and Jane's fraternal twin, Joe, who, although not directly involved in this project, have all equally contributed to who the Macombers are as a family and whom we love very much. At the time of this book's publication, we are all in our forties, with Rob being the oldest and Paul the youngest. And we are happy to report that both of our parents, Marge and Bob, are still alive and enjoying watching their children progress through adulthood.

In terms of ancestry, we're "American Mutts." As best as we can figure out, here's how our bloodlines break down: one-quarter Irish, one-quarter Italian, one-eighth Swedish, and a blend of Scottish, English, possibly some French, and perhaps even a tad bit of Native American thrown in the mix. All in all, we're just a pretty basic example of a family produced by the great American melting pot.

Where We're from—Castine, Maine

We were all born in a thirteen-bed hospital in a small Maine village of less than a thousand residents called Castine. Situated on the coast between Bar Harbor and Camden, it was a lovely place to grow up. With its seaside location, historic charm, and traditional architecture, Castine is the type of classic New England town that one often finds on postcards and in travel books.

All in all, Castine is the type of small New England village that you see in a Norman Rockwell painting. It has a grade school, Adams School, with fewer than a hundred students, sitting atop the Town Common. The kids play softball there during recess, with the flag-pole serving as second base.

With boating, beaches, and numerous surrounding islands to explore in the summers of our youth, the coast of Maine was, as they say, "God's country" during the warm months. And when the cold arrived, Castine became a winter wonderland of sledding, skat-ing, and snow forts in the winter. In short, it was truly a magical place to grow up as a child.

Castine is a town where everyone knows you, your dog, and your great aunt by first name—and what you had for breakfast. Yes, like most small villages, there's a *Peyton Place* element to the com-munity. (Our mother, a two-time "Miss Castine," was an extra when that movie was filmed in the late fifties, just across Penobscot Bay from Castine, in Camden.) But what really stands out in our mind about growing up in Castine is the real sense of community that was—and is—part of the fabric of its daily life.

Our Education

Although one of the poorest families in town, we were—thanks to generous scholarship programs—able to get much better educa-tions than our limited financial means ever would have allowed. We were fortunate to be able to attend many different private boarding schools and colleges on scholarship. Because of the philanthropy of others, six kids, whose father was a carpenter and a fisherman, had their lives changed immeasurably for the better.

Both of our parents instilled in all of us a deep appreciation for the importance of education. Our mother, Marge, however, made a special effort to see to it that we got as good an education as our academic abilities would allow.

Marge's emphasis on her six kids' education is perhaps best illustrated by the story that Jane tells about an interaction with a classmate she had as a high school senior:

When I was at Gould Academy during my senior year in high school, I was talking to a classmate in algebra before the teacher arrived. I don't recall exactly how the conversation started, but I began talking about how many siblings I had. He asked if they, too, went to private school. I said they did and started telling him all of the different prep schools and colleges that my siblings had attended or were still attending.

I was not trying to impress my friend, and he knew that. It was just a normal conversation. But after hearing how all of my five siblings had gone to, or were still going to, expensive private schools and colleges, he could only come to one conclusion, and said with awe, "Wow, your parents must be filthy rich!"

His jaw dropped completely to the ground when my response was, "Nope. Actually, it's just the opposite. We're dirt poor. We all got scholarships!"

My classmate could not believe that a poor family from a small Maine town could, or would even attempt to, put six children in college, never mind pricey boarding schools. That gives you an idea of my mother's dedication to our education.

Our Family Background

When we were growing up, our family just barely scraped by financially. With our dad's ability to earn a regular living severely hampered by his chronic addiction to alcohol, we were on welfare during much of our youth, sometimes had a phone in the house and sometimes didn't, and had a succession of very used cars that included those we nicknamed "The Rust Bucket," "The Oil-Burner," and "The Red Lemon."

Although the six of us children grew up poor in the material sense of the word, there was a great deal of love in our upbringing. In many ways, we were very lucky, for the sense of family that was instilled in us by our parents, grandparents, and aunts and uncles is something that has been an important part of our lives and continues to this very day. Indeed, the lessons we learned in our childhood about love, family, the value of education, and the importance of never giving up have everything to do with why we are writing this book.

CHAPTER 8

Jane Macomber: Who I Am

L et me begin by saying that you are going to find that I write with a *lot* of emotion. I'm sure that my frequent use of exclamation points, italicized words, and colloquialisms might raise the eyebrows of my former English teachers, but I'm just trying to write in a style that is as close as possible to what you'd hear from me if we were sitting down and chatting together over a meal.

I am a single mother of two teenage boys, Justin and Caleb. I work full-time as the assistant manager of the housekeeping department at a small inn in Massachusetts.

I am, and always have been, a very "hands-on" type of mom. I just plain like children in general. My sister Laura has often called me "The Kool-Aid Mom," the one who has the neighborhood kids over all the time.

When the kids were younger, it was not uncommon for me to be outside playing kickball with my two boys and their friends. Now that they are teenagers, my car has turned into the local taxi as I shuttle them to the mall, take them around to do errands, or make midnight snack runs. It is also not unusual to find five or six young boys asleep in our living room on any given Saturday or Sunday morning, as I have always tried to make their friends feel welcome in our home.

My Hobbies

I do have a couple of hobbies. The first is photography.

Our father is a self-taught photographer who has passed that interest on to me. He bought me my first camera (completely manual) and told me that, to be a good photographer, I must take pictures. And so for the past decade and a half, I have taken thousands and thousands of pictures. I have a special fondness for florals and, of course, for my children.

Another hobby of mine is collecting children's books. I have hundreds of such books and have derived immense joy from them.

My Lifetime Interest in the Unknown

On to a topic that has obviously become much more than a hobby for me: the unknown.

Ever since I can remember, I have been afraid of ghosts–but, at the same time, have been fascinated by them. I've always loved ghost stories, even some that were meant to be funny and not scary.

I guess you could say the unknown has always fascinated me, whether it was ghosts or just a good mystery book. I devoured every Hardy Boys book Rob ever owned. Later in elementary school, I started reading Ed McBain mysteries. I couldn't wait to finish one and race to the library to get the next one.

I also loved Stephen King books in elementary school. I was one of the first kids in my school to read Stephen King's *Carrie,* and then *Salem's Lot.* I have not read all of his work by any means, but he is a fantastic storyteller. I love the fact that he dares to explore the unknown. And he lives just an hour away from where I grew up. Maybe there's something in that cold Maine air....

And, as I mentioned, while loving this sort of thing, I was also scared to death of some of it, especially of ghosts and vampires. *Salem's Lot* was my favorite book, but I was terrified that a real vampire might show up at my window every night. To this day, if I have seen a scary movie or read a frightening book, I don't hesitate to sleep with the light on.

This all may sound crazy–I communicate with "dead" people, but I'm scared of them! What I'm afraid of is *seeing* them. Especially ones that are not so nice. It's one of life's age-old contradictions that we all deal with at times.

Although I believe this fear holds me back from frequently seeing "ghosts" or things on different planes, I have on occasion seen and heard some things. Not nearly as much as some people I know, but enough to make me scared, and at the same time, yearning to see more. There's that contradiction thing again!!!

I will not get into all of the specifics of my first encounters for personal reasons, but when I was around eleven years old, I saw the shadowy figure of someone on two different occasions in my home (it was the same "person" each time). I also heard someone during this same time period and believe it was this same "person" (ghost if you will).

Later in life, I became aware of aliens. I am still scared to death of them, yet fascinated at the same time. I would love to see a UFO, but would hate to be abducted. I don't see how we can be the only intelligent life in the universe. (And with the way things are going, I sometimes think we are the most unintelligent beings in the universe!)

Anyway, I have always been "into" the unknown. Anything to do with the supernatural has always intrigued me. I loved the stuff as a kid and still do.

My Education

Although I've just touched on a handful of my childhood experiences in school, I now want to walk you through my overall education. In hopes that they will allow you to get to know me a little bit, I'm going to include many unvarnished details about the path I traveled through my academic experiences.

The Adams School–Grades 1-8: Great Teachers, Great Food, Great Times

When I entered first grade, the Adams School was a four-room schoolhouse that had two bathrooms and an attic. Each room housed two grades: first and second together, third and fourth together, and so on.

Right from the beginning, I loved school. I enjoyed learning and seeing all of the other children. Looking back, I can see we were a privileged bunch of kids, with fewer than one hundred of us in the entire school.

I especially enjoyed the home-cooked lunches that were hand prepared by the wonderful Mrs. Helen Gray. I'm talking home cooking, with the absolute best macaroni and cheese in the world. And home-baked yeast rolls that any Castine student can still smell simply by thinking of them! (Just how much my siblings and I loved her cooking is illustrated by the fact that after Mrs. Gray passed away, our family was given her recipe book.)

We had wonderful teachers. Mrs. Danforth, Mrs. Howard, Mrs. Babcock, and Mr. O'Brien provided excellent instruction on all of the academic basics. Moreover, Marge Babcock was–and, to this day, still is–one of my favorite people in the whole world. It was easy to see she genuinely loved her job and working with children. She will forever remain one of the better parts of my childhood.

When I was in either seventh or eighth grade, my teacher, Mr. O'Brien, knew that some of my friends and I were interested in ESP. So, for science class he let us do some "scientific research" on ESP.

Mr. O'Brien got us some of those cards with the stars, wavy lines, and circles. While one student held up a card with the drawing facing him or her, another student would concentrate and try to guess what the card had on it. We also tried to control what numbers would show up on dice, using concentration and will power. I always got the highest score in these ESP experiments and loved my teacher, Wallace O'Brien, for letting us do something so cool!

My High School Years: Troubled Times...with a Happy Ending

When it came time for high school, my mother wanted me to go to private school. She felt that it would "broaden my horizons," so to speak. I, on the other hand, had no intention of leaving home.

I remember the interviews I had at four different boarding schools. I was not very enthusiastic about any of them. I remember in particular my answer when the interviewer at Milton Academy, where Rob had gone, asked if I was there because my mother wanted me to be. A big "Yup" came shooting out of my mouth. I was thrilled when all four schools sent rejection letters.

Because of low enrollment, the Castine High School had shut down years before. (My father remembers a commencement ceremony where his friend was the only one graduating!) After that, most kids were bussed to the high school in Bucksport, about half an hour away. But following in the footsteps of my sisters, Laura and Sarah (their high school experiences also ended up including boarding schools), I chose to go to George Stevens Academy in Blue Hill. Because it was a smaller school than Bucksport, my sisters and I thought it to be a better choice for us. Since there was no bus to Blue Hill, it meant our parents had to drive us. Eventually, we arranged to hook up with a bus from the neighboring town of Penobscot, thus reducing our parents' driving significantly.

Even though all of my friends from Castine were going to Bucksport, I did know some kids from Penobscot who attended

George Stevens, and I was thrilled to be going there. I loved it right from the start. I was enrolled in the upper level classes, Level Five, and really enjoyed them. The teachers were excellent. I also loved the social life and soon started hanging out with several kids from Penobscot, as well as classmates from other nearby towns, on a regular basis.

I got good grades in school, but was well into partying by then. In fact, my popularity at Blue Hill was due not only to my outgoing personality, but also to the fact that I supplied some of the best home-grown pot in the area (not grown by me, but by a good friend). It was not uncommon for me to stay after school to hang out with friends and get high. That, of course, meant I had to hitchhike home. I decided, however, that most of the time it was worth it, although it didn't sit well with my parents. I was usually home by late afternoon and had plenty of time to do my studies.

By the time my second year of high school in Blue Hill rolled around, I was beginning to go downhill academically. The first half of my sophomore year I did fairly well, earning mostly Bs. But the second half of the year saw a dramatic change as I slid into a deep depression and was drinking more and more. I drank so much that one friend nicknamed me "Sponge." My grades were slipping, and my attitude toward the whole learning process went out the window.

By the time the end of the school year came around, I had missed finals because I was sick. I had to take my exams on a day after everyone else was done with school. I didn't do very well on them.

For some reason, my parents couldn't pick me up that day. I think I must have lied and told them I could get a ride because they didn't like me hitchhiking. But that is exactly what I did.

I remember thinking as I was walking down the road that I was not going back to school the next fall. I had made my mind up on that matter already.

This was a big disappointment to my parents, as they had gotten me (and my brothers Joe and Paul) a full scholarship to a small private school, Kents Hill, outside of Augusta, Maine. Looking back, I guess that it must have been early on in my sophomore year, when my mental state was still somewhat intact, that I had initially agreed to go there. But, by the end of the year, I had no intention of going to any school. I was too involved with my misery and depression.

Having tried without success to get me to go to Kents Hill and Blue Hill, my mother decided to see if I would try Bucksport High School, where most of the other Castine kids went. Typical of adolescents sometimes taking school rivalries too seriously, I considered Bucksport to be "the enemy." But I relented and went there...for five days.

On the sixth day I purposely missed the bus. My parents got me in the car to drive me. I started whining about my stomach aching. My father hit the roof. But my mother, too tired to fight me anymore, consented at that point to my becoming a high school dropout.

At a loss as to what to do about the situation, my parents asked a local school counselor to come talk with me. After about five minutes, I stormed out on her too. But the counselor then had some very good advice for my parents: Let Jane work it out on her own.

I learned years later that my father, not knowing what to do, had even considered "locking me up" in some sort of institution. Had that happened, I can assure you I would be another suicide statistic. (Thank you, Mrs. Noonan, for your good advice to my parents about letting me work it out on my own.)

I moved out of my parents' house shortly after these incidents to help my cousin with her children for a few months. Despite my mental state, I did love kids and found great joy in helping out. Thinking back, I realize it was probably really good for me to have something so positive in my life.

My depression was still there, but by the time the next school year rolled around, I had come to my senses enough to know that I needed to go back to school. By this time, I was living with my parents again.

I chose to return to my first school, George Stevens Academy in Blue Hill. About two months into the fall, I quit drinking and doing drugs and aced the year. (I describe the spiritual experience that led to this decision a few chapters further on in the book.) I also decided that my last year of high school wouldn't be so bad at a boarding school. I even attended Phillips Exeter Academy in Exeter, New Hampshire, for the summer session after my junior year at Blue Hill. It was a great experience and a good primer for my senior year at Gould Academy, a private boarding school in Bethel, Maine.

When I arrived at Gould, I was one year sober and on top of the world. I fast became friends with many different types of kids, but tended to stick to the partying crowd. After all, just because I didn't drink anymore didn't mean I couldn't have fun. On the contrary, I had a lot more fun once I quit drinking and all that other stuff.

Gould was great! I had such a good time there. They totally accepted me, the new kid, the born-again Christian who was religious and all, but still liked to have a good time. (I still consider myself a Christian, but now believe that all religions have something to offer if one is interested in learning about spiritual matters.)

Every five years a bunch of my friends from Gould and I get together for the class reunions there. Some of the best people I know, I met at Gould.

College and Beyond

My brother Rob, always the academic, thought I should do a post-graduate year, just to have another year under my belt before I went off to college. I went along with it and had lots of interviews at various schools around New England. But, because no one that year could offer me enough financial aid, I went home after graduating from Gould and worked in the local grocery store.

I applied to several colleges for the following academic year and was thrilled when I was accepted at my first choice: Hampshire College in Amherst, Massachusetts. Hampshire is a great school, and I feel honored that I was accepted there. But, for reasons I wish to keep private, it did not work out for me.

I did not return to Hampshire the next fall. I worked for a few years and finally realized I needed to go back to school. Wanting to try a new area, I applied to several schools in California. But before hearing back from them, I ran into an old friend. We ended up having two children together, so I never finished my formal education.

Some say I should go back to school now that the kids are older; but I believe all that life has offered me has been an education beyond compare.

The Ideas Being Presented in This Book Are Suggestions

As I have come to understand it, the wide cross-section of varied experiences that I have had in life is one of the things that contributed to my being allowed the honor of helping to carry on Ruth Montgomery's work. From what she and the Spirit Guides have said, another factor is my longtime interest in "the unknown." Regardless of the exact reasons I have been permitted to be involved in this project, I consider it a great privilege to be bringing to you the recommendations for our world that Ruth and the Spirit Guides are sending to all of us from The Other Side.

The ideas presented in this book are suggestions–suggestions to put our planet on the track we say we want it to be on.

I am not going to use fear and say that if these ideas are not followed, then all hell and damnation are going to break loose. I believe the only Hell that exists is the hell we create ourselves. I will also say that I believe it is just as easy to create Heaven.

In a book I once read called *God's Underground*, the author de-
clares, as best I can remember it, that "if passion exists, even if that
passion is hatred, the possibility of love exists." I wholeheartedly
agree.

"Pop-Ins"

Let me touch on one more thing. Sometimes people I know
who have crossed over come through too. Sometimes we ask for
certain people, and they come through, and sometimes people (including people I don't know) just "pop in for a chat" while I'm doing
the automatic writing. When this happens, I often can feel the excitement of these souls, because they are so happy to be able to
make contact.

So, that's a quick snapshot of my background and me. I assure
you that I am not a nutcase looking for notoriety or anything else. I
simply wish to follow through on the assignment that I have been
given by Ruth and the Guides.

CHAPTER 9

Greetings from Paul Macomber

Like the rest of my siblings, I was born and raised in Castine, Maine. For much of my youth, I grew up in a two-hundred-year-old colonial house that was, shall we say, showing its age. I lived there with my parents, three sisters, two brothers, our three-legged dog, Honey, and numerous cats. It's true that we didn't have much money, but did have a lot of love among all of us. And what I've found interesting as an adult is that it's the memories of the latter that are by far the strongest.

My Early Thoughts on Spiritual Matters

I remember when I was probably about seven or eight years old that I started contemplating the thought of death and what happens afterward. I recall thinking that there had to be more to it than just living your life, and then when it came to an end, they'd put you in a box, bury you in the ground, and that was it.

How could you just stop being? It just didn't make sense to me that one day when I died I would cease to exist. I wanted to believe there had to be more going on after the death part. The thought that I would just be gone, and that was it, always led me to be looking and thinking about alternative possibilities to something after death.

Stories of ghosts both scared and intrigued me. I think that this was because if they did exist, it meant that there was some type of life after death...although it didn't seem as though ghosts had a very pleasant existence, at least not the ones you hear about when you're eight or nine. But it sure was a better alternative to being left in the ground with no future at all.

Like most everyone else, I heard talk of Heaven and God during the early years of my youth. Yet I never heard any stories about people who had any real experience of having been to the afterlife. At the time, it seemed to be more of a fairy-tale type of place where you supposedly went after death if you lived a good life and were a nice person.

When I was about ten or eleven, I remember hearing some people talk about reincarnation. It sounded nice that when you were done with this life, you would get to start all over again with another. On the other hand, I couldn't understand how people could transform from one person to another person. It seemed to me that you were who you were—and how was that ever going to change?

By the age of fifteen I still had no clear belief system about what happened after death. I did know that I felt there was something more to it than dying and being gone forever, but what that was I still didn't know.

Around the age of seventeen or eighteen, I read a few books on reincarnation, and they resonated as being true to me. It seemed to make sense and helped to fit the pieces of the puzzle together in terms of connecting the life and death part. I guess you could say that was the time when I started to embark on my spiritual exploration of life.

As you can probably surmise, I'm now fully on board with a strong belief in the reality of Heaven, ghosts, reincarnation, and life after death. In fact, those concepts that seemed so far out there when I was young are now the foundation of my belief system.

My Academic Background

After finishing elementary school at Castine's Adams School and attending Bucksport High School for a year, I received the remainder of my high school education at Kents Hill School, a private boarding school with just over two hundred students, located in central Maine, not far from the state capital of Augusta. My time spent there was a very enriching period in my life.

At Kents Hill, I was exposed to students from different parts of the country, as well as from various locations around the world. My schoolmates had diverse cultural and socioeconomic backgrounds that you didn't find in the everyday, year-round life of Castine.

I met some of my closest lifelong friends while at Kents Hill, many of whom I'm still in regular contact with today. Those were very formative years that prepared me well, not only for my time at college, but also for the path that lay ahead of me in life.

After graduating from Kents Hill, I attended Phillips Exeter Academy summer school and then took eighteen months off to work and save money for college. I attended Babson College, which is located in Wellesley, Massachusetts, twelve miles west of Boston. Babson is a small business and liberal arts college, with an emphasis on business education.

I wasn't in the top of my class academically at Babson like I had been in high school. In retrospect, I'm certain that it had a lot to do with my strong desire for social interaction, intertwined with my fair share of beer consumption. Nevertheless, I received a great education and had a good time doing so.

"...I ran into an old friend from Nantucket who invited me out to stay with him on the island for a weekend."

After college I lived in Boston for a couple of years doing odd jobs, not knowing what I wanted to do with my life. One day while walking down the street, I ran into an old friend from Nantucket who invited me out to stay with him on the island for a weekend.

While in college I had spent a summer working on Nantucket, and two of my best friends from Kents Hill came from there, so it had been a special place for me. As it was mid-July and about a hundred degrees in Boston, I took my friend up on his invitation…and the weekend turned into a five-year stay.

During those five years, I worked building houses and performing other odd jobs. I also became involved with drugs—cocaine, to be specific. Living on a beautiful, secluded island like Nantucket and using drugs allowed me to avoid facing the question of what I wanted to do with my life. It was a perfect escape, or so I thought at the time. Looking back now, I can see that it was just an easy way for me to postpone having to face my fears about what seemed to be the daunting challenges of trying to figure out a career and direction in life.

I have numerous fond memories of good times on Nantucket and made many great friends while living there. Because of my irresponsible attitude and involvement with drugs, however, I ended up in prison for a year.

I found out that I was in trouble with the law a few weeks after leaving Nantucket, just one day before I was scheduled to move to California and start a new life going into business with an old friend and roommate from college, Andrew Zenoff. I had to postpone my trip to turn myself in and retain a lawyer to defend me.

After returning to Nantucket to face my charges, I was released on bail and had one year before I went back to court to learn that I would be sentenced to a year in prison. I spent that year in California working with my friend in a new start-up venture. He had invented a new baby product called My Brest Friend that lends support to breast-feeding moms and had only recently launched the business. During that year, I did little else but work, read books, and exercise. At the end of the year in California, I returned to Massachusetts to face my charges and received my year-long sentence.

Although it wouldn't have been my first choice as a place to reflect and search my soul, prison ended up being a positive experience in many ways. I read dozens of books, most of which dealt with spiritual topics. I also wrote more letters than I have ever written in my life. But, most importantly, I was able to look deep inside myself to determine what was really important to me and what it was I wanted to do in life.

I came to the realization that my relationship with my family and friends was what was most important. I further concluded that, in addition to making a living, I also wanted to do something that would help people, preferably on as large a scale as possible. At the time, I envisioned developing a business that would not just make a profit, but also positively impact the lives of others as well. After being released from prison, I returned to California, where I have lived ever since.

My college friend and I now market the My Brest Friend nursing pillow, which he invented, to people all over the world. It has assisted hundreds of thousands of new moms to breast-feed successfully and, in doing so, has helped their little ones be healthier. We also subsequently started another new venture that is a retail concept. It provides most everything a new parent would need, all under one roof. We are currently in the process of expanding it and are growing both companies.

For all of the twists and turns in my travels along life's path, I hadn't even the faintest inkling that I would ever be involved in something like the book you are now reading…until it started happening. But before we get to that part of the story, my brother Rob will take over as narrator and tell you about himself.

CHAPTER 10

Some Details about Rob "Cuac" Totaro Macomber

You must be wondering where I got the nickname "Cuac"—or how even to pronounce it. You see, when I was in first grade, kids started calling me "Cucumber" because of my last name. By third grade, they had shortened it to "Cuke." When I went to write my nickname down for the first time, however, I spelled it "Cuac."

Not long afterward, as I was riding with my "Grammy Al" to Bangor, I saw a roadside vegetable stand that had the correct spelling of "Cuke." Nonetheless, I concluded that I liked my version better and would forever keep "Cuac" as the preferred, though phonetically mangled and decidedly unique, spelling of my nickname. Hence, you'll often see me referred to as "Cuac" in much of this book, though "Rob" and "Robbie" are also used to show how various family members and friends refer to me in our everyday lives together.

"Totaro" became a part of my name when I married my wife, Phyl, whose maiden name is Totaro. Since she had elected to add "Macomber" to her name, I decided to add "Totaro" to mine. In fact, when I announced this during a toast at our rehearsal dinner, the reaction that it brought to the faces of Phyl's parents, Bertha and Leonard Totaro, remains one of my life's most treasured memories.

Sports

Like many youngsters, I enjoyed playing sports as I grew up. So much so that, as an adult, I now sometimes read three different sports pages a day: *USA Today*, the *Boston Globe*, and the *Boston Herald.*

Basketball, golf, and softball occupied countless hours of my youth and left me with many special memories. Athletics was something that didn't require a lot of money (thankfully, junior golf club memberships were only $17.50 in Castine when I started playing at age six) and, as it has for millions of children from poor families, helped "level the playing field" for me as I was growing up—especially in my own mind. In short, I was a decent athlete, but certainly not an exceptional one.

Perhaps because of my height (6'4"), basketball became my favorite sport. Though I played in high school and, for a limited time, in college, my love of the game has always far exceeded my ability to play it. In fact, I am now one of those middle-aged guys who refuses to hang up his Converse high-tops. I still enjoy trotting (heck, I was slow when I was eighteen) up and down the court during a noon hoops game at Dartmouth College a few days a week.

How much do I enjoy playing hoops? Let's put it this way: I still have a recurring dream a couple of times a year that I can dunk the basketball again.

No, I wasn't any great leaper when I was young. I missed most of my dunk shot attempts and could only consistently "put it down" with the aid of a stickum spray called "Firm-Grip" that allowed my small hands to control the ball enough to slam it through the basket. But the thrill of every once in a while getting up high enough to "do it on my own" by stuffing it through the hoop with two hands (yes, it really is as much fun as it looks) is, I would speculate, the type of treasured memory from yesteryear that lingers on in the minds of many about days gone by. Although the specific memories may vary among different individuals, I would venture to say that, at least to a certain extent, most everyone beyond their teenage years knows the feeling I am talking about.

If you're in your teens, or are not even that old, but are a good enough reader to be holding this book in your hands, then please pay special attention. This isn't just some middle-aged guy going down memory lane in his mind. It's critical that you don't let the George Bernard Shaw (don't worry if you don't know who he is or haven't read anything by this acclaimed writer—neither have I) quote, "Youth is wasted on the young" end up applying to you. Make the most of your early years, appreciate the things you enjoy most, and, above all else, don't be afraid of life. As you will see later in this book, the spirits in Heaven who have given us the core information for this book say that you have a special role to play in getting this world put on the right track.

School

As previously mentioned, my siblings and I were extremely fortunate in terms of the educational opportunities we had. For me, it meant being given scholarships to attend a private high school located in Milton, Massachusetts, called Milton Academy, and Bowdoin College, a small liberal arts school situated in Brunswick, Maine. Being able to go to these two institutions was a true privilege and left me profoundly grateful to have been the recipient of the beneficence of other members of our society.

I will never stop being thankful for books. They have changed my life. I *know* that they can do the same for the many people around the world who've never had the chance to taste the magical powers of education, the ultimate elixir.

If there's a bigger believer on the planet in the importance of education, then I'd like to meet that individual...for I'm sure that is a person from whom I could learn a lot.

Food

No profile of me would be complete without mention of how much I like to eat–no, make that, how much I *love* to eat.

I mean you're talking about a guy with an eating resume that includes the following:

- After my Aunt Mary had filleted the catch from my first deep-sea fishing trip, polishing off an entire eight-pound haddock as a ten-year old.

- When I was in grammar school–maybe sixth grade, I would guess–wearing a white sweatshirt on which I had written on the back in big, bold green letters: "EAT, CUAC, EAT."

- On a bet, when I was sixteen, wolfing down four Big Macs in six minutes at a McDonald's in Brewer, Maine.

- Losing a radio-broadcasted pie-eating contest the following year because I slowed down midway through when I realized that I was tied for the lead only because I was swallowing the strawberries whole.

- Thinking that I needed to bulk up my slender 190-pound frame for basketball when I arrived at Bowdoin as a freshman and supplementing my double-helpings, three-meals-a-day diet with a daily intake of an entire loaf of peanut-butter-and-jelly sandwiches.

- In the midst of a weekend in Boston while in college, eating three-and-a-half large cheese steak subs late one night at one of Jay Leno's favorite old haunts, Buzzy's Fabulous Roast Beef.

- During another college road trip, devouring a dozen lobsters in forty-five minutes at "Custy's Restaurant" in North Kingstown, Rhode Island…and then having the establishment's closing time thwart my attempt to break their then-record of thirty-something lobsters in one sitting.

- After completing my final college exam, celebrating not with a traditional glass of champagne or bottle of beer, but by treating myself to an excursion to one of my favorite local haunts—the local Deerings ice cream shop. It seemed like a fitting way to toast the moment, as I figured that my college roommate, Rob DeSimone, and I had eaten more hot fudge sundaes in Brunswick, Maine, than any other two students in the history of Bowdoin College. After finishing my sundae (made with chocolate chip ice cream and extra whipped cream), I thought to myself: *That was good, but it wasn't nearly as much fun as having one with Rob. I think I'll have another one in his honor.* And so I did.

Oh, by the way, my all-time favorite ice cream flavor is Friendly's "Buttercrunch," and my top pick for a sundae is undoubtedly their classic "Jim Dandy." Here's how it's described on their menu: "There's divine decadence by the spoonful in this sinful split with five scoops of ice cream, strawberry, marshmallow and chocolate topping, a split fresh banana, sprinkles, walnuts and whipped topping."[1]

Although there are also plenty of food-related vignettes from my adult years, I think you get the point: Eating has been a big part of my life. So much so that I have often joked that, until Phyl and I got together, my idea of being healthy was not ordering extra cheese on my cheese steak subs. I'm sure that my fixation with food probably not only stems from the fact that it's just plain fun, but also has something to do with our family finances having made food a precious commodity when my siblings and I were growing up.

As one of my sisters once said to her college boyfriend, "Going grocery shopping was a really big deal in my family." I thought of this when I recently read an article in which *Wheel of Fortune*'s Pat Sajak explained that he's very grateful now to be able to buy anything he wants when he goes to the grocery store. It was nice to see such a privilege truly appreciated.

While I myself have certainly had to watch what things cost when grocery shopping as an adult, I definitely have not been underfed.

To the contrary, since my mid-twenties, my belt size has started with a "4" the majority of the time—once reaching 46" when my weight peaked at 267 in the mid-90s.

Although those numbers dropped to 183 and 36" respectively when Phyl and I got married in 1998, I then put on a quick twenty pounds during our two-week honeymoon and began my ascent back up the scales. As I write this manuscript, I'm tipping them at 236, with a 40" waistline. I share all of these weight-related details with you because for all of the funny "food" stories and memorable eating moments, I still have a hard time accepting the fact that I've spent most of my adult life overweight.

My sense of semi-disbelief about my weight underscores the degree to which, despite the many humorous eating anecdotes, food has become a very serious matter in my life. Perhaps the best way to illustrate how I feel about this subject is to share a memory with you from my childhood.

When I was eleven, I was reading *My Turn at Bat*, the wonderful autobiography of legendary baseball star Ted Williams. In it, Williams wrote:

> *From the time I was twelve years old I was a malted milk hound. Malted milk with eggs. When I started playing professionally, and could afford it, I'd have four or five a day. I'd like to know how many calories I put away in those years. I look at myself now, when a dish of ice cream means another notch in the belt, and I have to think that that skinny skeleton body belonged to someone else.*[2]

When I saw that, I thought: *That will never happen to me. I'm not going to be one of those guys who was an athlete early on in life and then puts on the pounds later when he gets older. I'll always exercise and keep in good shape.*

And then Life happened.

The bottom line is that I now find myself struggling on almost a daily basis to control my weight. Every evening I am reminded of just how troubling this issue is to me. Just before going to sleep, I try to do a brief review of the day and identify three things that I did "right," three things that I did "wrong," and the reasons behind those "wins" and "losses" for the day. Almost always, at least one of my daily entries in the negative column involves overeating. Often this produces feelings of self-loathing, disappointment with my own lack of willpower, and the now familiar admonition to myself: *How can a guy who considers life such a great privilege and professes to love his wife and family endlessly have a cholesterol count of 251 and yet still be out of control with his eating habits so often?*

Fairy Tales

Okay, how about we lighten things up a bit now (no pun intended)? How about we talk "Fairy Tales" for a bit? As someone who has a life-sized replica of a knight in shining armor in his dining room, this is a topic close to my heart. You see, this is a subject that has a lot to do with who I am as a person, the perspective my siblings and I have on life, and, perhaps most pertinent for you as the reader, how we have approached attempting to understand all of the information we have received from Heaven as we have gone about writing this book.

The importance of fairy tales providing a philosophical framework for my family and me is best captured in an excerpt from what we included in this book's dedication about our mother, Marge Macomber:

> Whenever a Walt Disney movie would be showing at the theater when [Robbie] was a child, his mother would always manage to find a way to get her children to see it. She felt that it was very important for them to have the opportunity to see these films of fantasy, magic, and fairy tales.

*While Robbie has irreplaceable memories of going with her to see **Pinocchio**, **Snow White**, **Bambi**, and a host of other enchanting classics, the thing that made the most lasting impression on him is that his mother was every bit as excited to see these movies as he and his sisters and brothers were. Her sense of enthusiasm for these timeless flights of fancy, the irrepressible youth of her soul, and her unshakable belief in happy endings are all part of Mum Marge's legacy to her son Robbie. To this day, his two favorite movies of all-time in the entire world remain **The Wizard of Oz** and **Peter Pan**.*

The extent to which these childhood classics have impacted my life can be seen just by looking at the license plates on the cars my wife Phyl and I drive. One of them reads "WIZOFOZ" and the other "PETRPAN." And then there's the corner of our living room that's like a mini-shrine to *The Wizard of Oz.* Oh yeah, when we got married in 1998, our wedding dance was to "Somewhere Over the Rainbow"…with Phyl wearing replicas of Dorothy's ruby-red slippers that my sister Sarah had made as a wedding gift for her.

Our "Grampa Paul" and "The Tin Man"

Although *The Wizard of Oz* has played an influential role over the course of my entire life, it wasn't until after I started writing this book and heard my mother tell a "Wiz"-related story from family lore that I fully realized where she had gotten some of her "unshakable belief in happy endings."

Ever since I was a young boy, I had heard Mum describe how, when I was just a year old, her father, Paul Allen, my "Grampa Paul," had held me on his lap so that I could watch *The Wizard of Oz* with him. I have no recollection of that experience because he died the following summer, leaving his wife Verna (our "Grammy Al") to bury him on her fiftieth birthday. What I do recollect, however, is that Mum had mentioned over the years that her dad had briefly known Jack Haley, the actor who had played "The Tin Man" in *The Wizard of Oz*. When I began work on this book and was seeking to understand my family background a little better, I came across a small nugget that shed some light on where, at least in part, the "don't-ever-be-afraid-to-try-anything" advice she has *always* given to us kids came from.

While tape-recording some conversations with Mum about a wide range of family history, I captured a brief vignette involving our Grampa Paul and "The Tin Man":

> *Cuac: You said at one point that Grampa Paul knew the fellow who had played "The Tin Man"?*
>
> *Mum: Oh, right. He worked at the Boston Navy Yard, and his helper was "The Tin Man" before he went to Hollywood. What was his name?*
>
> *Cuac: Jack Haley. Wasn't he Grampa Paul's electrician's assistant?*
>
> *Mum: Yes. He used to tell my father that he wanted to be an actor, go to Hollywood, and try to get into film. My father encouraged him and said, "Well, do it if that is what you want to do. You will never know until you try it."*

This little family story is not at all meant to imply that the reason Jack Haley became an actor is because of our Grampa Paul's encouragement. No, the point is rather that this short narrative illustrates the tremendous influence that previous generations have upon future ones. Our grandfather possessed an "anything-is-possible" attitude about life and instilled in his daughter, Margaret, that same sense of belief. And had she not passed that same sort of outlook on to us, it is doubtful, very doubtful, that this book would exist.

A Few More Miscellaneous Tidbits

So, what other things will give you a quick snapshot of me? Though by no means a complete summary or in any particular order of importance, here are a few more details about Margaret Allen Macomber's oldest child, Rob:

Favorite TV shows (old and new): *Lost, Alias, Medium, 24, Heroes, Magnum, P.I., West Wing, Commander-in-Chief, Ghost Whisperer, Joan of Arcadia, Touched by an Angel, Witchblade, Remington Steele, X-Files, The 4400, Hogan's Heroes, Gilligan's Island,* and *Mike Hammer*...to name just some of them.

Favorite fiction authors: Charles Dickens, Jules Verne, Kenneth Roberts, H. G. Wells, Robert Ludlum, Jeffrey Archer, Nelson DeMille, Jack Higgins, Stan Lee, and other countless comic book writers whose names I do not know. But regardless of what author I am reading, I've always been most interested in reading about the emotions being felt by the story's characters. Even when presented with Dickens's masterful passages describing settings and scenes, I found my eyes going into "skim mode" as I raced ahead to learn what was going on inside the characters' hearts.

Favorite memory in life: The weekend that Phyl and I got married. With five best men, nineteen ushers, one maid-of-honor, ten bridesmaids, two readers, two ring bearers, one flower girl, and numerous other family members and friends present, the recollection of Phyl and me together sharing the experience of our wedding with so many people whom we care about is a memory that time will never diminish.

I enjoyed our wedding so much that, after the ceremony was over, I suggested to Phyl that we get dressed up in our wedding clothes every year on our anniversary. And so that's just what we do. It's an absolute gas and has become an extremely special tradition for the two of us.

Phyl's got the tough part of that gig, though, as she has to fit in the same wedding dress every year. All I have to do, on the other hand, is head over to College Formals and rent a tux in whatever size I happen to be.

Old harmless habits I can't seem to break:

• Since age fifteen, I've been addicted to Chapstick. I keep tubes of it in all sorts of different places and get uncomfortable if I don't have one within immediate reach.

• I often get lost in thought while driving, causing me to miss exits and make wrong turns on a regular basis. Phyl calls this my "Float Mode."

I guess that's about it for openers about me, with one big exception: What I have done as an adult for work and how a series of severe business setbacks profoundly affected my take on the spiritual side of life. Although this part of the story and the way in which it led me to being involved in writing this book will be explained later in more detail, here's the short version.

An Open Mind toward the Mysteries of Existence

I must say that earlier in life, I never would have envisioned being on my present path of spiritual inquiry. Coming from a traditional academic background and having pursued an entrepreneurial career in business, I was, up until the early 1990s, leading a life oriented toward the mainstream that had as its primary focus the achievement of conventional success.

Rob DeSimone, my high school classmate and Bowdoin roommate, and I began our first business together at age nineteen. It was a small summer moped rental business called Mopeds of Maine in Bar Harbor, Maine, subsequently leading us to locate there year-round after college and become commercial real estate brokers and small-scale real estate developers.

On November 11, 1991, a major curveball came my way in business that served as a catalyst for my beginning to seek answers to the age-old questions of existence. Since then, I have increasingly endeavored to make some small inquiry about the spiritual aspects of our experience here on Earth. Although later on in this book I will explain more about the specifics of this business calamity and the effect that it had on my life, suffice it to say that the past decade and a half has witnessed a major transformation of my belief system.

Faced with what quickly evolved into a seemingly never-ending morass of litigation (from which I am still diligently trying to pick up the pieces), I sought to glean at least some slight bit of understanding about how a career that I had been working on so hard since age nineteen could have taken such a sharp detour. Seeking to gain at least a modicum of insight into why this might have happened, I slowly began to delve into the spiritual side of life.

After reading dozens of spiritually oriented books—most of my favorite nonfiction authors, some of whom we have quoted in this book, are now of this genre—I have come to the not-so-surprising conclusion that the first place to look when searching for reasons when something goes wrong in one's life is in the mirror. This is a pretty simple and basic lesson that probably should have been obvious much earlier on.

Although I consider myself to be a very spiritual person, you should know I am not what many would call an extremely "religious" individual in the conventional sense of the word. Although baptized a Catholic, I rarely attend church and do not feel I have found any one faith that seems to "have all the answers."

To the contrary, what I believe is continually evolving and subject to constant change. I guess you could say that whatever belief system I have is very "fluid" and that, more than anything, I have tried to keep an open mind about the mysteries of existence. Not surprisingly, this ongoing thought process usually leads to many more additional questions for me than it does answers.

In my pursuit of gaining some sort of spiritual perspective, I came across a number of books written by Ruth Montgomery. Or perhaps I should say, they made their way to me. As you shall soon see, Mrs. Montgomery's work ended up altering the course of my entire life and helped put it on the path that has led to my involvement with the writing of the book that you are now reading.

"When your views on the world and your intellect are being challenged..."

As influential as Ruth Montgomery's writings have been on my direction in life, it is in the words of another person whom I never met that I found the best description of how I have come to approach the "big-picture" questions we all ask ourselves in private moments.

More than a decade ago–and not too long after my business woes commenced in the early 1990s–I came across a quotation in a catalog for Bar Harbor's noted human ecology school, the College of the Atlantic (COA). The quotation was part of a dedication to a COA teacher who had recently passed away, Professor William H. Drury, Jr. Even though I had never met the gentleman or even heard of him before, it was obvious from the dedication in the catalog that he had been a great teacher, was revered by his students, and had touched the lives of many young people.

When I first read Professor Drury's words, they struck me as being very powerful. They made enough of an impression upon me that I immediately photocopied them so that I would always have them. I guess because I have always enjoyed learning and "being a student," William H. Drury, Jr.'s words really spoke to me and hit a chord deep inside. Here is what Professor Drury had to say:

> *When your views on the world and your intellect are being challenged, and you begin to feel uncomfortable because of a contradiction you've detected that is threatening your current model or some aspect of it, pay attention. You are about to learn something.*

CHAPTER 11

Why Our Family Experience Has Helped Us Write This Book

At the time of our brother Joe's marriage to his wife Bah on September 15, 1995, Cuac gave a toast that we think captures the essence of what our life as a family has been like (so much so, that he offered the same one when Paul married his wife, Sasha, on September 16, 2005). Here is what he said:

> Now that we are officially family, I would like to share with you what it means to me to be a Macomber. It means having many relatives who are intelligent, interesting people who are fun to be with. It means having relatives who are not just your family members, but who are also your friends. But most of all, it means that no matter what may be going on in your life, no matter what else is happening around you, you know, 100 percent certain, that there are a whole lot of people out there who will always be there for you and who will always love you—**unconditionally**. I hope that you enjoy being a Macomber as much as I have.

This is not by any means meant to suggest that our family life has not had its fair share of problems. Didn't we have fights and arguments with each other growing up as kids? *Of course we did.* Wasn't there a tremendous strain placed on the entire family dynamic because we were poor? *You bet there was.* Aren't there disagreements between all of us adults that continually arise? *Absolutely.* But beyond all of the individual differences, divergent personalities, and varying perspectives, we have always known that our ultimate safety net is each other.

Indeed, what has made our lives as Macombers so rewarding is that we have experienced firsthand the power of love to unify people possessing a wide range of interests with many differing opinions. And we know that, just as love has been the glue that has held us together as a family, so, too, does it for millions of other families all around the world. But too often many of us lose sight of the fact that the deep love we reserve for those closest to us in life also possesses the potential to literally change the world.

With our planet hurtling on a collision course with itself, it should be obvious to every single human being upon the face of the Earth that *love is the only possible answer* to the multitude of problems that now have us all too close to blowing ourselves up. Like a bunch of immature kids on the playground, we go through life pointing the finger of blame at each other when things do not go the way we would like them to—and then wonder why the world is such a mess. Come on, folks, let's go! It's time to wake up!!

That's why we're writing this book series—to deliver to humanity one of the biggest wake-up calls the world has ever known. This wake-up call is composed of messages sent straight from Heaven to Earth—messages *in their own words* from Ruth Montgomery and her fellow Spirit Guides. Simply put, they're offering us some words of wisdom to help us open our eyes and see what we need to do to solve the many problems that now vex our world and threaten our future.

PART II

The Passing of the Torch

"I then suggested to Jane that she ask Lily and Ruth if it would be possible for Jane to do what Ruth had done. Could Jane, using the information provided by the spirit realm's automatic writing transmissions, write a book?"

The pen promptly scrawled out a one-word answer:

"Together."

"Among the many curves and loops on the paper were written some words that could be made out without too much trouble. When I read them, I could scarcely believe my eyes:

'Lily is leelee...Ruth Montgomery... listen to me...listen, listen.'"

–Ruth Montgomery and the Spirit Guides

CHAPTER 12

Jane's Going to Get This Party Started

A s a child, I did not go to church much, although I do remember going to Sunday school so I could ride a little giraffe scooter! I recall my mother telling me that God was everywhere. At the age of three, I imagined little sparkling crosses floating everywhere. This is what I imagined God to be: brightly lit crosses floating about the world, emitting love to all people and creatures.

Unfortunately, this beautiful vision did not carry through as I grew up.

"The main thought on my mind was: *Should I kill myself?*"

It is not uncommon for *very* young children to start partying. I was one of those *very* young children. Although you've already read about some of my experiences with alcohol and drugs, the severe challenge they posed to me in my youth warrants further explanation.

I was nine the first time I smoked marijuana–and had been involved in drinking before then.

I started smoking cigarettes at the age of ten.

By the time I was thirteen, I had become seriously involved in drinking alcohol and smoking pot. In fact, the summer I was thirteen, I was drinking and smoking pot on a daily basis.

By the age of fifteen, I was trying speed and LSD. I continued to drink heavily and would pretty much do anything else that was offered to me. Fortunately, being in a small town didn't afford more than a hit of acid once in a while or some speed now and then.

My self-confidence was not high to begin with, so all of this activity led to extremely low self-esteem. I was at a point where I thought there was no hope. I started to contemplate suicide as a way out of my miserable existence.

For the next two-and-a-half years, the main thought on my mind was: *Should I kill myself?* I felt little power inside myself and almost no control over anything.

My friends and I started playing with the Ouija board late at night when we would stumble into one girl's kitchen completely drunk (we usually stayed at her house). I remember feeling power then and only then. I could make the heart-shaped piece from the Ouija game move around the board by myself.

The trouble was, we were getting "bad" spirits a lot of the time. I remember letting their negative energy enter me. I welcomed it and enjoyed it–because it scared my friend. I'd get this wicked look on my face, and she'd ask me to stop, saying that I was scaring her. I'd wipe the look off my face, but inside I was laughing wickedly, like the Devil himself. I liked having some sort of control over someone. I enjoyed making my friend scared.

"It was as if God whispered in my ear and, for one split second, I listened."

Somewhere in the midst of all this, however, that little bit of control wasn't enough. I don't remember when or where, but at some point I started talking to God.

I had pretty much shut my family out, quit high school, and alienated a lot of my friends. But God was always there. He was a good listener and didn't talk back, at least not in a conventional way.

I know now that God was probably talking to me, probably more than I was talking to Him. He must have been, because during the two-and-a-half years that I was contemplating suicide, I also had several private counseling sessions with God in that same period of time. In the end, He won out.

At the age of seventeen, I had a profound spiritual experience when I gave up drinking and doing drugs. As I have just described, it actually began before then, but that was the defining moment for me.

My path toward self-destruction all came to an abrupt end while I was strolling around in the hallways of the Castine Community Hospital late one night, waiting for a friend to get his head stitched up. A bunch of my friends were partying on Halloween night 1981. One friend ended up in the hospital getting stitches in his head. He had gotten into a fight with another friend.

Can you guess the reason for the fight? If you're thinking alcohol, then you're correct.

I had been trying to put some perspective in my life and had been sober for three weeks prior to that night. That night I drank half a glass of beer.

After that, the fight and the whole hospital thing took place. It was at that moment that it all became very clear to me: The entire situation was due to alcohol. If I wanted my own life to take a turn for the better, all I had to do to start in that direction was to quit the booze and drugs.

I decided that everyone else could continue to drink and do drugs, but the best thing for me was to stop. It was as if God whispered in my ear and, for one split second, I listened. I was thinking: *Why didn't I do this years ago?*

"I literally went from dark to light overnight ...and know that God has many good things in store for us all."

I've been sober ever since. What astounded me was how simple the solution was: Just stop. (I believe the human race could decide in the same way that we want to be a peaceful planet. It really isn't as hard as we make it out to be.)

Giving up that way of life and getting sober seemed so easy... because that is what I had decided I wanted to be. No thinking about it or talking about it, just *being* that.

I literally went from dark to light overnight. I was always happy and found the most joy in helping people and being nice. My friends couldn't figure out what happened; but they were happy that drunk, slobbering, broke Jane wasn't always bumming their booze and annoying them. As soon as I got my license, I became the designated driver!

I finished high school and used to be so overjoyed at living that I wrote "GOD LOVES YOU, JESUS IS GREAT" all over my notebooks. I was so thankful to be alive that I could think of nothing else—except all of the good things in life. Some people thought I was fanatical, but most were just happy I had stopped my wicked ways.

Since then, I have realized that no one can be happy all of the time, that life is a balance—there are good times and bad times. But through it all, one thing has remained constant—my faith in God and my undying commitment to His cause.

Since that night a quarter of a century ago, I've been open to spiritual matters and am fascinated with life—on any plane or level. I've also been clean and sober for that long but am not your conventional recovering alcoholic.

I don't go to AA; it doesn't bother me to go to a bar or someplace where people are drinking; and I don't find it hard to socialize without the booze. *Au contraire*!!! I love people, loud music, dancing, and just plain having a good time.

And for the past twenty-some years, if someone needs a designated driver and I'm around, I gladly accept the job. Not that I go out all the time, but if I want to, I am not held back by the fear of: *What if I pick up a drink?* That is because the desire to drink completely left me that Halloween night.

My life has not been easy since my youth. Since my sobriety, I have been anorexic, overweight, had bad relationships with men (all alcoholics), and am presently a single mother of two boys. But through all of the frustration, pain, and anger, I have always known that God is with me and that I need to keep going on, growing, and learning. I constantly pray for myself and others—and know that God has many good things in store for us all.

CHAPTER 13

Paul's Spiritual Background

"The earth is a schoolroom for the soul's development.
Our bodies are like the blue Tiffany box that holds a gift.
Once the gift is removed, the box is discarded.
The treasure remains."[1]

—Mary T. Browne, *Life After Death*

One of the first "spiritual" books I read was given to me in the late-80s when I was in college by an aunt of ours, Lara Allen. The daughter of our Grammy Al and sister of our mother, Lara has been an avid reader throughout her life and is always eager to share the results of her learning. Titled *The Magus of Strovolos: The Extraordinary World of a Spiritual Healer,* it is a fascinating nonfiction work by Kyriacos Markides, a sociology professor at the University of Maine at Orono, telling the story of a very advanced spiritual healer named Daskalos.

Daskalos lived in Professor Markides's native Cyprus and had the ability to cure people of supposedly incurable illnesses. Able to heal the sick in ways that defied the known methods of modern medicine and reported to be capable of leaving his body at will, Daskalos and his teachings offered insights into many of life's greatest mysteries. Reading this book piqued my curiosity about the "spirit world," this other realm where we supposedly came from before incarnating on Earth—and to where we apparently return after leaving our physical bodies here on this planet.

"Why are we here? What's Life all about? Is there a meaning to any of this?"

I began to read many other books of a spiritual nature. I did this because I began to find that what they had to say seemed to address many of those big questions we always ask ourselves, like: *Why are we here? What's Life all about? Is there a meaning to any of this? Is there life after death? What about reincarnation?* Such books have given me some modest amount of insight into framing a clearer and better understanding of what we are truly doing here.

The common thread I found in most of these books was that we, as spiritual beings, have a temporary human experience. We come down here to Earth with a veil of forgetfulness to further advance our spiritual selves. Because of this veil of ignorance about the past, we have no recollection of previous lives. This is because, if we did, we would be worried about things we had done in previous incarnations and would not be able to concentrate on what it was we were here to do this time around.

It seems that before we come to Earth, we choose the lessons that we want to learn in order to "work on our soul" and make it more whole and complete. The way I understand it to function is that we each have a unique soul that needs work on various "rough edges"—be it love, forgiveness, patience, kindness, etc.—before it is perfected and rejoins God for all eternity.

Prior to coming "down" to Earth, we supposedly each pick what it is in particular that our soul needs to learn in order to make us a better spiritual being. We choose our lessons and head off to "School-house Earth." We come to learn to be better souls and to make the planet and the universe a better place to live.

It Starts with You, Me, and *Everyone*...

It's as if the wisdom contained in each lesson is a small piece of a larger jigsaw puzzle that is our life. The more pieces I put together, the clearer the picture becomes—and the more meaning my life seems to take on, as I realize that there really is more to life than just living and dying.

We're here for a reason. We're definitely, as the saying goes, all in this thing called "Life" together. We need to learn to get along, communicate better, and help one another in whatever ways we can.

It's my belief that this world can be an amazing place for all who live here, but we obviously have a long way to go. It starts with you, me, and *everyone* doing our parts to make the world a better place. No one person alone is going to save the world, but together we can truly turn things around.

CHAPTER 14

1992–1996:

An Inferno of Litigation, Non-Stop Fear, and a Search for Answers

---

"There is no 'sin' as such since there is no eternal punishment. There is only experience. All human souls will eventually be redeemed through the law of Karma, maturation, and the assimilation of knowledge and wisdom. Today's murderer will become tomorrow's master of enlightenment. Christ's parable of the Prodigal Son cryptically reveals to humanity its own destiny: return to the palace of the loving father after the trials and tribulations of earthly lives."[1]

–Kyriacos Markides, *Homage to the Sun: The Wisdom of the Magus of Strovolos*

C uac here again. I'll pick up the story in 1991, the time of the business mishap I mentioned earlier.

The Business Side of Life

By this time, Rob DeSimone and I had begun to develop a pretty grandiose vision for a motel property in which we had acquired a 50 percent interest in 1988. We were going to call it the "Bar Harbor Oceanfront Resort" and create a project that was a cross between a make-believe castle straight out of a fairy tale and a grand old turn-of-the-century hotel from the Gilded Era.

Excitedly envisioning a stately exterior of pristine white and a red roof featuring numerous turrets, we intended to incorporate design elements from three classic American hotels: the historic Mount Washington Hotel in New Hampshire's White Mountains, Walt Disney World's famed Grand Floridian Beach Resort, and the San Diego area's magical Hotel Del Coronado. (Interestingly enough, we later learned that the Hotel Del Coronado was built in 1888 and was a favorite of L. Frank Baum, author of *The Wizard of Oz*, who did a lot of his writing there and reputedly modeled the "Emerald City" after his beloved lodging establishment.) Rob and I also had plans to include a lighthouse containing luxury suites in the project, using as a model the oft-photographed Pemaquid Point Light in southern Maine.

11-11-91

On November 11, 1991, I received a phone call from our lawyer that totally changed my life. Up until that point, my career was progressing steadily along a life path Rob DeSimone and I had set up when we were nineteen and first became business partners. During that fateful phone call on 11-11-91, however, our attorney informed me that what had been expected to be a fairly routine legal dispute (on a transaction we had attempted to broker for my "Grammy Al" as she sought to sell her inn to a prospective purchaser) had erupted into a major piece of litigation.

Although I did not realize it at the time, this brief November 11, 1991, telephone conversation would be the beginning of a seemingly endless odyssey through the court system that would consume the next decade-plus of my life. Little did I know then that I would one day look back upon 11-11-91 as the date from which numerous lawsuits, involving literally dozens of lawyers, would spring, transforming my business career into "a train wreck."

Anticipating that we would secure financing to buy our partners' 50 percent interest in the motel, Rob DeSimone and I had previously put down nonrefundable monies toward the transaction. When the aforementioned litigation mushroomed, we lost our financing for the deal. This, combined with the financial drain that had resulted from that litigation, left us unable to continue making our bank payments as of the end of 1992. By the spring of 1993, the bank had begun foreclosure action in court and placed the motel property under receivership. This, in turn, precipitated yet more litigation in the form of legal troubles with our partners.

Our litigation nightmare continued to snowball during the next eighteen months, as suits and countersuits flew back and forth, with more and more law firms entering the fray. This period of time witnessed a constant financial struggle for Rob DeSimone, Jeff Butterfield, and me. Jeff was—and is—a dear friend and longtime business colleague who was involved in all of our ventures and whose life was inextricably intertwined with Rob's, Phyl's, and mine. Just for us to have enough money to eat and keep the utilities turned on was tough during much of this time.

Rob, Jeff, and I were working literally full-time on the multiheaded litigation monster, as we sought to salvage the motel project and protect the equity that we had worked since age nineteen to build. Enmeshed in a mystic maze of lawsuits that many of the lawyers involved termed the most complex cumulative legal matter that they had ever seen in their careers, the two of us struggled to digest the voluminous amounts of documents and to help our attorneys sort things out.

Phyl, continuing to work all this time in the special education field, had maxed out her credit cards, borrowing tens of thousands of dollars in an effort to help us attempt to protect the project's future. Jeff, who was to be our partner in the project if it came to fruition, worked side by side, year after year with Rob and me, even borrowing money against his automobile to help the team survive the storm.

At one time, money got so scarce that the four of us were forced to use my Grammy Al's Mobil credit card for two months so that we could eat out of the local convenience store. The low point, however, was when we had run out of oil at the home office where Rob DeSimone lived and where he, Jeff, and I worked in what we referred to as "The War Room." The pipes soon froze and remained that way for two days, as the three of us worked huddled together indoors with our winter jackets on. Because of a pressing court deadline for written briefs in one of the cases, we weren't even able to take the time to find someone from whom to borrow $50 for a minimum delivery of oil.

At the end of 1994, Rob and I reached a settlement that concluded the part of the litigation involving the original real estate transaction that had begun our legal woes. Although this provided us with some much-needed financial relief, it was not enough to stop the foreclosure action on the motel.

The litigation surrounding the motel raged for nearly two more years. At one point in 1995, Rob, Jeff, and I thought we had all of our problems solved when a business colleague introduced us to SunAmerica. The financial firm made arrangements to buy out our partners' interests in the project, put funds in escrow, and was ready to help us complete development of the property. Alas, it was not to be, as final deal points between the parties could not be worked out.

In February of 1996, the 50 percent interest in the motel belonging to Rob and me went up for auction. After our partners ended up as the high bidders, more litigation followed during the next several months. The result was that the auction sale was not consummated, and an agreement was reached by all parties that seemed to make sense for everyone involved: We would split the property, our partners would keep the existing motel, a new bank would come into the deal, and, after two years, we would get the vacant shorefront land upon which to build the Bar Harbor Oceanfront Resort.

On August 24, 1996, settlement papers were executed by all of the feuding factions, finally putting to rest years of turmoil for all involved. After stacks of legal documents were signed, we gathered beside the motel's pool with our former partners and drank a glass of champagne together, toasting a future that seemed designed to allow everyone to flourish.

Finally, the fighting was over. No more bitter litigation. And although the years in the court system had left Rob and me with major legal bills and other financial obligations that would take a while to pay off, our long-term financial future seemed at last secured. Life looked good.

But What Was Going on Inside of My Soul Back Then?

As just recounted, the phone call I received from our lawyer on November 11, 1991, ended up being a curveball in my business career that set in motion an extended series of events that drastically altered the game plan I had established for my life. I had intended to work very hard until I was forty, and then spend my forties doing things with the fruits of my labor for the individuals and institutions that had been so good to me in my life. I most especially wished to be able to help the many relatives of both my immediate and extended families, as well as to do something significant for both Milton Academy and Bowdoin College for the wonderful education that those schools' generosity had provided me. At fifty, I had planned to begin a long-held desire to study the spiritual aspects of life.

As my journey into "Lawyer Land" unfolded, I started asking myself why such a change in plans could have happened after so much hard work and careful planning. As I reflected about this more and more, words from my early days at Milton came back to me.

You see, during one of my first days on campus, I can remember my all-time favorite academic teacher, A. O. Smith, saying to our freshman English class, "Nothing in a work of art, whether it is a novel, poem, or painting, happens by chance, but by design."

Reasoning that Life is the ultimate "work of art," I gradually found myself seeking answers in my attempt to understand the bumps in the road I was encountering. In short, my interest in exploring the spiritual part of existence got moved up on the schedule in my self-styled personal syllabus.

When the Student's Ready, the Teacher Appears

A couple of years before I received the fateful 11-11-91 phone call regarding the business litigation, our Aunt Lara gave me a book that became the starting point for my investigation of spiritual matters. It was the same one she had shared with Paul: *The Magus of Strovolos*, Professor Kyriacos Markides's book about the spiritual healer named Daskalos. Up until that point, the vast majority of my reading–at least since I had gotten out of college–had been about the business world. For instance, when Donald Trump's first book, *The Art of the Deal*, came out in 1987, I read it twice over and immediately bought multiple copies to give to relatives and friends.

Because my overriding focus was on making progress in my career, I didn't feel like I had the time to do the type of "pleasure reading" that had formed such an integral part of my youth. Other than reading an occasional novel by Robert Ludlum and allowing myself the rare treat of escaping into a few comic books now and then, almost all of my reading as an adult had been geared toward helping me learn about various aspects of business.

Well, when the universe began to sprinkle its little bag of surprises down on my carefully constructed life plan, I had no choice but to "find the time" to read. If I was going to have any chance of surviving the litigation conflagration and avoid having a complete nervous breakdown, then I needed to see if there was any information out there that could help shed light on why things were going so wrong.

And so it is against this backdrop that Lara's gift found its way into my hands. When I had first picked up *The Magus of Strovolos* two years prior to this, I had no idea what impact it would have on my life. Still feeling guilty about spending time reading anything other than business topics, I initially thought I would read only the beginning of the book–out of politeness, because it had been a gift.

After several pages, I said to myself: *This stuff's pretty interesting. I think I'll read some more.* By the time I had finished a few chapters, I was thinking: *This book is helping me get a little insight into how life works. I'm definitely finishing it.* Once I had completed Professor Markides's story about Daskalos, I felt like I had learned more from it than any other book I had ever read. Simply put, it seemed like I had found a roadmap for existence.

Betty Eadie's *Embraced by the Light* Blows Me Away

"Above all, I was shown that love is supreme....
We are here to have love for every person on earth."[2]
                                        –Betty Eadie, *Embraced by the Light*

As I wove my way back and forth between struggling to survive the raging legal inferno and attempting to understand a little more about spirituality, 1994 brought another book into my life that really resonated with me: Betty Eadie's fascinating narration of her near-death experience, *Embraced by the Light.* Although there were many books I was reading (sometimes a few at the same time) as the full fury of my business litigation unfurled itself, *Embraced by the Light* was one that I ended up going through over and over again.

An incredibly detailed chronicling of what the author learned and experienced when she visited Heaven after clinically "dying" during a hospital stay, *Embraced by the Light* gave me renewed hope as I tried to cope with my professional career being turned upside down. *Embraced by the Light* provided me a lot of positive things to cling to at a time when I was having trouble just getting out of bed each morning. The book made facing day after day of fighting the wars in court and scrambling for money to keep the bill collectors at bay a little bit more bearable. Some of the things that really stood out to me in *Embraced by the Light* were:

- Confirmation that there was indeed a purpose for literally each and every thing that happens to us in our lives—all ultimately designed to further the spiritual advancement of our souls.[3]

- An explanation of how unconditional love awaits us all in Heaven.[4]

- An insight into fear that I had never before heard, but instantly, and instinctively, recognized as containing a very important truth: "*...fear is the opposite of love...*"[5]

- *Embraced by the Light* also explained that fear is "Satan's greatest tool."[6]

I wasn't certain whether I believed in the existence of Satan, but I knew for sure, based on my own experiences in life, that the basic principle Betty Eadie was explaining sure made sense to me: that fear was the most powerful weapon of whatever or whomever one wishes to call the negative forces at work in existence.

Just as I have since learned many of Betty Eadie's other readers did, I bought additional copies of *Embraced by the Light* for family members and friends whenever I could afford it. The book brought such a persuasive and dynamic message of love and tolerance that it made me want to share it with as many people as possible.

At one point, I even daydreamed about how, if I were to win one of those big $100 million dollar plus lotteries, I might be able to use a significant portion of the proceeds to buy a copy of *Embraced for the Light* for every family in the country. At the very least, perhaps such a fortuitous turn of events would make it possible to buy prime-time television airtime on all the major networks simultaneously so that the entire nation could hear what Mrs. Eadie had to say. Farfetched musings, perhaps, but they underscore the dramatic effect that her book was having on my life.

Although written from a Christian perspective, I felt that the information Betty Eadie brought back from her visit to Heaven contained knowledge of universal importance to people of all beliefs–or nonbeliefs. Indeed, even if one didn't share the author's spiritual perspective or accept her experience as "valid," I thought that being exposed to *Embraced by the Light* would be a thought-provoking and exciting exercise for anyone.

I Assign a Value to My Emerging Spiritual Education

As I sought to glean some modest degree of understanding about what had been going on in my life during the mid-1990s, I began to develop a knowing in my heart about just how important my inquiry into spiritual matters had become to me. I began to realize that I would not trade whatever modicum of insight I had gained about our existence here on Earth for all of the business success I had anticipated having achieved by that point in life.

The Stage Has Now Been Set

So there you have it. You now know where things stood on both the personal and the business sides of my life as of the fateful summer of 1996. I am going to turn things over at this point to my wife, Phyl. Not only did she live all of this with me, but, from the moment of this book's conception, she has been the fourth participant in this endeavor. Indeed, Jane, Paul, and I have relied on Phyl's support, involvement, and assistance from the very beginning of this wonderful odyssey.

And so, without further ado, here's Phyl to give you some background information about herself, a take on our life together from her perspective, and a description of what happened next. What she is about to tell you is a very pivotal part of the Macomber family's voyage into the unknown.

CHAPTER 15

Phyl's Story: Family, Friends, and Florence

My name is Phyl Totaro Macomber. I am the oldest daughter of Bertha and Leonard Totaro.

This warm and kind couple couldn't have children after they had married in 1953 and so adopted me on September 16, 1961, my "homecoming" from St. Joseph's Orphanage in Scranton, Pennsylvania. The nuns at St. Joseph's saw me come into this world seven weeks earlier and took care of me until the day I became a Totaro. Ever since I wailed endlessly as my parents carried me down those stone steps on the grounds of the orphanage, my Mom and Daddy knew I would have a lot to say in life.

I was raised in Old Forge, a small, predominately Italian town in northeastern Pennsylvania that is the self-proclaimed "Pizza Capital of the World." Not many kids could say that their grandmother lived with them and helped raise them, had their Uncle Chick's barbershop in their home, and, because of his love of music, knew the words to many popular Frank Sinatra songs by the age of seven.

When I was younger, I thought everyone had the type of home life that I shared with my family. I truly believe—now that I think back to that time—that I thought *everyone* lived in an Italian neighborhood. That's all I knew. It was the type of place where older gentlemen smoking cigars would hang out on street corners and kitchens smelled of fresh-baked Italian bread, with large pots of spaghetti sauce bubbling on the stove.

I grew up Catholic and, thanks to the hard and dedicated work of my parents, attended parochial school through eighth grade. The two of them always emphasized the importance of religion and education.

As far back as I can remember, when my father would return home from his work at the Texaco Oil Company plant with his pay, he and my Mom would close the bedroom door and apportion the money for the family's bills. But what I didn't realize back then was that they took money from each paycheck (and that wasn't an easy task) to set aside funds for both my sister's and my college education.

As I grew older, I came to embrace a far broader and more diverse view of spirituality that went beyond Catholicism. I could never understand why one religion claimed to be "right." How could all the others be "wrong"? So, as I progressed along my spiritual journey, I adopted varying views of what felt right to me. And what "felt right" were concepts that consistently fell under the umbrella of love and kindness.

My Daddy always told me that when faced with a decision, I should not do something because I *thought* it was right. Rather, he advised that I should do something because I *felt* it was right. Simply put, my father was the first person to teach me to follow my intuition and inner voice. That advice has served me well over the years.

"Islands are romantic. Magical. Where dreams come true."

—A quote from a magazine article lost long ago

Beginning at age four, I talked about moving to New England. When playing with the kids in my neighborhood, I used to pretend that I was a businesswoman. I'd carry around a piece of cardboard as a briefcase, saying that I was "moving to Boston to own my own business!" My mother used to shake her head and exclaim, "Where does this child get this stuff from?"

Something—even at that young age—just felt "right" about going to New England. Something was drawing me farther north. I now believe it was my connection to Cuac. No, I *know* it was my connection to Cuac.

When I was in graduate school, I was persuaded by my schoolmates to go on a camping trip to Bar Harbor, Maine, which they said was located on someplace called "Mount Desert Island." I say "persuaded" because I was exhausted from taking summer courses and wanted to recuperate prior to the start of the fall term. I relented, however, as one of them was counting on my supposedly reliable vehicle to make the trek north. Her name was "Margie," the green Chrysler Newport that was my trusty steed throughout my college days.

The idea of going to a part of the world that was supposed to be so beautiful sealed the deal for me. My college roommate (who had recently been diagnosed with M.S.) and I arrived in Acadia National Park around 11:15 at night on August 16, 1986. It was a clear night. I had never seen so many stars in the sky.

We were looking for Blackwoods Campground to meet the remainder of our friends. I attempted to turn left onto the Ocean Drive Park Loop Road when Margie lost her steering. At 11:30 P.M., I started to walk down the road with a flashlight to go to a phone at the visitor's center. Then I saw headlights coming toward me.

It was Cuac. He stopped and said in his rather unusual sounding accent, "May I be of some assistance?" I stared into his blue eyes and, well, I guess you can gather that these are the same blue eyes I gaze into every day.

A Tip from "Coach"

Although I refer to my husband by his longtime nickname of "Cuac," my personal nickname for him is "Missing Piece," taken from Shel Silverstein's wonderful story, *The Missing Piece*. That is because I felt, when Cuac and I began seeing each other in 1988, I had finally found the part of life that made me whole as a human being.

Soon realizing that I couldn't be apart from Cuac, I moved to Maine in 1989. Living there for eight years with Cuac was a wonderful experience—despite the significant business challenges that we faced.

I enjoyed maintaining a regular exercise regimen—especially during the long winter season—and was quickly getting to know people in my new "neighborhood." A woman I dubbed "Coach" taught my favorite exercise class. Coach's real name was Wendy Sumner, an energetic, kind, funny, athletic instructor who conducted challenging fitness classes at Fitness East Health Club.

Wendy and I became fast friends. It felt like we had known each other forever. As you will see, the two of us formed a connection that was literally life changing.

You may be familiar with the concept of "six degrees of separation," the term used to describe how people are often connected in some way. Well, Wendy knew Cuac from his hometown of Castine. She knew all the Macombers! And, unbeknownst to her, I was Cuac's girlfriend!

Wendy was related to two of Cuac's childhood chums. One was his dear friend, David Bowden, and the other, Bruce Bowden, his longtime grammar school classmate. Bruce had died in a tragic car accident when he was in his late teens. Bruce's father (Wendy's grandfather), Ormy Bowden, was a former Castine fisherman who was good friends with Cuac's father, Bob, and his uncle, Bill Macomber. "Small world," as the saying goes.

Looking back, I can see that Wendy and I became connected for a reason. As time went on, we both engaged in a continuing dialogue about spirituality and worldviews at the gym.

And then Wendy introduced me to a woman who was about to change my life. Her name was Wanda Adkins.

"Who is going to Florence?"

I will never forget standing in the weight room that Saturday afternoon when Wendy enthusiastically shared with me the visit that she had had with a retired nurse named Wanda Adkins. Wendy explained that Wanda was a psychic who had the ability to see images and get messages from The Other Side. Wanda had explained to Wendy that she had had this gift since she was young and that, after retiring from the nursing profession, she had decided to do readings for people for free.

From previous conversations we had had, Wendy knew that Cuac and I were interested in having a psychic reading with the well-known psychic George Anderson, who lived in New York. Consequently, Wendy thought we might both be interested in meeting Wanda Adkins.

Between repetitions and multiple sets of bicep curls and tricep dips, Wendy shared her experience of the long visit that she had had with Wanda in the psychic's living room. Wendy was fascinated that Wanda, whom she had never met prior to that visit, was sharing details about past and future events related to Wendy's life—including very accurate, specific, personal information about *and from* Wendy's long-dead cousin, Cuac's boyhood friend, Bruce Bowden. (Bruce, interestingly enough, was the person who gave Cuac his long-standing nickname when the two of them were in grammar school together.)

The detail that stopped me in my tracks, however, was when Wendy told me that Wanda had inquired who "Florence" was. Wendy went on to explain to Wanda that she did not know any "Florence."

Wanda then paused and corrected herself, saying, "Not who. It is a place. Who is going to Florence?" Wendy replied that she had a friend who was planning a trip to Italy. Wanda responded, "Tell your friend that something significant is going to happen to her when she is in Florence."

As you have probably guessed, I was the friend going to Italy. I was planning a trip with my father and my sister and would be leaving in August. Florence was the last stop in our two-week itinerary. And Wanda Adkins had never even heard of me before.

"It will change your life."

My first visit with Wanda was on July 18, 1996. After I got her phone number from Wendy, Cuac called, made an appointment, and was careful not to reveal any details about the two of us.

I honestly did not have any high expectations about this meeting that turned out to be an experience to remember. In fact, I was quite cautious about my interactions with this woman. It was, however, the quantity of unique and meaningful messages and symbols conveyed by the spirit world to this retired nurse that made me realize this was the real deal. When receiving a message or a symbol from The Other Side, Wanda would share it with me, sometimes asking me what it meant. Since she explained that she was simply passing on messages, I would then validate the information with a short response.

An example of this was when Wanda shared a vision that she saw of two elderly people who came to her—a man and a woman—with their heads turned in toward each other. As Wanda demonstrated the body posture to me, I knew that it was my maternal grandparents. You see, the only photograph that I had of my grandparents together was on the summer porch of the home on

Oak Street where I grew up. Wanda had, unbeknownst to her, demonstrated to me their exact pose in the photograph.

My maternal grandfather, Caesar Scaccia, was a barber. In fact, his barber chair serves as the centerpiece of our living room. A hardworking man, he longed to own his home free of debt. Around the time that the final mortgage payment was to be made to the bank, my Grampa Caesar had a massive stroke in his barbershop and died that evening. It was New Year's Eve 1948. The last photograph that had been taken of him and my grandmother together was just prior to his passing.

Wanda did not know any of this information. In fact, Wanda knew nothing about me.

When describing her vision of this couple, Wanda went on to say that she needed to inquire about something that didn't make sense to her. Wanda asked, "Why would this man be holding a pair of scissors?"

Well, needless to say, Wanda had my ear from that moment on.

Without any mention of it at all from me, Wanda inquired about Florence. Before I had the chance to respond, Wanda stated, "I see a plane go up and I see a plane go down. Who's taking a trip?"

Wanda then reiterated the same message she had gotten when Wendy had visited, saying that a significant life event was going to happen to me when I visited Florence. In fact, her words were, "It will change your life."

During the reading, Wanda explained that she was seeing repeated images of hundreds of clay pots around me. She asked if I was a potter. I replied that I was not. Wanda went on to ask if I was taking a trip down south in the near future. She said that she saw lots of magnolia trees above my head and wondered if I might be going to the Carolinas. I replied that I was not. Wanda then said, "Take it with you, dear."

As you can guess, when I left for Italy on August 29, 1996, I could not get out of my mind Wanda's words about my upcoming time in Florence. The long plane ride over the Atlantic offered a time for me to share this story with my sister and father. Although fascinated by the details, the focus of this trip for them—and for me—was to meet our family in Manfredonia and to tour Rome, Venice, and Florence. The first stop was Rome.

After spending three days in the Eternal City, my father returned back to our room at the Grand Hotel with a brochure outlining a day trip to the island of Capri. Although this was an unplanned journey on our itinerary, my sister and I were eager to take the ferry to this magical place. Having learned about the Blue Grotto from the famous Sophia Loren movie, *It Started in Naples*, we quickly agreed with Daddy's suggestion and headed off with him.

After touring the island's two towns, Capri and Anacapri, our tour group stopped for a hearty Italian lunch at a small café. As we exited the establishment to return to the boat, my sister rushed me along so that we could meet back up with the group and not lose them.

As I turned around to joke with Rosie, I stopped dead in my tracks, staring at my sister in disbelief. A puzzled look came over her face as she observed the strange expression on mine. I didn't hear a word my sister was saying to me. My gaze was fixed on the hundreds of clay pots behind her and all of the blossoming magnolia trees above her head.

"Maybe Wanda was just plain wrong."

Visiting my paternal grandparents' homeland in Manfredonia—walking the streets where our father's mother ("Nana Zusep") had sold fish, touring the old church that our grandparents had attended as children, and gazing out at the Adriatic Sea—was an emotional experience for all of us.

Many tears were shed when we presented to our non-English speaking Totaro family a large framed wall hanging, marking the date my grandparents' names were added to the wall at Ellis Island, commemorating their immigration to the United States. Although our Italian relatives and we didn't speak the same language, it was evident to me that love can be expressed without words.

After experiencing the magic of Venice for three days, my excitement on the train ride to Florence was hard to contain. Sitting in the dining car, eating a biscotti and drinking a cappuccino, Rosie and I wondered when a "Wanda-ism" would pop up and, more significantly, how it would change my life.

Our time in Florence was filled with appreciating art and architecture, drinking Chianti, and eating great food. The night before we left Florence, Rosie and Daddy were busy packing and getting ready for the train ride back to Rome the next day, which marked the conclusion of our trip. I, on the other hand, was sitting on the rooftop terrace of our hotel, The Baglioni—with a view of the magnificent Duoma so close it seemed like I could reach out and touch it.

As I gazed out onto the city of Florence, I was reflecting back to Wanda's words about how something was going to happen while I was there that would change my life. Although a wonderful ending to our two-week journey, nothing *significant* occurred while I was in Florence—certainly nothing "life changing."

I thought to myself, *Well, maybe it will happen another time that I am here...or, maybe Wanda was just plain wrong.*

CHAPTER 16

Meanwhile, Back in the U.S.A.

Paul here again, folks. In April of 1996, I had moved off of the island of Nantucket and was visiting with family members before I was to move to Mill Valley, California, in May to work with my friend Andrew Zenoff. I found out I was indicted on the drug charges the night before I was scheduled to fly to California, while visiting with my niece and mother in New York City.

After discovering the very serious situation I now found myself in, I had to postpone my trip, research and retain the appropriate attorney, and then surrender myself to the Nantucket Police Department. It took me over six weeks to find who I thought was the right lawyer, so it was now the beginning of June before I departed for California. I knew I would have to return to face the charges at some point, but my attorney said we would apply for continuances when my court dates came up. It would probably be at least a year before my trial would begin.

After the previous five years of living on Nantucket, exercising very little and partying quite a lot, I wasn't in the best physical, mental, or spiritual shape. I was forty to fifty pounds overweight and had only read a few spiritual books during my entire stay on Nantucket.

When I arrived in California, I was determined that this would be the beginning of a new life filled with health and spirituality. I knew I needed a complete change in lifestyle if I wanted to achieve the happiness and goals I wanted in this lifetime.

My college friend Andrew suggested I take the rest of the summer off before starting my job so I could get in shape and do a little soul-searching. I agreed it was a good idea, so I bought a new bike, joined a gym, and starting reading as many spiritual books as I could get my hands on.

On a typical weekday that summer I read in bed when I first woke up, had breakfast with my friend, biked to the gym, worked out for two hours, and then rode my bike, exploring Marin County for another four to six hours. Upon returning home, I'd have dinner with my friend, chat for a while, and then retire to my room to read for two or three hours before going to sleep. On weekends we would usually spend our days relaxing at the beach, reading books, and sharing conversation.

I Find My First Ruth Montgomery Book

By the time September rolled around, I had lost forty pounds, read dozens of inspiring spiritual books, and was ready to begin work with my friend in his new start-up business. It was during this period that I found my first Ruth Montgomery book.

I was living in Mill Valley, literally right around the corner from the public library. Having not worked all summer and living mostly off the generosity of my old college buddy, I didn't have a great deal of money for the many books I was reading and would often go to the library to find my next one. And so it was there at the Mill Valley Public Library that I came across my first Ruth Montgomery book, in what must have been late July or early August of 1996. It was *Strangers Among Us*.

I found the book's subject matter to be absolutely fascinating; it was, as you know, about Walk-ins. *Strangers Among Us* also spoke of catastrophic Earth Changes in the not-too-distant future and humanity's need to start uniting as a race. Ruth Montgomery's book explained that we needed to learn to work together better so that, when these changes take place, we will be prepared to deal with them.

Strangers Among Us seemed to say that we all have a choice to make. On the one hand, we can keep going down our present path: destroying the only place we have to live, Planet Earth, and killing one another as we squabble among ourselves like a bunch of immature kids. The end result of this course will be that things will continue to deteriorate for both the Earth and ourselves, with catastrophic results for both. Or, in the alternative, human beings can start sharing in the abundance that is here. There is more than enough for all of us. To me, Ruth Montgomery's book quite clearly says that we need to start taking care of the planet and to appreciate everything that it provides for all of us.

I Wanted to Share It with My Brother Rob

After having found *Strangers Among Us* to be so interesting, I wanted to share it with my brother Rob, who by then was interested in discussing a broad range of spiritual topics.

I soon sent Rob a copy of *Strangers Among Us*. Then, after just having read another one of Ruth Montgomery's books, *Threshold to Tomorrow,* a follow-up to *Strangers Among Us*–again, about Walk-ins and the parts they are playing here on Earth to make the world a better place–I sent him a copy of that one as well.

After reading the first two books by Ruth that I had discovered, I eagerly searched out the other books she had written with the help of her Spirit Guides through the automatic writing process. Each one of them was as riveting as the first two. It wasn't long before I had read most of them.

Both before and since reading the Ruth Montgomery titles, Rob and I have traded books with each other that we have found to be of interest. Most of these have had some type of spiritual theme, leading us to countless questions, making for many hours of interesting phone conversations about a wide array of subjects and causing us to explore and exchange our views on many different matters. It is like an ongoing adventure with a best friend, who also happens to be your brother, investigating the biggest mystery of all: Life itself and why we're here.

CHAPTER 17

And While Phyl Was in Italy

I t's Cuac back at the keyboard.

Although I was truly thrilled for Phyl that she was away on this "once-in-a-lifetime" trip with, as I call them, "Dad Totaro" and "Sister Rosie," I also missed Phyl's companionship in the routine of our daily life together in Bar Harbor. And because it had only been a week since we had at long last ended the many years of bitter litigation, I was more than a little bit sad to see her go, just when it seemed like we were resuming a normal life. During Phyl's absence, I ended up doing a lot of aimless walking around Bar Harbor's shopping district, causing a friend of ours to say subsequently to Phyl, "Cuac looked lost while you were away. I was wondering if the two of you had split up."

Several days after Phyl departed on her trip, my brother Paul sent me a copy of a spiritually oriented book that he suggested I read. Although I had been doing a good deal of reading on this topic, Paul had been doing more—and was always interested in sharing materials that might be of interest. Time and time again, I would go to the post office and find yet another thoughtful, generous gift of a book from my youngest sibling waiting for me.

When I got the package from Paul that arrived shortly after Phyl left for Italy, I strolled down Bar Harbor's Cottage Street and opened it up as I walked back to the apartment where Phyl and I lived. I noticed that it had been written by a lady named Ruth Montgomery. The name rang a bell in my head. *Wait a minute. Wasn't that the author whom the psychic, Wanda Adkins, had recommended to Phyl and me?*

"This stuff's pretty far-out—even for me."

When I got home, I looked through some papers in the home office that Phyl and I shared, to see whether I could find the piece of paper on which I had jotted notes during our visit with Mrs. Adkins. I found a scrap of paper from the amazing evening we had spent with that wondrous lady and, sure enough, there was the scribbled name "Ruth Montgomery." I then remembered having thought to myself at the time that Wanda had enthusiastically brought up Ruth Montgomery's name as a leading author of spiritual material. *Huh, I've come across a fair amount on this topic, but I've never heard of this lady.*

I would later realize this musing to myself was a telling indicator that I didn't know as much as I thought I did, how important it is to always keep an open mind about new knowledge in any area of life, and the vast quantity of information available to all of us if we are truly interested in venturing into unexplored territory, whatever our area of inquiry happens to be.

I then turned my attention back to the Ruth Montgomery book that Paul had sent me. It was called *Strangers Among Us*. As I read the back cover and flipped through a few pages, I was a little put off. *Walk-ins? Soul transferrals?* I remember then thinking to myself: *This stuff's pretty far-out—even for me.*

The copy of *Strangers Among Us* that Paul had sent me seemed destined to soon head to the bookcase and join the crowded ranks of unread books.

And then, just a few days later, Paul sent me another one of Ruth Montgomery's books, *Threshold to Tomorrow*. With it, he enclosed a note that said something along the lines of: "Rob, I don't know if you've had a chance to look at the first one I sent you by this woman, but I hope that you'll read these books. I really think that this lady's got some important things to say."

That did it. I respected my brother too much not to follow up on his suggestion. If Paul had read some of this writer's stuff and felt like it contained information worthwhile enough to send me two of her books, one right after the other, then how could I not read them?

An Unlikely Messenger

As I read through *Strangers Among Us* and *Threshold to Tomorrow*, I soon realized that Mrs. Montgomery's books contained much more than the radical concept of Walk-ins. Indeed, although I found the possibility of transference of souls more compelling than I had expected, what I found most persuasive about these two books was their explanation of how the Earth itself is a living being that is being forced to respond to mankind's horrible treatment. Although I had previously heard of this notion of "Earth Changes," I had never paid much attention to the whole idea.

The case that Ruth's Guides made for humanity having to, in my own simplistic karmic terms, "pay the piper" for our ongoing and intensive abuse of the planet's natural resources just plain made sense to me. In *Strangers Among Us* and *Threshold to Tomorrow*, I found the spirits' argument that *everything* is interconnected—including our well-being as a race to the "health" of the Earth itself, as well as all of us human beings to each other—to be rooted in good old-fashioned common sense.

To paraphrase Popeye, the idea that "Mother Nature's had all She can stands and She can't stands no more" seemed pretty logical to me. If our own bodies can end up on overload and throw up when we get sick or abuse them by overindulging with food and drink, why wouldn't it stand to reason that mankind's non-stop assault on the environment should produce similar results from Mother Nature?

What I read in Mrs. Montgomery's books just *felt* right. There's no other way to explain it. Although I had read plenty of other books that dealt with reincarnation, karma, and other spiritual topics, there was something about the information she conveyed from her Spirit Guides that had an incredibly powerful impact on me.

As a businessperson who had long looked at land from a real estate perspective, with development potential and future profits in the forefront of my mind, I had never seriously considered the possibility that the Earth itself was anything but a resource for man to use for his chosen endeavors and personal pleasures. Although I firmly believed that owners have a civic responsibility to develop their property in a tasteful, aesthetically pleasing manner, I was also a strong proponent of private property rights.

In short, I was not a card-carrying "tree hugger" who might be deemed a perfect candidate to be moved by messages from Heaven about the need to save the environment. The bottom line is that I was more interested in cutting trees down to maximize development potential and open up water views than I was in saving them.

Earth Changes

In spite of seeming to be an ill-suited recipient of such news from The Other Side about the growing potential for significant Earth Changes resulting from humanity's abuse of the environment, I found Mrs. Montgomery's writings touched something deep inside the core of my being. Her Guides warned that the turn of the century and the change of the millennium brought with them the threat of tremendous upheavals of the planet in the form of major earthquakes, increased volcanic activity, and violent storms with dangerously high winds and torrential rains. Most disturbing were the Guides' prediction that some portions of the world's existing coastlines would be submerged under water as a result of the anticipated Earth Changes.[1]

During the same few days that I was reading the two Ruth Montgomery books Paul had sent me, I was also watching some tapes of the A&E channel's *Ancient Mystery* shows that I had accumulated but never gotten around to watching. One of them included a segment on a futurist named Gordon-Michael Scallion who made predictions based on visions he had.

Like Ruth Montgomery's Guides, Mr. Scallion saw difficult times ahead for our planet, including a shifting of the Earth on its axis, with expected Earth Changes around the turn of the century producing major upheavals all over the globe. Scallion, however, was even more specific about the geographic areas that would be most affected than Mrs. Montgomery's Guides had been—he had produced an actual map depicting which parts of the world would end up being submerged under water and which would not.

Gordon-Michael Scallion's future map of the world had the coast of Maine moved considerably inland. If the predicted Earth Changes were to take place, then Bar Harbor would be history. Although it defied all conventional logic, something inside of me told me that Phyl and I needed to move away from the water.

I decided that, when Phyl returned from her trip, I would tell her about the information I had been exposed to while she was in Italy and explain that I thought we needed to hedge our bets. I resolved to attempt to persuade the love of my life that we should uproot our entire existence and relocate somewhere else. Although I intended to keep working on the resort project and to split my time between Bar Harbor and wherever "somewhere else" turned out to be, I was totally committed to getting an inland base established away from the coast of Maine...where I had spent virtually my entire life.

But what would Phyl think about such a wild idea? About moving from Bar Harbor just when it seemed that my business career was back on track? About leaving a successful private practice in special education she had built in her own professional life?

I wasn't sure what Phyl would think about all of this, but I knew that I was going to talk to her about it when I picked her up at Logan Airport.

CHAPTER 18

"I Trust You
with
My Life"

Phyl here again.

I arrived at Logan Airport the evening of Friday, September 13, 1996. As the wheels touched down in Boston, I thought to myself how grateful I was that Cuac and I were finally on the path to resolving his long-term business problems and beginning what one would call a normal life.

You hear about those moments in life that touch you in a way you will never forget. Well, there in the distance, I saw an imprint in my mind that will forever be there: My Missing Piece—the one who made me whole—smiling with his blue eyes twinkling, yet looking a bit off-center.

I ran into his arms, buried my face into his chest, and squeezed him ever so tightly. And then, I looked up at his face, and Cuac said in a serious tone of voice, "Little Girl, I missed you. I am so happy you are home. I need to talk to you."

Flocks of people were passing us in the crowded corridor as the smile started to fade from my face. Cuac went on to say, "I do not

114

think that we are meant to live in Bar Harbor. In fact, I think that we need to move."

Puzzled by Cuac's statement, I looked at him quizzically. It was clear to him that I did not understand. I felt disoriented and started to realize I had not yet even gotten my luggage for us to head out of the airport.

At this point, Cuac started explaining to me that, in the previous several days, he had read some books by Ruth Montgomery that had changed his life. After a few minutes of discussion, intertwined with gathering my luggage from baggage claim, I interrupted him and took his hands in mine. I looked up at him and said, "Piece, I trust you with my life."

"It looked like Wanda Adkins knew what she was talking about after all."

I knew that we were entering an evening of long discussion at the historic Parker House Hotel, the establishment where Boston cream pie originated and where John F. Kennedy proposed to Jacqueline Bouvier. We were staying there before heading back up the coast to Maine the next day. Over dinner and drinks that night, Cuac explained all the information he had read concerning Earth Changes.

As I digested all of this, I came to understand that my life had indeed changed while I was in Florence. In piecing together the previous week of Cuac's activities in Bar Harbor, we both realized that he had read Ruth Montgomery's books during the exact time period in which I was in Florence, Italy. It looked like Wanda Adkins knew what she was talking about after all.

"We were both perfectly placed at that very time in life in September of 1996."

As you now know, we had spent the previous four years swimming upstream in Cuac's draining business situation in Bar Harbor.

During this time, he would often say to me, "Just another thirty days, Little Girl..." as a way to offer a ray of hopeful light at the end of the litigation tunnel.

When I had left for Italy, it had seemed that the scales were starting to tip in our favor and that our future together in Bar Harbor would be measured in decades. And now we were making a decision that was about to take our lives to the other side of New England.

Although I did not yet know at that time what my own mission was, something about Cuac's belief that we needed to relocate just "felt right" in terms of what we should be doing in our life together. In retrospect, I am absolutely certain about one thing concerning the few days he was in Bar Harbor, Maine, and I was in Florence, Italy: We were both perfectly placed at that very time in life in September of 1996.

CHAPTER 19

Cuac and Phyl
Head for
the Hills

I t's me, Cuac, resuming the role of narrator again.

The latter part of 1996 was a soul-searching time for Phyl and me. Were we really just going to pick up and leave Bar Harbor at the very time the litigation had finally ceased? Was it possible that we were going to relocate just when the dream of being able to make the "Bar Harbor Oceanfront Resort" a reality would be realized at long last?

As Phyl and I contemplated the gravity of the move to which we were beginning to commit ourselves, I decided to read some more of the books Ruth Montgomery had written. The more I digested of her Guides' transmissions about various topics, the more convinced I was that they were disseminating important information about mankind, our world, and the laws by which the universe operates—lofty subjects to be certain, but presented in such a practical, easy-to-read style that I found myself thinking: *What this Ruth Montgomery lady and her Guides are saying is filled with so much common sense, how can I possibly not take this stuff seriously?*

In addition to reading more Ruth Montgomery books, I also sought to learn if there were other materials that spoke about Earth Changes. In so doing, I soon found out that Nostradamus, the famed sixteenth-century prophet, and Edgar Cayce, the acclaimed twentieth-century clairvoyant, both had predicted some form of Earth Changes would occur around the turn of the century. *Maybe something very unusual was ahead for humanity. I just knew that getting a foothold somewhere inland away from the water felt like the right thing to do.*

On the other hand, I was reinvigorated by renewed hope that a groundbreaking ceremony for the long-envisioned resort project was just around the corner, as Rob DeSimone, Jeff Butterfield, and I rededicated ourselves to advancing our development plan. Although we were still hamstrung financially, we started scraping together some modest amounts of money so we could pay for the necessary professional fees to restart the architectural and engineering part of the process on the business endeavor that we all believed represented lifetime financial security and a dream come true.

When I broke the news to Rob and Jeff about the move Phyl and I were planning to make and the decidedly unconventional catalyst for our decision, the two of them couldn't have been better friends or more respectful of my feelings. I explained that while Phyl would be living full-time in our new location, I would be splitting my time between wherever "there" turned out to be and Bar Harbor and remaining active in our joint business affairs. Although Rob and Jeff said they thought I was having an extreme reaction to what I had read, they did not at all try to interfere with what Phyl and I intended to do.

But precisely where were we going to move? To help us figure that out, Phyl and I purchased a copy of Gordon-Michael Scallion's *Future Map of the World: 1998–2012.*

As we looked at Mr. Scallion's map and sought to determine what seemed like a "safe" area to consider for our relocation, we reviewed where he predicted the new coastlines of North America would be as of 2012. As Phyl and I studied Scallion's *Future Map of the World,* we developed a short list of what was important to us in selecting a place to which to move:

- We both liked the personalized lifestyle of living in a small New England village.

- Although the coast of Maine was a fun place to spend time in the summer months, Bar Harbor was a tourist town and, to a large degree, literally boarded up during the off-season. I was used to this from having grown up in Castine, but the long, quiet winters had always been a little difficult for Phyl. The two of us decided we would pick a place that was more of a four-season area, where things were open year-round.

- We wanted to be closer to Phyl's family in Old Forge, Pennsylvania. Because Bar Harbor is an eleven-hour drive from Phyl's hometown, we only got to see her family a couple of times a year.

- Being located closer to Boston was a priority for the two of us. Although we thoroughly enjoyed life in a small community, every once in a while we enjoyed getting, as Phyl puts it, "an urban fix."

"Woodstock it would be."

Based upon these criteria and the "safe areas" indicated on Mr. Scallion's map, Phyl and I decided that Vermont would be our choice. I told her that I knew of two communities in the state that were supposed to be very nice places to live, Woodstock and Stowe.

After looking at a map of the state and seeing that Woodstock was closer to Pennsylvania, Maine, and Boston than Stowe, we concluded that Woodstock is where we would go. It is a lovely small New England village that is open year-round. It is also equidistant from our two "home" areas, being located six-and-a-half hours from both Old Forge and the Bar Harbor/Castine area, and is only about two-and-a-half hours from Boston. Woodstock it would be.

Rough Waters Ahead

It's Phyl again, to continue the story.

In July of 1997, Cuac and I took a break from our moving plans and scheduled a second visit to see our new friend, the psychic, Wanda Adkins. Wanda greeted us warmly on a beautiful summer evening and invited us into her cozy living room, where we had met with her during our previous reading.

Within minutes of sitting down, Wanda turned her head swiftly, looked at me, and said, "Who's moving?" She went on to explain that she saw a pair of shiny new shoes at my feet, indicating to her a significant change or transition to a new place. I started chuckling, smiled at Cuac knowingly, and began to fill her in on our recent decision to relocate.

The three of us began to discuss Ruth Montgomery's work and some of Ruth's predictions for the world. (At that point, I had not yet read any of Ruth's books; after moving to Vermont, I read her last two.) Wanda stated that she herself was considering a move because of her own concern about Earth Changes.

Wanda, however, received no guidance from The Other Side that she could share with Cuac and me about the wisdom of our move to Vermont. It seems that we were being required to take a leap of faith in making such a dramatic change in our lives.

Wanda did tell the two of us that she saw more battles ahead in Cuac's business life. In fact, she stated that she saw "rough waters ahead–like white-water rapids," but that, just like floating down a river in a raft, we would reach "calm waters" again.

I questioned Wanda on this. I simply did not want to accept this prediction. We had had the settlement with our partners in August 1996. This was not supposed to happen. No more fighting. The litigation had ended. Our life was on a new track. Finally, peace...

Wanda explained to us that she tends to see things "around the bend." I found myself getting angry about this–and getting somewhat anxious. In fact, I said to myself that Wanda was dead wrong and refused to acknowledge that there could be fighting ahead for us.

CHAPTER 20

More Rough
Waters:
1999–2000

C uac back here with you on the keyboard.
Phyl and I followed through on our relocation plans and made
the move to Vermont in late 1997. For the next year, I shuttled back
and forth across New England, spending one week in Vermont and
the next in Bar Harbor, as Rob DeSimone, Jeff Butterfield, and I
made plans for our hotel development.

As 1999 began, it seemed our long wait to break ground on our
Bar Harbor Oceanfront Resort project was about to be over. Although our vacant shorefront land—which was serving as back-up
collateral for our former partners as part of resolving the initial litigation—had yet to be released by the bank that had provided the
new financing, our prior partners had decided that they wished to
sell the existing business and their portion of the real estate. Perhaps
it might still be possible to develop the property in its entirety.

Since our finances were still feeling the impact of being ravaged
by the previous years of litigation (the effects of which I feel to this
very day), Rob DeSimone and I were in need of a partner with a

strong balance sheet. So we approached the hotelier to whom we had sold the Bar Harbor Inn back in 1987, David Witham.

Over the years, we had come to recognize that David was an incredibly astute operator who had multiple lodging establishments and possessed a better understanding of the quantitative aspects of business than anyone we had ever met. Even more importantly, since he had sold his Hampton Beach, New Hampshire, properties and moved to Bar Harbor, Rob and I had come to view David as a good friend whom we could trust.

In early 1999, a series of business arrangements was struck between the various parties that would transfer control of our former partners' interest in the lodging property to David Witham, Rob DeSimone, and me. Initial documents were executed, preliminary development plans were sketched, and future financial projections were run. But, alas, it was not to be. For various reasons that ended up being the subject of yet more litigation, the deal never closed.

Later that year, our former partners didn't make their final bank payments for the season, plunging the motel property back into foreclosure. Since the vacant development land on which Rob, Jeff, and I intended to build the new hotel was still subject to the bank's mortgage, that meant our financial lives had been thrust back into the court system.

The words of Wanda Adkins had proved to be prophetic—my business life had entered "more rough waters."

How Could This Be Happening Again?

But what about the dire Earth Change predictions made by Ruth Montgomery's Guides with the coming of the twenty-first century? Although the Indonesian tsunami, Hurricane Katrina, and other natural disasters have certainly had a devastating impact on the lives of millions of people around the world, the predictions of Ruth Montgomery's Guides thankfully did not happen. No widespread geophysical calamities such as record-breaking earthquakes one right after the other or unprecedented volcanic eruptions occurred–nor did the dreaded "Y2K" disaster, involving the possibility of the world's computer systems crashing when the year 2000 rolled over on computers around the globe. Although I was quite aware that these things, which had been predicted, had not happened, my more immediate attention was on the chaos into which my business life had once again descended.

As the year 2000 got underway, I was back in "litigation mode"– full-time. Much to my great regret, I was revisiting the "Lawyer Land" that I thought I had left behind. Back in court with our former partners and desperately fighting the foreclosure action that threatened to auction off my dreams, the new millennium brought with it a level of personal fear the likes of which I had never before seen.

How could this be happening again? What had I done wrong? I thought that the 1996 settlement with our former partners had been a fair business deal for everyone and one that was morally correct. Why was this happening to me?

CHAPTER 21

2001– A Year of Change

D etermined not to lose virtually everything I had worked for since age nineteen, I was consumed with all of the legal issues surrounding the situation. These court battles took the vast majority of my time and virtually all of my mental energy. In short, I thought about little else. Even during the infrequent times when I might be going through the motions of doing something else, my mental attention was still mired in case details and legal strategy.

At one point, our father mentioned to me that his brother, our Uncle Bill, had asked him, "Why is Robbie spending so much time and energy on all of this stuff?"

I knew full well that implicit in my godfather's question was a very astute observation: *After all the spiritual exploration that Robbie has done, he should know better than still to be so preoccupied with the business world.*

I also knew that Uncle Bill was right. I felt in my heart that my uncle's words of concern were right on target and that I had allowed myself once again to get into a single-focus mode of life. The fog of fear in which I was enveloped had blinded my ability to reason with myself.

In spite of what my instincts were telling me, I kept thinking about how close I had come to building my long-sought Bar Harbor Oceanfront Resort development—and how I needed to scratch and claw to do everything I could to prevent my dreams from being sold off at auction.

Wondering Whether Ruth Montgomery Had a Successor

As 2001 rolled along, I decided to adopt a more balanced approach to life and develop a better sense of appreciation for all of my blessings. Sometime in August of that summer, I had a thought about a question that had never previously entered my mind: *Had Ruth Montgomery's Guides ever mentioned her having a successor when she passed on and moved to The Other Side?* After all, when Ruth had put out her last book in 1999, she had been very specific about the fact that *The World to Come* was her swan song.

Ruth's books had made it quite apparent that Lily, her principal Spirit Guide, was a very strong-willed fellow. It just didn't make sense to me that if Mrs. Montgomery died, Lily was going to be content to clam up and say to himself, "Well, we had a good run while it lasted. I guess Ruth's last book was over and out to all."

The more I thought about it, the more it seemed logical that Lily and his fellow Spirit Guides would want to keep transmitting information that they, from their perspective in Heaven, knew could be of great benefit to the world. Their partnership with Ruth had opened so many people's hearts and minds about the wondrous workings of the universe—why would they want to stop helping humanity at such a critical time in Earth's history?

As I mused about the concept of Ruth Montgomery having a successor, I halfheartedly wondered whether there was even a remote possibility that I might have the potential to help Lily and friends when Ruth moved on from this life. I immediately had another, more concrete thought: *There must be thousands, no millions, of people around the globe who would be eminently more qualified than I am to have the extreme honor of serving as an intermediary for Ruth's Spirit Guides.*

And then I had another thought–no, a feeling, *a knowing*–deep inside my soul: *In the highly unlikely event that I was ever lucky enough to have the privilege of carrying on Ruth's work, I am certain I would see the project through to its completion.* I can't describe what I felt any better than to say that there wasn't even one millionth of one percent of doubt anywhere inside of me that, if I were ever given the chance to help Ruth's Guides carry on their collective work, I would take the responsibility with the utmost seriousness and make it my own life's work. No matter how long the odds, how preposterous others might say it was, or how many obstacles were placed in my path, nothing, absolutely nothing, would prevent me from carrying out my assignment. Not no way, not no how!

Quickly dismissing the idea that I would ever be worthy enough to step into Mrs. Montgomery's shoes, I was still quite curious to learn whether her Guides had ever said anything in their automatic writing transmissions about anyone succeeding her. I decided to try to contact Ruth and ask her whether Lily et al. had ever made mention of this topic.

Not wishing to have any letter I might send her get lumped in with lots of fan mail, I didn't want to send anything in care of her publisher. I figured that if I could somehow locate her home address, then perhaps there might be a chance she would personally respond to my inquiry.

I knew from her books that Ruth lived in Naples, Florida. I also figured that, if I could find her date of birth that my business partner, Rob DeSimone, could probably track down her home address in his capacity as a part-time police officer. I decided to get on the Internet to see whether Mrs. Montgomery's birthday was anywhere to be found.

As I navigated my way around the Internet, I was initially pretty frustrated because I couldn't locate anything about Ruth's date of birth. And then I was jolted by something stunning: Ruth Montgomery had passed away earlier that summer. Just two months earlier, on June 10, 2001, Ruth Montgomery had died in Naples, Florida.

I sat there in sadness and shock. This pioneer of the psychic field, whose books had touched so many lives, including my own in a very profound way, had moved on from this earthly existence. As I digested this news, I resigned myself to the fact that I would never know whether Ruth's Guides had suggested the possibility of anyone carrying on in her stead.

September 11, 2001

Although I was certainly saddened by the world's loss of Ruth Montgomery, the end of the summer of 2001 also brought with it a looming business loss in my own life: the lodging property, in which I had first become a partner in 1988, was scheduled to be auctioned off on September 11th.

Rob DeSimone and I put forth a Herculean effort to avoid having the auction take place. We enlisted our would-be investor, the hotelier who owned the Bar Harbor Inn, David Witham, to attempt to stop the foreclosure proceedings. Despite his offer to the court system to pay off the bank and all junior creditors in full, apparently nothing could tame the litigation monster, which seemed to have a life of its own. At one point David, a very spiritual individual who has quietly donated millions of dollars to various charitable causes, commented in a somber, puzzled tone of voice, "Maybe this property's got bad energy surrounding it. I believe in that stuff, you know."

Bad energy? Individual and collective karmic destinies? A twist of fate? Whatever it was, when September 11, 2001, arrived, Rob DeSimone and I were wearily resigned to losing the project on which we had spent the vast majority of the previous thirteen years.

On the morning of September 11th, I was scheduled to meet Rob at his place in Somesville, a picturesque little village on Mount Desert Island, where he had just recently moved. From there, we had planned to make the fifteen-minute drive over to Bar Harbor to attend the dreaded auction. In what seemed to us to be cruel irony, the foreclosure sale was to be held on the specific part of the property we were to have received according to the terms of the 1996 settlement agreement.

When I arrived at Rob's and walked into his living room, the television was turned on. The World Trade Center's Twin Towers in New York City were on the screen. He explained that a plane had just hit one of the towers and the media wasn't certain how it had happened. Like so many viewers were that day, I was just numb with emotion at what I saw on the television.

One of the initial things I said to Rob was that my guess was someone had hijacked the airplane and flown it into the building on purpose in a suicide mission. Thinking that perhaps I was being a bit of an alarmist, Rob wasn't so sure. And then the second plane hit.

As my boyhood friend and I watched the horrific scene play out in Manhattan, it instantaneously put things in perspective. Sitting in a mystified daze, Rob and I quietly stated the obvious to each other: *We didn't really have too much to complain about in the overall scheme of things.*

Although the tragic events of terrorism that day caused the auction to be slightly delayed, it did go off as planned. The property ended up being sold for a price that resulted in a significant surplus left over. Since title to the entire property was still in our former partner's name as part of the 1996 settlement between the parties, I knew that none of those funds would be headed into our account. Although I realized it would take yet another round of difficult litigation to see about that (which, as of this book's publication, is still ongoing), I ended up walking away from the site of the auction—a place that had held so many dreams for so long—with a very unexpected feeling surfacing in my heart from a day filled with an unprecedented mix of emotions: gratitude.

Like it did for so many of us, September 11, 2001, had me looking at the world differently than I ever had before.

I Finally Start Paying Attention to the Signals Life Had Been Sending Me

I emerged from 9/11 knowing that not only had our world been forever changed by the events of that day, but also that my own future no longer included the possibility of finishing the resort project to which I had devoted more than a decade of my life. Although I knew that yet more litigation loomed ahead as I pursued money damage claims regarding the auction proceeds, I was also starting to give further consideration to how I had been approaching life in general.

Despite having been exposed to a good deal of spiritual information and making some adjustments to my imbalanced approach to life, I still had a track record of too often reverting back to being consumed by events in my business life. As it did for countless people around the globe, what played out on September 11th had me taking stock of my life as never before.

As "I took my own inventory," so to speak, during the fall of 2001, it was difficult to avoid concluding the obvious: For years on end, I hadn't been paying attention to the unmistakable signals that life had been sending me. My dogged pursuit of my development dreams had been, time and time again, buffeted up against the rocks by the stormy sea of Life. After experiencing repeated aborted transactions involving the same piece of real estate, years upon years of life-sapping litigation, and enough emotional crash-and-burns to make me a shell of my former self, when was I going to admit to myself that I was ignoring telltale markers being left for me by my own life's path?

Being persistent is one thing, but I had clearly been going against the flow of Life—and I knew it. If I truly subscribed to the fundamental truth that Daskalos and so many others have long espoused as a basic principle of existence—that ultimately, "Life is the greatest teacher of all"— then I needed to begin learning my lessons a little better. But if I hadn't been on the right path, where should I be directing my attention?

CHAPTER 22

Cuac Decides to Reach Out to the Spirit World

In going through this process of self-analysis, I kept returning to the notion that it just didn't add up that Ruth Montgomery's Guides would want to stop communicating with the people of the world. I might have been a pretty persistent individual in my litigation wars, but from what I had observed in Ruth's books, this Lily chap was a soul who was in a league of his own when it came to determination.

The longer I toyed with the whole notion that it was only logical that there must be a successor somewhere on the planet for Mrs. Montgomery's work with the Guides, the more curious I became about the concept. Thinking about the matter, however, became an exercise in frustration for me.

Ruth was dead. Her husband had also passed on before her. I had even mailed a letter to a woman named Liz Nelson who had been listed in one of Ruth's books as head of a support group for folks who identified with the Walk-in concept. After several weeks, the letter was returned to me with a notation saying it was not deliverable. (I later learned that this lady had also apparently passed away, although I could not confirm this.) I didn't know of anyone else I could contact who might shed light on the subject. Why should I waste any time or mental energy wondering about a question that simply couldn't be answered?

Finally, after having the matter bounce around in my head for weeks on end, I had what seemed like a pretty wild idea: *Why don't I give the automatic writing a try to see if anything happens?*

Even though I wasn't confident that anything would happen, I decided I would sit down and attempt the automatic writing process. I looked through a couple of Ruth's books to re-familiarize myself with how I might go about trying to contact the spirit world–and then began.

Sometime in November of 2001, as best I can reconstruct, I shut the ringers on the phones off, sat down at my desk in our home office, took a pencil and held it lightly to a blank piece of paper, closed my eyes, said a short silent prayer for protection from any negative energies, meditated briefly, and then just waited to see whether anything was going to happen. After the ten minutes for which I had set the timer on the microwave oven in the kitchen, I heard a "beep-beep-beep" signaling the end of my first attempt to make contact with the spirit world. Nothing had happened.

Over the next week or so, I gave the automatic writing a few more halfhearted tries. Each time I ended up just sitting in silence with the pencil remaining motionless in my hand. As I hadn't really expected anything to happen, I wasn't all that disappointed. After all, I was a person who had always had great difficulty even doing a simple meditation. If I couldn't even keep my mind still enough to do such a basic exercise, what were the chances I would be a suitable candidate to receive automatic writing transmissions from Heaven? *Not too likely.* At least that's what I thought.

First Contact

Though I failed in my initial attempts at automatic writing, I just couldn't get the idea of trying it again out of my head. It seemed like such a long shot, but something inside me compelled me to make another, more serious effort to see if there were any spirits "out there" who might be interested in trying to communicate through me.

This time I approached the automatic writing process with more patience and resolve. Knowing that Ruth had come up empty in her early exploration of automatic writing, I decided to sit down on a daily basis for a couple of weeks to see what would come of it.

Although I missed a session or two here and there, by and large I attempted the automatic writing process daily for ten days or so. Same results. Zippo. Nothing. Although it was sort of relaxing to turn the phones off and just sit in silence, it appeared that I wasn't capable of having any direct contact with the spirit world. Nonetheless, I was determined to continue my little quest to see whether there was anyone in Heaven interested in writing through me.

After about two weeks or so, I felt the pencil move ever so slightly during one of my daily sessions. Although I was very conscious of making certain I didn't do anything myself that would cause the pencil to move in my hand, I still figured I must have had an unintended twitch. I kept my eyes closed and the pencil resting lightly on the paper for the remainder of the allotted ten minutes on the microwave timer. When I opened my eyes, I could see that the pencil had made a faint, tiny mark of about an eighth of an inch long on the page. I was intrigued by the fact that it was the first time I had opened my eyes and wasn't looking at the same blank piece of paper, but I chalked the small pencil mark up to an involuntary muscle spasm.

Although I figured that the previous day's lone little scratch was of earthly origin, I have to say I had a heightened sense of curiosity when I sat down at my desk the following morning for the next attempt at automatic writing. Within the first couple of minutes after I closed my eyes and gently rested the pencil on the paper, I felt my hand just barely move. Yet nothing else happened for the rest of that morning's session. But once again, when I looked down at the paper, there was a light marking on the paper about an eighth of an inch long. I wondered whether anything unusual might have happened, but the movement was so limited that I again attributed it to some sort of accidental spasm.

In spite of my inclination to dismiss any potential significance of the prior two days' minute markings, when I punched in my ten minutes on the microwave the following morning, I found myself more intrigued than ever about automatic writing. As I settled into my seat, closed my eyes, and lightly rested the pencil on the paper, I made an extra effort to make certain to keep my arm and hand perfectly still.

Not more than a minute had gone by when, all of a sudden, I experienced a moment that I will never forget: Some sort of energy gently surged *into* my arm. My immediate reaction was: *WHOA! This is a feeling unlike anything I have ever experienced in my entire life. I know this isn't me moving the pencil this time. But it also feels sort of strangely natural.*

Slowly, but firmly, this "external" energy now inside of my arm moved my hand across the page in pretty much a straight line. And then it suddenly stopped.

I sat there for the remainder of my usual ten-minute session, waiting to see if anything else was going to happen. It didn't.

As soon as I heard the beeper on the microwave go off, I opened my eyes and looked down at a line on the paper a little over an inch long. It had really happened! I was staring at a pencil mark that had been made by some unseen force emanating from outside of me.

My reaction? Awe. Excitement. Wonderment. I was simply amazed by what had happened and couldn't wait to tell Phyl about it when she got home that night.

Hen-Scratchings from Heaven?

When I described to Phyl that night how the pencil had moved on its own in my hand, she was fascinated and encouraged me to continue with my daily attempts at automatic writing. Getting this encouragement from her reinforced my own sense of enthusiasm for what I was doing and made me determined to press on with my efforts to see if the spirit world had anything to say to or through me. Indeed, when I went to sleep that night, I could hardly wait to get up the next morning to see whether anything would happen in the next automatic writing session.

When I sat down the next morning, I wasn't sure what, if anything, was going to happen. I didn't have to wait long to find out.

Almost immediately after closing my eyes and putting the pencil down on the paper, I felt energy enter my arm and begin to move my hand. I sat there just letting the pencil crawl haltingly over the surface of the paper. Although it initially started out on a straight line, it then started to move in a here-and-there fashion.

For the rest of the ten-minute session, the pencil moved in starts and fits around the page. Sometimes the movement would stop altogether, but then gradually resume its scribblings. Scarcely able to believe what was going on, I tried hard to–and, if you have ever attempted meditation, you will know what I mean–"concentrate on not concentrating." Starting to sense that the invisible energy found it easier to move my hand when I was not focusing on what was actually happening, I did my best just to keep my mind as blank as possible–which was much easier said than done, believe me.

When I heard the beeping sound from the kitchen telling me that I had reached the end of my ten minutes, I stopped, opened my eyes, and saw a collection of markings the pencil had made in seemingly haphazard fashion on the page. Although there was not any sort of detectable pattern to the squiggles, such as a circular motion or figure eights, one thing I am completely certain of is that

I wasn't the one who had moved the pencil. As the saying goes, "I know what I know."

Needless to say, I went forward from that point with an enhanced sense of enthusiasm for my 8:30 A.M. ten-minute automatic writing sessions. (I waited until after Phyl had left for work so the house would be as quiet as possible and usually settled into the automatic writing between 8:30 and 9:30 in the morning.) To my great delight, the pencil continued to move whenever I would sit down and increasingly gained "strength" as the energy in charge of the writing gradually seemed to establish a better "connection" with me.

As the days went by, the automatic writing seemed to progress. The energy pushing the pencil around the page slowly started to make the circles and figure eights that often appear in the early stages of automatic writing transmissions. Heartened by the evolving nature of my regular ten-minute sessions, I was hoping soon to see some words begin to form on the paper.

Throughout these initial sessions, during which the pencil moved around in my hand on its own, I kept wondering whether this invisible energy could possibly be emanating from the spirits of Lily and the rest of Ruth Montgomery's Guides? Or perhaps even from Ruth herself? I just had no way of knowing.

I knew I was interested in helping them continue the wonderful work Ruth and the Guides had done while she had been alive. With this in mind, I decided that I was going to write them a note before my next attempt at automatic writing to spell out my feelings in very clear, concise terms.

On December 20, 2002, I wrote the following in the spiral notebook I was using for my efforts to contact the spirit world:

Dear Lily, Art, Bob, Ruth, and Guides of the Group,
    I would like to receive communications from you through automatic writing. If it will be of benefit to the spiritual evolution of the

Earth and the Universe, I would like to be a successor to Ruth and write books based upon your communications and my own experience.

Thank you.

Rob Macomber

After writing the note and sending it out from my heart to its intended recipients, I began another automatic writing session. Although I couldn't sense any immediate difference that day, the ten-minute contacts with the spirit world on the following couple of days seemed to produce a change in what the pencil was doing on the paper. The unseen energy was making more of a concerted attempt to move in a pattern that showed it was trying to write through me in longhand. Instead of going every which-away, the pencil was trying to form individual letters. It also seemed to be attempting to "write" in a left to right direction.

Perhaps just as significantly, I was also beginning to develop a sense that the energy really was coming from the Guides and Ruth Montgomery. Indeed, when I finished my December 22nd session, I wrote another note to them before Phyl and I departed Vermont for the Christmas holiday. Here is what it said:

Dear Lily, Art, Bob, Ruth, and Guides of the Group,
  I will return for my appointment with you at 8:30, Thursday morning on December 27, 2001. Thank you for coming through to me. I am interested in learning if I should spend time on the computer or if that is premature.

Rob Macomber

CHAPTER 23

A Little Macomber Family Christmas Dinner Conversation

Phyl and I then traveled down Interstate 91 to Amherst, Massachusetts, where the Macombers were gathering for the holiday. (Although we see both of our families every Christmas, we alternate each year where we spend Christmas Day.) As we were having Christmas dinner, I told everyone about what had been happening with my automatic writing sessions.

Now, you may think talk of attempting to communicate with the spirit world is pretty bizarre conversation for a family to be having at the Christmas dinner table. That may be true for many folks, but not for the Macomber family. Although we had never talked about anything quite like this before, no one looked at me like I had three heads or suggested I was nuts.

Because most of my siblings had at least some experience reading books about a wide cross-section of spiritual and metaphysical topics, it was not at all unusual for our family get-togethers to include discussions about things ranging from aliens to reincarnation. Although our father is pretty skeptical about "supernatural" things and our mother is open-minded but not persuaded, I don't remember either of our parents ever discouraging us children from exploring unconventional avenues of inquiry.

Does that mean all we talk about is far-out subjects dealing with the paranormal? Far from it. The majority of the time, meals around the Macomber dinner table center on the typical topics of daily life that most people discuss: what's going on in each other's lives, what movies we've seen lately and enjoyed, when is the next time we might see each other, etc. But it's okay to bring up unorthodox stuff as well.

Perhaps the best way to illustrate how nontraditional topics of conversation are treated in the Macomber family is to share with you what I recall about the reactions I got when I brought up my automatic writing activities at Christmas dinner: I can't remember one specific thing about what was said. I would guess that my siblings reacted with responses like, "That's pretty neat" or "So what was it like?" But the fact that nothing stands out in my mind about that particular conversation is probably the most telling indicator of how my foray into the world of automatic writing was received at the Christmas dinner table.

Paul's Recollections about Christmas Dinner 2001

I remember the first time Rob told the family he had tried to do the automatic writing himself. It was Christmas of 2001. We were sitting around the dinner table, and Rob announced that he had been trying to channel Ruth Montgomery's Spirit Guides through automatic writing.

Rob first gave everyone at the table a brief review of who Ruth Montgomery and her Spirit Guides were and what type of writing they had done. He said he had recently attempted to make contact with them through the automatic writing process and that, while the pen did seem to move on its own a bit, it wasn't any more than some scribbles.

Rob seemed very enthused about the fact that the pen had moved on its own, but seemed disappointed that he was not able to communicate clearly with the Spirit Guides. I remember him saying something like, "Wouldn't it be amazing if somehow we could continue the work Ruth Montgomery was doing with her Spirit Guides?" As I recall, most of my family didn't say much more than, "Yeah, that would be quite something."

I have to admit that, even though I was very much a believer in all the good Ruth's books had done and was very interested in the exploration of that side of life, I didn't think twice about the possibility of anyone in our family being the successor to Ruth Montgomery's spiritual work. Not believing at the time that it was even a remote possibility, I think my response to Rob's question was something like the rest of my family's answer: "Yeah, that would be truly amazing." I didn't give it a second thought after that. Luckily, Rob did!

CHAPTER 24

The Passing
of the Torch

C uac with you once more.

After the holidays were over, I resumed my efforts to communicate with the spirit world. I could feel that "the energy" was moving my hand with a definite sense of purpose. Even though nothing distinguishable or readable was being formed, it was plain to see that whoever or whatever was moving the pencil around with my hand was clearly endeavoring to form written words.

The results of my automatic writing reminded me of the way, when I was three or four and had not yet learned to write, I used to make out "pretend checks" with our Grampa Austin's checks from closed bank accounts when he was Castine's town treasurer: You could tell I knew some of the shapes that were used to form letters, and I realized that things should go from left to right, but that was about it. There wasn't even one letter that could be identified.

As another New England winter got underway, I continued with my ten-minute scribble sessions. In fact, the month of January 2002 is when I was the most diligent in keeping my morning appointments with those spirits who I increasingly believed were Ruth Montgomery and her Guides. Nothing readable was coming through the automatic writing, but I remained enthused about the experience.

Although my attention sometimes got so distracted by my litigation work that there were plenty of days when I didn't do any "writing," I still managed to do it a few times a week. On the days I "missed," I sometimes still wrote the Guides a note to let them know I felt badly about not making it for our morning session. The following are a couple of examples of such *mea culpa* messages I jotted down in my notebook:

January 11, 2002

Guides,

I apologize for missing another appointment with you. Please do not give up on me. I will be back at the desk at 9:30 A.M. EST for another appointment. Please continue to come through to me.

January 23, 2002

Dear Lily, Art, Ruth, Bob, and Guides of the Group,

I will return for our 9:30 appointment on Monday, January 28, 2002. Please be patient and do not give up on me.

During the month of January, I had also been trying the automatic writing on the computer. Although I had kind of figured that my very modest progress with the pencil didn't bode well for receiving spirit communications on the keyboard, I had, nonetheless, begun on December 27th to give it a whirl two or three times a week.

Unlike my "handwritten" automatic writing sessions, my attempts on the computer went nowhere. Although I could feel the energy making an effort to do something, only a few individual keys got pressed once in a while. The results were so skimpy that they could easily have been the result of involuntary motions. In any event, my initial fascination with the automatic writing process was definitely wearing off.

I Just Can't Read "My" Writing

By the end of January, I was starting to become frustrated with the fact that my automatic writing abilities didn't seem to be progressing any further. Although the sessions continued to produce plenty of scribbling, most of it in a relatively straight line across the page from left to right, there was still no "writing" that was readable.

Although it was certainly fascinating to have unseen energies move the pencil around the paper, I started to get a little discouraged. The frequency of my morning ten-minute automatic writing exercises began to wane. Things just didn't seem to be improving. Frustrated by my apparent inability to be a very good receiver for the Guides to write through, I felt more and more like my otherworldly hen-scratchings weren't really leading anywhere.

On January 31st, I wrote out a question to the source providing the unseen energy; it's a telling indication of my desire to see more progress with the automatic writing project:

Lily, is this you and the Guides?

And then, just as I was beginning to think that the morning sessions with the pencil weren't leading anywhere, I had a conversation sometime in late February or early March with my sister, Jane, that knocked my socks off. So, at this point, I'll let her fill you in on what had been happening on her end of things.

Jane Picks Up the Pen...and the Plot Thickens

Hi! It's Jane here.

As you've just learned, after Ruth Montgomery passed over, my brother Cuac wondered whether there was supposed to be someone to carry on her work. He faithfully tried the automatic writing process, and although the pencil moved some for him, it never produced anything readable.

Prior to Cuac trying the automatic writing, I had read only one of Ruth's books, *The World to Come*, and wasn't too familiar with automatic writing. But over Christmastime, while Cuac was visiting, he told me he'd been trying to do some automatic writing. I instantly knew that I could "do it." Being as busy as I am, however, I didn't actually try it for a little while.

Sometimes I wake up in the early morning and can't get back to sleep. One of those winter mornings, I decided to put pen to paper to try it. I closed my eyes and rested the pen on the paper. It "automatically" started writing: figure eights, scribbles, etc. I did it for forty-five minutes or so, until I was tired and had filled several pages with "my" doodling.

The first time I did it, I thought, "Wow, this is wild!" Yet, at the same time that it seemed totally amazing, it also felt like the most natural thing in the world. After that, I did it here and there, but didn't think too much of it (at least not in the way I think of it now). Eventually, I started trying it more and more. Initially, the pen just made the scribbles. And then "It" started to form words.

One day when my sister Laura and I were all done with work at the inn where we are employed, she said, "Let's go upstairs in one of the rooms, ask 'It' some questions, and see if 'It' actually writes something back!" We proceeded to go to Room 33.

I grabbed a small notepad that was in the room. "It" started out by doing the normal scribbling. And then "It" wrote what appeared to be the word "leely." It wrote this several times. Laura said, "Hmm. Maybe that's 'Its' name."

Laura then asked, "Who killed Andrew Borden?" "It" wrote,

"Lizzy is a murderer!" (Lizzy Borden that is!!!!)

We asked "It" other questions, but I honestly don't remember what they were. Some intriguing things came out, but I was still very new and not completely trusting. I know my own thoughts got in the way of some of the stuff. Before each question, however, the pen repeatedly wrote, "leely."

As the winter progressed, Laura and I continued to ask "It" questions. When we did, "It" started writing answers. But "It" continued to start by writing the word "leely."

I now know, of course, that Lily, Ruth Montgomery's principal Guide, was the name "It" was trying to write. It makes sense that in the early stages of my automatic writing the letter "e" would come out instead of the letter "i." It is easier to write "e" since it has a more continuous flow than the sharp point of an "i."

"I kept the writing to myself for a while."

I kept the writing to myself for a while. I did not want to share it, especially not with Cuac. My sisters Laura and Sarah were the only ones who knew. (It's not exactly the kind of thing you bring up with everyone during coffee breaks!) I remember that I did also tell a friend about what I was doing. I told her that I purposely did not want to tell Cuac, that it was my gift, and that I wanted to keep it to myself for now.

I knew Cuac would be so excited and gung-ho—and would want to do something with it. I wasn't ready for that. I wanted to let it gel, so to speak, and get used to the idea before beginning anything formal.

Anyway, I eventually told Cuac. He was ecstatic.

By then, Laura had figured out that "Leely" was really "Lily," Ruth Montgomery's principal Guide. And by that point, the Guides had started to drop hints that they had a little more on their minds than providing my sister and me with paranormal entertainment for our personal amusement. For instance, they scrawled out the following two statements during these early automatic writing sessions:

Leely is the man and he is much greate[r] than you real-
ize. Lily is here and great ones are coming.

I'm going to turn you back over to Cuac again, but before doing so, I'd like to tell you a little bit about what the words look like when I receive automatic writing transmissions with the pen. The spirits write in longhand in one continuous motion, with no capitalized letters or punctuation at all. Although I consciously stop my hand when I get near the right-hand edge of the paper and move down to the next line, the spirits don't dot their "i"s or cross their "t"s. I have to do that "manually" after I've finished receiving a transmission. The material is then properly punctuated by whoever (usually Cuac) is transcribing it and inputting it into the computer.

As the book goes on, I'll be giving you more details about what the whole experience of getting these communications from the spirit world has been like for me. We've taken very seriously the responsibility of accurately conveying the information we've received from the spirit realm. For example, when you see a quotation from Ruth or the Guides, that means they've actually "said" those words through the automatic writing transmissions. In some instances where it seems they've left out letters or words necessary to complete a thought or sentence, we've inserted them and indicated that we've done so by bracketing any added letters or words.

It has also been extremely important to us to attempt to present, as clearly as possible, the personal experiences we've had along the way in becoming messengers for our invisible co-authors. That is why you'll sometimes see us give an estimated timeframe on when something happened in our lives. Piecing together the sequence of events has been quite an exercise for us—because one often feels like a pinball being bounced back and forth and shot all around in the game of Life. Describing what happened when, and what was going on during different periods of our lives, has been much more difficult than we ever imagined.

But enough about the process of how this story was written. Let's check back in with Cuac and let him continue the telling of it.

The Torch Is Offered

Cuac here.

"Ecstatic?" You bet I was.

When Jane informed me about what had been happening with the automatic writing and that the names "Lily" and "Ruth Montgomery" were appearing in the transmissions, I was very excited. *Could it be that Jane had really made contact with them?*

Jane suggested that, next time I was in Amherst, we should sit down together so that I could see for myself what was going on in her communications with the realm of spirits. Not too long after that, in what I believe was mid-March of 2002, I realized that Phyl and I were soon going to be driving by Amherst during a trip to see her family in Pennsylvania. I called Jane, set up a day and a time to meet with her, and eagerly looked forward to our get-together.

When we arrived at Jane's for the appointed meeting, we all gave each other hugs, exchanged initial greetings, and then she said, "You want to do some writing?"

Jane took a piece of blank paper, closed her eyes, and set the pen down on it. Then her hand immediately started moving all around the page. As I watched in fascination, I could see that the pen was making a lot of loops and curves as it meandered around the paper, but it was also forming words every now and then.

After a couple of minutes, Jane stopped and opened her eyes. Among the many curves and loops on the paper were written some words that could be made out without too much trouble. When I read them, I could scarcely believe my eyes:

Lily is leelee...Ruth Montgomery...listen to me...listen, listen.

I then asked Jane whether she could mentally ask the spirits what I should do next in my professional life. This had been a subject I had been thinking about a lot that winter. In fact, during the month of February, I had asked the Guides this question in my own automatic writing sessions no fewer than seven times. The basic question I had written out in seven different variations between February 4th and February 28th was "What should I do next for a job?" The problem was that none of the responses I had received in my automatic writing transmissions were legible.

Jane closed her eyes and put the pen back down on the paper. As the pen resumed moving back and forth in her hand, it alternated between writing words and making more curved markings of a random nature. When she stopped again, we peered down at the paper and read the following response:

Find another job....Teacher is the answer.

I then suggested to Jane that she ask Lily and Ruth whether it would be possible for Jane to do what Ruth had done. Could Jane, using the information provided by the spirit realm's automatic writing transmissions, write a book?

The pen promptly scrawled out a one-word answer:

Together.

Wow! But exactly what did that mean?

As we were on a pretty tight time schedule that day, at that point Phyl and I needed to get back on the road. We expressed our amazement to Jane at what we had just witnessed and agreed that we would make plans to meet all together again to observe more of her automatic writing abilities.

The Torch Is Accepted

After Phyl and I returned to Vermont from our visit with her family in Old Forge, we quickly fell back into life's regular routine. Although we were both amazed at what had happened in Amherst with Jane's automatic writing demonstration, our focus was soon diverted by the daily demands of everyday life. For me, that meant dealing with my ongoing legal battles.

At that point in the legal process I kept thinking about the fact that there would eventually come a time when the litigation would be over and I would have to decide what to do with the rest of my business career. At some point—win, lose, or draw—my decade-plus journey through "Lawyer Land" would be over, and I would need to figure out what I was going to do next.

Prior to witnessing Jane's automatic writing transmissions, I was planning on taking one of two routes once the dust on my legal woes had settled:

- On the one hand, I felt that Rob and I could get adequate financial backing to begin another development project in Bar Harbor. Since we knew the local real estate market there and its players, politics, and regulatory environment, this seemed to be the logical direction to go. The problem was that it would require me to continue commuting back and forth to Maine every other week—not a long-term lifestyle that Phyl or I was crazy about.

- The other alternative was to attempt to get a real estate project going in Vermont or New Hampshire, which would allow me to spend more time with Phyl. I sensed that the local marketplace was strong and that the area would continue to grow in popularity as a second-home and relocation destination for urban dwellers from the Northeast and elsewhere. These factors, combined with the steady expansion of Dartmouth College and Dartmouth Hitchcock Medical Center, which were propelling the local economy forward, made getting a new deal together on the western side of New England seem feasible. The problem was that I knew full well that it can take years to get to know the ins and outs of a real estate market well enough to succeed in a new venture.

Those seemed to be the two primary options for beginning to rebuild my business career once I concluded my long and perilous escapade through the legal system. Or so I thought.

As I continued to navigate my way through the litigation maze during the spring of 2002, my mind continually returned to images of the automatic writing transmissions Phyl and I had watched emerge from Jane's pen. The writing had said that the answer to my dilemma about what to do next was to become a "teacher." Although I had always enjoyed academia and loved the atmosphere found on school campuses, what I kept coming back to was the answer Jane had received to the question about writing a book based on information provided by the spirit realm: *Together.*

Could that mean I was supposed to team up with Jane and "together" write a book that would share with the world new information from Ruth Montgomery's Spirit Guides? Was it really possible that Ruth had now joined them and that my sister and I were supposed to pick up where she had left off? It just seemed too fantastic to consider.

Although my own attempts at automatic writing were less frequent by this point, I nonetheless asked the Guides about this specific issue. In my automatic writing notebook, I wrote the following question:

> *Should I go to Amherst regularly to work with Jane on automatic writing in order to help her write books?*

The only reply I received was the customary scribbling, which contained not even any distinct letters, never mind readable words. Apparently, I was not meant to receive legible transmissions. Yet I still kept *feeling* that I should be working on some sort of book project involving the transmissions that Jane was apparently receiving from Ruth Montgomery and her Guides.

Despite my internal quandaries about the plausibility of actually writing such a book, something inside of me kept returning again and again to the concept. I repeatedly attempted to dismiss this fanciful notion of redirecting my professional life toward a career of writing. The argument with myself usually went something like this:

How can I even consider making such a career change when I haven't even written one book?

Every author has to write that first one.

Okay, but many folks who write books have had at least some previous experience writing before they tackled their first book. Look at all the authors who started out as writers for newspapers and magazines.

Fair enough. But hasn't the past decade of litigation seen you write voluminous amounts of letters and memos. Out of necessity, hasn't your experience in "Lawyer Land" required you to draft countless documents and help attorneys craft one brief after another? Hasn't the whole process of being plunged full-time into an arena in which you had no prior experience forced you to stretch your abilities? Haven't you had to learn how to digest vast quantities of new information and then articulate well-reasoned conclusions?

All right, I admit that I've written a lot more in the past ten years than I ever did in high school or college. But we're talking about a book that is going to be based upon what some unseen spirits are saying...come on!

Sure, it sounds pretty out there, but examine what has happened to you since all of the litigation began, since your business career imploded, and since you started exploring the spiritual side of life. What has this experience taught you about yourself?

As I went around and around like this, I gradually became more honest with myself about how I felt about what had been happening in my life.

All of the fighting, fear, and stratospheric levels of stress in my business life had not at all been enjoyable. I hated it. As a person with an intense dislike of conflict, wasn't I kidding myself about what resuming a career in real estate development was going to be like? Even after the litigation was over, wouldn't I be returning to a profession that involved lots of legal wrangling and explosive issues on a regular basis?

Contrasted in my mind against the stark reality of what jumping back into the development game would be like were the wonderful things that had happened since my real estate endeavors had blown up in my face.

With the worst of my business fears realized and my long-sought objective of developing the resort of my dreams lost, I almost certainly would have been on a never-ending collision course with myself had Phyl not been there to rescue me from the flames of my own personal hell. Without the benefit of her presence in my life, I never would have survived the previous decade with my sanity intact. At best, I would likely have grown into a bitter, resentful individual who would have condemned himself to a life of endless blaming. But, because of Phyl, I was surviving the ordeal and, though definitely battle-scarred, was emerging as a person I liked a lot better than the "old" version of myself. Was I really going to plunge Phyl and myself back into a pressure-packed lifestyle that, by its very nature, had conflict as a central daily dynamic?

As I reflected on the healing and protective love that Phyl had provided me with during the long years of litigation, I also recognized that some of the best times of the previous ten years had stemmed from my involvement with spiritually oriented books. Whenever I had made the time to read such materials, I had just plain felt good. I had also tremendously enjoyed the occasions on which I had engaged in discussions with friends and family about the various ideas and concepts I was coming across in the books.

What I had gotten the biggest kick out of, however, was sharing the books themselves with others.

Whether it had been Betty Eadie's *Embraced by the Light,* Professor Markides's books about Daskalos, Mary T. Browne's *Life After Death,* Dannion Brinkley's *Saved by the Light,* Ruth Montgomery's books, or any one of dozens of other books I had come across in my readings, one fact was inescapable to me: Books about spiritual matters had given me the most joy when I gave copies of them away to others. Knowing how much they had helped me with my own struggles, I had found true satisfaction in passing along information I thought might be useful to people I knew.

Was this desire to distribute copies of spiritually oriented books a sign of things to come with respect to the book that you are now holding in your hands? I can't really say for sure. I do know, however, that I remember the sense of excitement I would get whenever I would pass along one of these books to someone else—the same feeling I have right now as I sit here writing the words you are reading.

Looking back, I realized I had enjoyed sharing meaningful, interesting spiritual materials with others to such a degree that I sometimes had gotten carried away and spent more on them than our budget would responsibly allow. So much so, that Phyl had sometimes given me Borders gift cards for my birthday or at Christmas. As she observed the gratification I was getting out of buying multiple copies of different works and passing them along, she had begun to realize that one of the best things she could do for me (and for the balance in our checking account) was to support my growing habit at the bookstore in this fashion.

As I ruminated on all of this during the spring of 2002, I thought back to an open-ended question Phyl had once asked me years before: "If you could do anything in the world, what would it be?"

My response had been, "Aside from the unrealistic possibility of being good enough at basketball to play in the NBA, what I would most like to do is be able to sit in a room and just think. I don't know exactly what about, or what it is exactly that I would be doing, but that would be it."

The more I tossed my answer to Phyl's question around in my mind, the more I kept coming back to the idea of trying to collaborate with Jane on writing a book…"*together.*"

Finally, in a moment when instinct prevailed over logic, I talked to Phyl about how I was feeling. Sometime in late May or early June of 2002, I said to her: "I don't think that I'm meant to make real estate development my life's work when the legal stuff is over. Although it defies all conventional reason and may not seem to make any sense, my gut is telling me that I am supposed to write a book with Jane and continue Ruth Montgomery and the Guides' work."

Phyl's reaction was both supportive and matter-of-fact. She replied, "If that's what your gut is telling you to do, then go for it. We'll be seeing Jane over the Fourth of July in Castine; why don't you talk to her about it then?"

So that's what I did when our family gathered in Castine for our annual Independence Day get-together in our hometown. I suggested to Jane that we attempt to write a book "together"—with each other…and with Ruth Montgomery and her Guides—so that we could help them continue their efforts to help humanity. Jane was most agreeable to the idea and said she'd be interested in giving it a try. And as I recollect, Paul was also involved in our conversation and was curious to see where all of this would lead.

And so this project was born.

PART III

---◆---

Heaven Unleashes a Flood... of Information

---◆---

"We can see from our perspective that God wants nothing more than peace on Earth and in the Heavens...and even if man is unwilling to listen, we will keep talking until he does."

–The Spirit Guides

"Evil does not want this to happen."

–The Spirit Guides

CHAPTER 25

Heaven Speaks: "This mission in life is the most important thing."

After our July 4th family reunion was over, Jane returned to Amherst and soon sat down to see what was going to happen next with the automatic writing process. Now that we had decided to follow the spirit world's suggestion to write a book "together," we were curious to see where the project was going to lead us.

We didn't have to wait long to get our answer. On July 11, 2002, the Guides started unleashing what would soon become a torrent of information about what they stressed were Earth's most pressing problems. As Jane commenced regular automatic writing sessions with these unseen spirits in Heaven, they started spewing out information at an increasingly rapid rate.

It soon became evident that the Spirit Guides had all sorts of pent-up knowledge they desperately wished to impart to our world. When we made the decision to write a book using Jane's automatic writing, it was as if we had opened the floodgates on a dam that was about to overflow.

Having no sense about what type of material might result from the Guides' transmissions, we were simply floored by the ambitious scope of their aims. Not only that, but many of the topics they started writing about were subjects about which we had little prior interest, never mind knowledge or expertise.

The Early Days

So you can get as good a feel as possible for how this project took shape when it was very much in its infancy, we are going to walk you through some of what the Guides wrote in the early transmissions on a day-by-day basis. As you read these communications from the spirit realm, try to imagine what it was like for us to receive them.

Day #1–July 11, 2002

When Jane put pen to paper upon her return to Amherst, the Spirit Guides wasted no time in saying what they wanted to write about. Never having been shy when he was writing through Ruth Montgomery, Lily immediately let it be known what was on his mind through Jane's July 11, 2002, transmission:

> **Lily is the one who wants to write [a] book on [the] Third World. Ruth Montgomery is the one to write about.**
>
> **Third World parties are in danger of losing their identities and they need a voice. They possess many rituals that are true and sacred to the earth. Their mission in life is to teach another form of love—and poverty teaches humanity and what it means to appreciate life. Love is their meaning and they are on the path to glory. Third World countries need to be put on the map. America needs to help them capitalize their uses, not just money.**
>
> **Tell Rob about everything, including teenagers in the world.**

Love is the only thing.

The Third World countries need to be recognized. That is the most important thing we can say. Third World countries are an important piece of the puzzle in helping the world to overcome the immense problems we face as a universe and world. The end result is putting up a secure place for our nation and people.

Day #2–July 12, 2002

There is much work to be done for the world. Third World countries are the major concern right now because they are the ones that hold the most and get the least. They are powerful in their own right and we can learn much from them and they from us.

Together we can provide everyone in the world with harmony and peace. This is no joke. The ability to achieve world peace is within our grasp.

Here are some thoughts: hunger overcome; providing everyone with meals; having a place for every child in the world to learn and grow; women having equality; homes for everyone; men and women getting along.

There is enough room on the planet for everyone. We need to stop being greedy and give of ourselves. Love is the key to salvation.

There are specific problems Americans need to address. They are: crime, violence, greed, poverty, class distinction, and money.

Many Americans are too greedy. We need to share ourselves, as well as money and resources. There are children who need homes and parents and friends. We can make this work together.

Tell Rob he can help by doing his share of groundwork, okay?

There are many issues we need to discuss. Let this lesson be a major part of world unity. Ruth Montgomery is here with us.

Janey, you may take a break and clean up.

We love you all.

Day #3–July 13, 2002

There is a man who can help you on this road to recovery. His presence will be known in time.

Don't worry about the small things. The most important thing is to get the information down as fast as you can. We will guide you where to go with it.

All your thoughts and ideas about things is [*sic*] true. We are instilling this knowledge in you because you are the best choice for the job. You are a very good human and an even better spirit.

You and Rob and Phyl have had a chance to experience the good and the bad; and that is why you are so good and you have a pure heart.

To be pure of heart, you must love all humans and spirits– and you do. To get this done will take little because you want it so much.

Rob is the organizer and Jane is the pothole [portal] to the issues and knowledge. Rob's intelligence and gentle manner will succeed in helping get the knowledge out.

Please get as many people involved as you can. Please put up a pleasant place for humankind and all will benefit. This mission in life is the most important thing. It can do good things for us all.

I am protecting you all so nothing can interfere with our plans.

We love you.

Yes, we need a place to put our love down and we need

you to do whatever you can. We need this information to be spread. Please put your guard down.

There is a man who will help you on the way. His name is Jesus the Lord. He will do everything he can to help you, Jane.

Don't get discouraged. The inn [Jane's place of employment] is not an end for you. You will write many stories, so please keep going and you will be rewarded for all of your hard work.

The most important thing is to get balanced in your life and take care of your kids who will be spiritually okay. Justin [Jane's son] is a good boy who needs you to be compassionate and understand they are going to be okay because you will make their lives better by doing this.

As for Rob, he is so excited that he could zoom off the Earth, but we need him to stay on Earth for a bit longer.

This planet sustains life when it is treated properly and maintained in good order. There will be enough vegetation to provide the world over with enough food for all beings.

We need to tell you to keep the rain forests alive. They need to be kept alive so humans can be kept alive. There are every kind of plants available for the medicinal uses you need and HIV and AIDS can be gone if you keep the rain forests alive. Life without them is going to be difficult if you don't stop them from being destroyed. They hold magic in their leaves for the world and we can accelerate the life of these plants without too much effort. To get the rain forests back, not all is lost yet, so you can make a difference. It is crucial to have the rain forests' medicines. The holy men will know where to go to get them and will teach their uses to the doctors who are pure of heart.

I see a lifting of veils as we reach this critical time, and we need to help it along the way. Simpler is better; it is the very state of mind we need to get the world in.

> The very essence to peace is the belief it can happen and a good head is a clear head. To accomplish this, we must put an idea in the world that the possibility for peace really does exist. It can happen with enough people believing it can happen and we can put a plan in order to do it. There are many people in the world who know this. It's important to find them out. Get up and please let our voice be heard.
> This is a good start.

Jane here. When I first started doing any serious writing, I used to sit in my bed at five o'clock in the morning, before the kids got up. I would sit up, bunches of pillows stacked behind me, with pen and paper ready.

I wanted to be sure this was real, so I would close my eyes whenever I did the writing. I needed to validate this stuff to myself. I wanted to be certain I wasn't guiding my hand over the paper. It was painstaking, but I did not trust it completely. If I had opened my eyes, I would not have been completely convinced that I wasn't just crazy.

In the first days of the writing, when a lot of this information about Third World countries started coming through, I was really excited. At the same time, however, I thought: *This is corny.* Yet the more I thought about what the Guides were saying, the more their words just plain made sense.

"We felt it was important for you to see what the transmissions are like in 'raw form.'"

Now that you've had a chance to review a few of the communications from the Guides, there are a number of things about the transmissions we would like to share with you:

1. The Spirit Guides obviously jump around a lot from topic to topic. This was a little disconcerting for us at first, especially when organizing the material as we were writing this book. Snippets

of information on certain subjects would be given during transmissions occurring on different days, initially making it somewhat difficult to get an overview of the Guides' recommendations for humankind. As time went on, however, and the Guides transmitted more and more communications, their Heavenly perspective rounded into shape nicely.

2. You can see that the Guides sometimes wrote as a group and referred to themselves as "we" in the automatic writing. When transmissions come through in the first-person singular ("I"), that is Lily speaking as an individual spirit.

3. The Spirit Guides use the word "and" a lot, as they dash from one concept to the next. Excited that they had established contact with people willing to help them disseminate their information to the world, they paid little attention to run-on sentences. Hence, as we integrated the Guides' writings into the manuscript for this book, we often simply had to leave out a lot of "ands" in order to have proper sentence structure for their communications.

4. The Guides' writings sometimes seem a little stiff and formal, as if in the style of a bygone era, making some of their sentences and phrases sound odd at times. We have retained their words and not changed their verbiage, but have sometimes added a few words in brackets to make their transmissions more readable.

5. The Guides often repeat the themes, concepts, and ideas they think are especially important for us humans to grasp. Since we ourselves very much believe in the power of repetition as a learning tool, certain points will be emphasized more than once. (Just look at how effective the repetition of the chorus line in a song over and over again is at getting its main point etched into the memory of the listener. Don't you find yourself almost automatically remembering words to a song you haven't heard in years

when you hear the beginning of a tune familiar from days gone by?)

6. Because Ruth and the Spirit Guides jump around a lot from topic to topic in any one automatic writing session, we have often woven together information from different transmissions not only chronologically, but also according to subject.

7. Lily and the rest of the Guides have sometimes communicated things about us and our family that tend to come across as overly flattering. We considered not including any such remarks they made, but concluded we would like you to understand, to the greatest extent possible, what our experience has been like. Our take on such remarks by our invisible co-authors is that they were likely intended to give us a confidence boost as we prepared to thrust ourselves into the public eye with such seemingly fantastic material.

8. The Guides definitely didn't waste much time in letting us know that doing this project was our mission in life.

9. And what about the Guides' amazing statement that Jesus Himself would be helping Jane? Did we think that could possibly be true? *Yes.* As people with a Christian background, we certainly didn't doubt that He would want to help with this project. On the other hand, we also realized that if we had come from a different faith, then maybe some other spiritual figure—Mohammed, Buddha, angels, etc.—might have been mentioned by the Guides at the outset of this endeavor.

10. Throughout this book we have referred to God in the masculine gender. Although we firmly believe that God is just as much "female" as "male," we have used masculine references for the sake of simplicity and in keeping with traditional usage. Please know, however, that we will be exploring the feminine side of God in a future volume of this book series.

CHAPTER 26

Cuac Is
Reduced to Tears

C uac here.
After getting back to Vermont from our annual family reunion in Castine, I was on the edge of my seat to see what was going to happen with Jane's automatic writing. Now that we had decided we were going to attempt to write a book with the Spirit Guides, I was really juiced to find out what they might have to say.

During each of the first three days–July 11th, 12th, and 13th–that this project formally began, Jane called me and read what had come through in her automatic writing sessions. I could hardly believe my ears.

The Guides were right on target about my feelings as Jane read the results of her daily communications to me: I was downright beside myself with excitement. To think that we were really being given the privilege of carrying on the fascinating work on which these spirits and Ruth Montgomery had collaborated made me so revved up that it was initially difficult for me to focus on anything else. Could this really be happening?

I quickly decided I wanted to be there in person for one of these incredible automatic writing sessions that Jane was having with the Spirit Guides. I called my sister and set up an appointment to meet her on the afternoon of Sunday, July 14th. As much as I eagerly awaited my trip to Amherst, I was totally unprepared for the experience that I was to have that day.

"Evil does not want this to happen."

When I arrived at Jane's place that summer afternoon, we gave each other a hug and immediately began talking about what had been happening the past few days. She told me she had done some more automatic writing earlier in the day and that I could read through the morning's transmissions as she began another session with the Guides.

Jane handed me the pages from that morning's communications from the Spirit Guides. They were filled with line after line of continuous cursive scrawl that was anything but easy to read. And to make deciphering it even a little more difficult, Jane's "eyes-closed" sessions with our unseen spirit friends tended to slope down and off to the right as her hand worked its way toward the bottom of each page. Nonetheless, by going over each line slowly, I was able to make out the words from the Guides' morning message. Here is a portion of what it said:

> **This is for real Jane.**
>
> **Things will fall into place, they always do. Your mother will be instrumental with the kids. Rob and Phyl are very excited.**
>
> **Today you and Rob need to try to formulate a plan for the future in how to go about the things that need to be done. He can give you lots of time if he pursues this diligently and takes his assignment seriously.**
>
> **We need to act on love and generosity of others, because it takes a lot to get a book done, but know you can do it. Please remember as you go along that we need as much love and understanding from as many people as possible. So don't get discouraged; they will provide for us.**

Paul needs to get involved because he holds great spiritual wealth and can take us places we need to go.

The purpose for this is to create wealth and happiness for everyone. Not money, so much as happiness within ourselves. Money is just a benefit from your work and we hope to see lots of love stem from the efforts you are giving.

Please help us by doing everything you can. All of our questions and information will come in time.

Tell Rob his mother is good and she needs him. To put a price on her love is not good. She is love itself, as many of you know. This is not a criticism; she just needs to be recognized.

Tell us they…we mean to say, we will tell all people about your efforts in our book.

Power can be good if people use it wisely and not gain for only them to become powerful.

This is a book about love and understanding and compassion and helping others. People need each other and can make a difference.

Only power from within is the real power. The only power we need is to help the planet and it will give us its power. The power of the Earth is great and it is a living creature who needs to be taken care of. We need to nurture her, for to gain her power back and she will give us her power for our good causes.

Ask of a world and true beliefs will come true.

The meaning of life is to love and help and grow spiritually, for we are all spiritual beings having journeys to different places.

Mankind is basically good, but evil has stepped in and we need to get along with each other and remember to love one another.

There is one other thing we need to tell you: please be careful when traveling and we will guide you where you go, but evil does not want this to happen. So know we will be there and be watchful for evil. And use caution, because we need your faith and belief in us to watch over you.

Fear is nothing more than wasted time. But you can still be cautious and use your instincts, because you have good ones and your faith will carry you far.

Janey, you have been chosen because of your goodness and true to heart knowledge of God and the ability to see good even where evil exists. It is your greatest asset and will buy you far more riches than money ever could.

Use it well and beware of the evil while extracting the goodness.

Goodbye for now.

"I just can't believe it, Janey, I just can't believe it."

As I was reading through these incredible statements of the Spirit Guides, Jane had started another session with the Guides. Seeing how quickly and smoothly the pen began moving in her hands was remarkable. Even though my sister had her eyes closed, the pen moved very deliberately from left to right with no hesitation. Unlike the brief automatic writing demonstration in the spring, during which the Guides had delivered the prophetic one-word message, *"Together,"* there were no big curves or loops.

Reading through the transmission Jane had received earlier that day, I felt a strong surge of emotion as I attempted to digest its implications. For one thing, it warmed my heart to hear the Guides' kind words about Paul and the importance of his involvement with the project, for he had been the person responsible for our family coming in contact with Ruth Montgomery's writings in the first place.

After I finished reading, Jane handed me more messages that she had just received from the Guides:

This is for real. Do not neglect the assignments we have chosen for you. Not a joke.

It is pertinent information that the Earth be taken care of and that the Earth's people be taken care of. It will be a good time for all and everyone will be rewarded in ways you did not think possible.

Rob, you are not meant to be in real estate. You have too big a heart to be a businessman. In the likely event you should ignore this, don't.

Rob, this is true. We need to get Third World countries involved in politics and have them wield the power they have within so they can be a part of making the world a better place. Please be patient and know that this is real.

The AIDS question is top of the list. There are people who can cure diseases with their know how and purity of heart.

You can help save the world from many bad things and we are here to tell you so we can wage war against the bad things.

This cannot happen overnight and we need to let many souls go so we can be here with you and please do not give up.

Third World countries are powerful people. They are self-less by nature because they came here to teach sympathy and compassion. They are the true heroes of the world and their suffering is not a mistake, but a lesson for all of us to learn from—and we will be better off in the future.

We need to get a computer for Jane. The one she has now is okay, but if we can another one, do it.

Please focus on Third World, Jane, and get the job done.

When I finished reading the latest words that the Spirit Guides had directed to us, the extreme emotions that had been welling up inside of me made me simply crumble. I started sobbing uncontrollably, saying over and over again, "I just can't believe it, Janey, I just can't believe it." Never having seen me quite like this before, my youngest sister gave me a comforting hug that I will never forget.

What exactly was I feeling that made me so overcome with emotion? In a word, *gratitude.* I was deeply thankful that Ruth Montgomery and the Spirit Guides actually felt like my family and I were worthy of the task of helping them help humanity–so much so, that, as you have just seen, it was initially hard for me to accept that it could be true.

Besides feeling grateful, I was also hard hit by the admonition of the Guides: "In the likely event you should ignore this, don't." They were obviously very aware of my long history of too often allowing business pursuits to overshadow everything else, especially the most important things in life.

And what did Jane make of my reaction to the events of the afternoon of July 14th, 2002? I'll let her tell you herself.

"What am I getting myself into?"

Jane here on the keyboard again.

Going back to when I started doing something formal with the automatic writing, I remember the first time I did it for Cuac. He was so in awe–crying, fascinated, and bewildered. His reaction was a little overwhelming for me. But, of course, it was new for him and not for me.

I was excited, don't get me wrong, but it's like seeing a really good movie for the first time. I'd already seen the movie, more than once. He hadn't.

And I have to be very honest here–part of me was like, "What am I getting myself into?" I was thrilled on the one hand to have this extraordinary gift and overwhelmed on the other, thinking, "Now I have something else to add to my plate!"

"My brother was as excited as a little kid at Christmas..."

It's Paul back with you.

I remember Rob's reaction after he saw Jane's automatic writing for the first time once this project formally began. I don't think I had ever heard him so excited about anything in all my life. He called me after having visited Jane in Amherst and witnessing the automatic writing.

I believe the first words Rob said, very enthusiastically and nearly shouting, when I picked up the phone were something like, "She can do it—she can really do it! I just came back from Amherst and saw Janie do the writing, and it was really Lily and Ruth who came through!"

My brother was as excited as a little kid at Christmas who had received absolutely everything he had put on his wish list—and then some. It was as if the seed he had tried planting some months before—when he tried to make contact with the Guides himself—had now somehow mysteriously started to grow, but not in the place where he had planted it.

I don't recall the conversation we had verbatim, but I do remember Rob suggesting that maybe we really were somehow meant to continue Ruth Montgomery's spiritual work with the Guides. I must admit I was also very excited at the thought that Jane was possibly channeling Ruth's Guides, and maybe even Ruth herself, but I had more reservations than I did convictions at the time.

I remember thinking then that it was a very exciting possibility, but it could also very well be that maybe Jane had been the one doing the writing, wanting to think it was channeled from the Guides. At that point, I still needed more proof before I was willing to believe that my sister Jane was actually channeling Ruth and her Guides.

Although I had read scores of books on similar topics about channeling and the spiritual experiences people have had, it was always something that happened to people you read about in books, not your own family members. Over the next few months, however, Jane received communications and information from the Guides that she would have no other way of knowing herself. She also channeled friends and family who had passed.

Getting messages, via my sister's automatic writing, from deceased friends in Heaven with details that were right on—and which my sister could not possibly have known about—was what closed the deal for me and got me on board one hundred percent. After that, I remember thinking: *Wow, this is actually happening to my family. Could it be that maybe we really are supposed to play some part in a spiritual journey with Ruth and her Guides?*

Needless to say, I have long since known the answer to that question I posed to myself a few years back.

"Finally, I was going to do something with my life that was truly meaningful."

It's me, Cuac, back with you.

As I drove out of Amherst that day on Route 116 and headed to get on I-91 to go back to Vermont, I was still reeling from the emotions of what I had just experienced with Jane. Although my mind was racing all over the place as I attempted to process what had happened, there were two things of which I was absolutely certain.

The first was that I knew in my heart I had at last found what it was that I had come here to Earth to do. Finally, I was going to do something with my life that was truly meaningful.

The other thing I was positive of as I made my way back to the Green Mountain State was that I was definitely "in" for the project. I mean "whole-hog," "let-it-rip" kind of "in." Not that I'd ever had any doubt about my desire to help Ruth and the Guides continue on with their work, but you never really know how you're going to react to a situation until the reality of it stares you square in the face.

Oh yeah, I was most definitely "in," especially after having learned from the spirits in Heaven that "evil does not want this to happen." How could a guy for whom fairy tales had played such an influential role in his life not be "in" for a challenge such as this? To put it in poker parlance, I knew that day that I was "All-In."

CHAPTER 27

The July 14, 2002, Transmissions:
Some Commentary on Their Importance

C uac still here.
Because the transmissions of July 14th, 2002, contained some very fundamental building blocks for this project, I am going to provide you with comments and explanations about some of the specific messages the Spirit Guides conveyed through Jane's automatic writing that day. For the sake of simplicity, you will see that I have taken several of their statements out of order and, instead, have grouped them together by topic.

Some Ground Rules for Cuac

"Today you and Rob need to try to formulate a plan for the future in how to go about the things that need to be done. He can give you lots of time if he pursues this diligently and takes his assignment seriously....Rob, you are not meant to be in real estate. You have too big a

heart to be a businessman. In the likely event you should ignore this, don't....Tell Rob his mother is good and she needs him. To put a price on her love is not good. She is love itself, as many of you know. This is not a criticism; she just needs to be recognized."

The messages the Spirit Guides directed toward me on July 14th, 2002, really hit home. I had asked for the opportunity to help them carry out the work they had begun with Ruth Montgomery...and Lily and colleagues were letting me know what would be expected of me now that my request had been granted.

The Guides showed they knew my schedule would allow me to commit significant blocks of time to this project; they also knew full well about my prior tendency of too often letting my conventional business concerns overshadow everything else in my life. Yes, they were certainly speaking to our family as a whole with their blunt statement, "Do not neglect the assignments we have chosen for you." But I also knew they were right on target with the words they had chosen to direct specifically to me. Indeed, their statement–"In the *likely* event that you should ignore this, don't"–underscored the extent to which these spirits were well aware that they were placing a lot of faith in someone who had repeatedly failed to place enough emphasis on the truly meaningful aspects of life.

Ever since July 14th, 2002, I have thought about that one line over and over again–and countless times it has helped me to keep my attention properly focused on my "assignment." That's not to say there haven't been instances since the inception of this project in which my longstanding litigation hasn't consumed significant chunks of my time. Much to the contrary, my legal issues continue to be a constant presence in my life. But the Guides' admonition of July 14th, 2002, has never been far from the forefront of my mind ...and never will be.

One of the things of which I had been guilty far too often up until that point in my life was letting my business affairs interfere with spending time with my mother and doing things with and for her. Never having been reticent to "call 'em like they see 'em" with Ruth, the Guides' tradition of being straight-talking taskmasters looked like it was still intact. And although I am very aware that I could still do a better job of being a good son to our wonderful mother, I also know that the Spirit Guides' counsel in this matter has helped me make improvements in this area of my life.

Encouragement and Inspiration from Our Invisible Co-Authors

"It takes a lot to get a book done, but know you can do it....Please help us by doing everything you can....All of our questions and information will come in time...we will tell all people about your efforts in our book....This cannot happen overnight and we need to let many souls go so we can be here with you and please do not give up."

Right from the early days of this project, the Guides wanted us to know not only that they believed in us, but also that we needed to believe in ourselves and our ability to take on this project. They knew that we had concerns about doing something we had never done before, but kept urging us to press on and not to worry about things. They would provide unseen help that would guide us in the right direction as the project progressed.

As you can see from their use of the phrase "our book," Lily and friends wanted us to know we were involved in a collaboration between the spirit plane and the physical world and that they would be with us every step of the way. Their reassurance was not only comforting to us, but also reinforced the sense of responsibility we felt to do our part and follow through on our assignments.

Our invisible co-authors' statement that they needed "to let many souls go so we can be here with you" made a huge impact on me. I took this to mean that there were numerous other souls—perhaps both alive on Earth, as well as those that had already passed over to

The Other Side, whom the Spirit Guides would have been working with were it not for their belief that our family would follow through on our "assignment."

The Guides' words about having "to let many souls go so we can be here with you" is another line from their early transmissions I have come back to time and again since the birth of this project, especially during the many instances in which I have felt frustrated about how long it has taken to get this first book finished. And I have come to respect the Guides' assertion that "it takes a lot to get a book done," more than I ever realized I would. But along the way, knowing what a tremendous priority these esteemed spirits were making of their collaboration with us has been an ongoing source of inspiration—and one that has repeatedly kept me focused on making certain I don't let them down.

Good and Evil...Love and Fear

"This is a book about love and understanding and compassion and helping others. People need each other and can make a difference...

"Mankind is basically good, but evil has stepped in and we need to get along with each other and remember to love one another.

"There is one other thing we need to tell you: please be careful when traveling and we will guide you where you go, but evil does not want this to happen. So know we will be there and be watchful for evil. And use caution, because we need your faith and belief in us to watch over you.

"Fear is nothing more than wasted time. But you can still be cautious and use your instincts, because you have good ones and your faith will carry you far.

"Janey, you have been chosen because of your goodness and true to heart knowledge of God and the ability to see good even where evil exists. It is your greatest

asset and will buy you far more riches than money ever could. Use it well and beware of the evil while extracting the goodness."

As Jane's contact with the spirit world really got underway in July of 2002, the Guides came right out of the gates with talk about good and evil. As I've already explained, the fact that they soon said "evil does not want this to happen" was part of what made me realize I had to make a lifelong commitment to this project. If the stakes involved in this project with the Spirit Guides and Ruth Montgomery were that significant, then my family and I obviously had a significant responsibility to help them combat "evil."

Framing things in terms of good and evil seemed to make sense to my siblings and me. Wasn't that how one sorted out the "good" from the "bad"?

On the other hand, the Guides' assertion that "Mankind is basically good" was something each of us instinctively felt in our hearts was an accurate statement.

Furthermore, the spirit realm's remark to Jane that "the ability to see good even where evil exists…will buy you far more riches than money ever could" was a concept that seemed immensely significant.

And then there was the Spirit Guides' claim that "Fear is nothing more than wasted time." Although not directly on-point, it nonetheless brought to mind what Betty Eadie described in *Embraced by the Light* as one of the great truths she had learned in her visit to Heaven: "fear is the opposite of love."[1]

That Lily and friends said right away "This is a book about love" was not at all surprising; that's just the sort of thing we would have expected them to say. But the fact that they quickly started talking about "fear" was something that definitely grabbed our attention.

How did all of these concepts fit together? Was it even possible for us to sort all of this out?

At this stage of the game we didn't have much sense at all about where this project was going to lead.

CHAPTER 28

Arthur, Bob, and a Protector Named Jesus

Although it was hard to say just where the Spirit Guides were going to take us on our journey with them, one thing was quite evident after Jane and Cuac's July 14th meeting: Cuac needed to start the time-consuming process of transcribing Jane's handwritten transmissions by entering their contents into the computer.

Though not always easy to figure out, the Guides' distinctive scrawl was definitely readable once one became accustomed to the lack of punctuation and the way in which the words all ran together, with no spaces in between. If a book was going to be written using the results of Jane's sessions with them, then the first necessary step was to get the material into a format where it could be easily understood and organized. Since Cuac had been assigned the role of "organizer" by the unseen forces behind Jane's automatic writing, this seemed like a logical place for him to start.

Jane sat down the next night around eight o'clock and checked back in with our newfound friends on The Other Side. As she was exhausted from a particularly long day of cleaning rooms at work and the daily routine of being a single mother of two young boys, the Spirit Guides sensed that she might not be up to doing any automatic writing that evening:

Jane, you can write tomorrow A.M. if you're not too tired.

Jane responded by saying mentally that she felt bad for being tired but that she loved them. To which the Guides said:

We understand. We love you too. Feel like writing Jane?

(Persistent spirits, these Guides, aren't they?)

Arthur Ford and Bob Montgomery: Present and Accounted For

Continuing on, our phantom partners in this project wrote that July 15th evening:

Tell Caleb and Justin we love them and appreciate their patience when you are writing.

And then the Guides came across with a message directed to her sons themselves:

Please be good to each other. Love, Lily, Art, and Bob.

This last sentence represented a significant event in the transmissions. For the first time, the Guides were letting us know that Arthur Ford, the famed medium and dear friend of Ruth, was still one of the Guides and that Ruth's husband, Bob, was also present and accounted for in "Lily's Legions." This was exciting stuff and only served to heighten our sense of wonder at what was happening.

We Learn Paul Has "The Gift" Too

Jane then mentally asked these Guides if anyone else in our family had the ability to receive automatic writing transmissions, to which they replied:

Paul. And Rob, a little.

Although we already knew that Cuac had received a number of illegible transmissions, learning that Paul was also capable of doing the automatic writing was a major development. Clearly, the scope of this project was beyond anything we had ever imagined. It seemed that the spirit world was full of surprises for us.

And then, as if to reiterate just whom it was we were in touch with and to emphasize how important it was for us to help them, the Guides wrote:

> **Lily is here. So are Art and Bob and Ruth. Please write what we say. We are real.**

"Jesus Christ is protecting you....Please speak out."

Stressing the urgency of the task at hand, these insistent spirits continued on:

> **We need to put this together. Jane, you will do this. Put [in] an hour a day. Three if you can, please.**

And then the Spirit Guides returned to what they kept reiterating was the world's single most pressing concern–Third World nations–and America's special responsibility to do more to help our sisters and brothers living in these countries:

> **Third World reform will prove to be a bright spot to you. Third World countries need to have basic rights. American people need to help this come around–and be proud to be Americans...but also be proud to be of this world. A part of this entire world, so everyone will be happy.**

Realizing that the magnitude of what they were asking regarding the Third World was more than just a little bit intimidating to Jane, the Guides then reassured her that she would be getting plenty of unseen assistance from a chap who has a pretty impressive track record of helping the less fortunate inhabitants of our world:

Jesus Christ is protecting you. This will be okay. So just go along with this and help us Jane. Please speak out.

So speaking out we are. But getting the things done that these spirits in Heaven say hold the key to turning our world around is going to require more help than even Christ Himself can provide. It's going to take *your* help and the help of whatever Higher Power you believe in.

You may be a Christian; you may not be. Two-thirds of the people on Earth are not. So, please, ask Whomever or Whatever you believe in to do everything possible to put this planet on the right track toward addressing the problems that currently threaten the very survival of *all* of us.

And if you don't believe in anything or anyone other than what can be verified by the five known senses, then that's fine, too. In fact, we think all that is needed to honor Heaven's call to action is for more of us to simply take heed of the wise words of a noted American atheist (and pretty fair actress):

"I'm an atheist, and that's it. I believe there's nothing we can know except that we should be kind to each other and do what we can for each other."[1]

–Katharine Hepburn

CHAPTER 29

The Guides
Go on a Roll

Invigorated by the inspiring transmission of the previous evening and mindful of the Spirit Guides' request to devote as much time as possible to this project, Jane got right back at it the next day. Beginning at 6:20 A.M., she settled in for another session with Lily and company.

Whereas Ruth Montgomery's automatic writing with the Guides had normally been at the same time each morning, Jane's role as a single bread-winning mother of two children has made it difficult for her to maintain that type of precise routine with her own automatic writing. On the other hand, whereas the length of Ruth's messages from the Guides was normally limited to one to three pages a day, the transmission of July 16th witnessed the beginning of something that would soon become a regular occurrence in Jane's "Angel Writing," as her boys dubbed it: page after page after page of Heaven-sent advice for our world pouring out from the spirit realm.

The Special Role of the World's Children— Especially American Youth

As the Guides got uncorked on the morning of the 16th, they wasted little time in spelling out what one of the key ingredients in their recipe for a successful future for humanity was: the youth of the world. And these Heaven-dwellers were very emphatic about the need for children in the U.S. to play a pivotal role in bringing about some much-needed changes to our planet:

> **We need to get the youth of America involved in doing good things for the people of the world. They are a huge piece of the puzzle because they have tremendous resources and energy, which is better spent helping other people.**
>
> **We need the youth of America to change the future of the world because they have the know-how and the need and the want to help their fellow man. The programs that exist are not the right ones. We need to put in place a plan of action to help them realize their focus and utilize their human qualities, while spiritually awakening themselves and helping to put Third World countries on the map.**

The Spirit Guides were quick to point out, however, that children all around the globe possessed the ability to help heal our world. But in order to fulfill their potential, they need to have love outwardly expressed to them more often by their parents and other family members:

> **We can start by telling our children we love them and helping them understand we will all be better off if love is around. Every child needs to know they are loved and needs a place of safety. Children need to learn to help the ones who have problems, because children can relate better to each other; they both will be learning from each other.**

Pretty basic stuff, right? Kids need to feel loved in order to achieve their potential. What's new about that? *Nothing.* But, as with so many other things that need fixing in our world, it's an area of life in which major deficiencies continue to persist. Despite how obvious and glaring a problem this is, it's one that all too often goes ignored.

Telling kids that they are loved. Shouldn't that be an easy enough thing to do? Yet too often adults are held back by their own fears and remain silent. Or they assume that they should raise their children the same way their parents raised them. In other words, "If it was good enough for me, it's good enough for them."

Well, what the Spirit Guides are trying to get us to focus on is the undeniable fact that the way things have been done to date is not working. And we all know it. Don't we?

"The prison system in the world is atrocious."

One of the most visible symbols of the extent to which the youth of our world are getting a raw deal is how many of them end up in prison, especially in the United States. While not ignoring the importance of individual responsibility, Lily and company addressed the issue of many young people spending much of their lives in American jail cells. They showed us how prisons everywhere serve as a mirror for a core issue in our society and that, as a whole, we have allowed our government to hide our problems rather than fix them, locking away our youth rather than rehabilitating them:

> [Troubled kids are] not criminals in their own right, but influenced by what George Lucas calls "The Dark Side." Hatred and crime are born of fear and are not man's true hearts. Together we can help them with their problems and they can help us with ours.
>
> Dangerous criminals need to be good to each other first, then to the rest of the world. They need to share their responsibility for their crimes with each other, like an AA meeting so they can get back on the road to goodness.
>
> That's why it's important that criminals help each other, because they can understand one another. Not hate, but why these things come to pass: poverty, class distinction, more names bigger than the rest. We need to put up a system

where every person's qualities are utilized so they will feel good about themselves and not want to hurt other people. Everyone in the world holds a quality that we need.

The prisons are so full of people that can make a difference—people that can help save each other from further destruction. The prison system in the world is atrocious. The guards are worse than the prisoners in many cases because they were abused or mistreated and want to do the same to other people legally. Not all guards are bad, but we need to teach compassion and be able to help each other—not hurt each other.

Together we can make a safe place for everyone. The key to starting is implementing people's skills with each other. Goodness is the predominant quality in us, not evil. We just get sidetracked because of our inability to understand.

The Big Picture

These spirits in Heaven concluded their lengthy automatic writing session with Jane that day with a hopeful message about our collective future as a race...if we will only follow their plan:

> We need to impart on you one more idea before you go. Urgency is only the beginning. Once we get going, we need to stick to the plan and become unified. We need to come together and stay together, because we are all in this together, not alone.
>
> No one was put here to be alone. Loneliness is not our purpose. Togetherness is our purpose. Loneliness on people's terms can teach, but only for small amounts of time, not all the time.
>
> We need to understand human beings and be together on love. The love of us all, not the love of one man or one person or woman. The love of more than one. The love of all families

together will bring the love of the world to us. Mother Earth is calling and waiting patiently because we all belong together.

We need to get back to the basics of life and forget materialism and money and get back to giving love, not competing. Everyone will get things and be rewarded with gifts from Heaven. We do need money, but more people [who] help, more peace—with the help of people who truly care about each other.

The world was not made for one man only or one idea. It was made for the whole of humanity to enjoy; not one person or a select group, but all people. Enough suffering has gone on. Now it is time to enjoy the benefits of life.

We can see a good bright future for the Earth if we can get people to help with the cleanup of the Earth. Playing games is not our business. Getting the job done is.

A Couple of Remarks from Cuac

Although I will soon turn the keyboard back over again to Jane, there are two things I'd like to explain as the first week of this project came to a close:

1. At this point in the process, I was almost on emotional overload. I bounced back and forth between being excited beyond description about being given the opportunity to collaborate with the spirit realm on their plan for Earth, on the one hand, and feeling overwhelmed with the enormity of what they were asking us to do, on the other. I was still in the process of trying to get my own business life in order—and here Heaven was asking me to help deliver a message to the entire world. Sensing my conflicting emotions, Ruth's husband, Bob Montgomery, soon came through in Jane's automatic writing with some words of reassurance for me:

Bob tells Rob to keep chin up. They are good friends, with a mutual respect for each other. This is going to be a great adventure for us all.

2. By this time, Jane's automatic writing connection with The Other Side had become firmly established. As evidenced by her multipage transmission of July 16th, the information was really flowing from the Guides by then. With each succeeding day, Jane was getting more and more "plugged in" to the spirit world–so much so that she soon began to develop the ability to receive the spirit realm's automatic writing transmissions via computer. And here she is to tell you all about that experience.

CHAPTER 30

A Multifaceted Gift

Jane back here with you.

Not only did the July 16th transmission reveal a wealth of specific information about this project, but it also directed me about the way in which I should receive the information. You will recall that the Guides didn't take long to prod Ruth to use her typewriter in their automatic writing sessions with her, so that they could transmit more information quicker and easier. Well, they soon let us know that I should start working on the computer keyboard in similar fashion.

"The letters and the entire page seemed to be laughing at me."

In the spring of 2002–after I originally started trying the automatic writing with pen and paper–I had wondered whether I could do it on the computer. At first I was excited, as I was when I started to do the writing manually. It was so real, yet so unbelievable. My fingers started to fly around the keyboard with a life of their own. There was obviously a lot of energy being put into my hands, but no control over it whatsoever. It was the equivalent of the way the manual writing started off with figure eights and big loops.

I stopped after a few minutes, excited to see whether any real words had appeared. Much to my dismay, the only thing staring back at me was a page of nonsense: letters, numbers, and symbols, but nothing readable. I carefully examined each line just to make sure that my "silent partners" hadn't imparted some great wisdom or knowledge in the hodgepodge of letters staring me in the face.

Instead of finding any such thing, the letters and the entire page seemed to be laughing at me. Why, I wondered, couldn't these great Guides just do it? I was putting time and energy into this and felt that the computer should be a freebie of sorts. They should make it easier for me.

I was frustrated to the point of exasperation. I wanted to yell at the computer and the Guides! It was like a child learning to ride a bike without training wheels and expecting never to fall, to start peddling away with all the balance of a Tour de France winner.

After realizing that my attitude was quite infantile, I calmed down. I decided that the best thing to do was to stop and try another day. I was the one putting the pressure on myself. I realized it wasn't the end of the world and that I should leave it for the time being.

"Janey, let your fingers do the talking."

–Phyl Macomber, summer of 2002

After the project had "formally" begun, it seemed the Guides were anxious I make another try with the computer. On July 12th, 2002, the day after the project officially began, they addressed this topic right away:

> The computer is okay. We will learn to key in on it. For now, keep writing because your train of thought is high....We need to get a computer for Jane. The one she has now is okay, but if we can get another one, do it.

I have to admit, I liked that they said this because I was working on quite an old computer. I knew Cuac and Phyl would do what they could to get me something better and soon loaned me a laptop.

On July 16, 2002, Lily and company again mentioned that I should key in transmissions on the computer. Here is what the Guides communicated that day:

> **We need to talk to you, Jane, as much as possible. The boys' computer will be okay for now if you can get it straightened out. Please get going on the computer. We can put down more information if we can teach Jane to let us do the writing. On that, don't confuse your own thoughts with ours. We are in control.**
>
> **We love you, too. You are a good person, so let's rock 'n' roll. Goodbye and blessings. Go now to help your kids, Jane. We can talk later.**

I often impart messages to the Guides mentally when they are writing through me. When you see a message like the one above where the Guides say, "We love you, too," I have obviously shown my gratitude with a thought and they have responded to that through the writing.

"By themselves the words are nothing, but with the book in place, we will be able to impart a lot of knowledge to the world."

My next attempt on the keyboard met with more success than the initial one. July 17th, 2002, was the date of the first formal computer transmission from the Guides. Here, in "raw" form, is how it came though:

> **jjjjaaaaaannne this will be ddifficult aaaaat firsrbutwe caaaaaaaaaan help you get adjusted. We needyou to help us by devoting as mussssssh tine as you can,please be caaareful**

when decipheing the injormation we give you. We will be aat
this a while. Let oour fingers do most of the work for you., we
wll continue to get the words out as much as we can, ruth
took a lingtime as well we thinkk we can get this done if we
want to . How ddo you feel about this timing jane?OK. Please
be the one to tell the world aboout this idea of ours and we
will be happy to rewaaeadd you.kdaorjjdkvnn
kkkkkkkkssssssss;;;aeiffedddd dddjaaaaaa;;;;eodm]]]]. You can stay
on the computer jane we will help you in time.this is a
fascinaaaaaaatng lesson on its own fdont you
thinkjane?dkkkkkwoa;;;;;;;;;; cddddkkjjjjfssssselwwwwwweijjjfbby
themselves the words are nothing bu t withthe book in place
we will be able to impaaaaart a lot o fknowledge in the world.do
you want to continue writing janee?

NOt right now thank you.

Now, here is that same transmission cleaned up with proper punctuation and spelling:

Jane, this will be difficult at first, but we can help you get
adjusted. We need you to help us by devoting as much time
as you can.

Please be careful when deciphering the information we
give you. We will be at this a while. Let our fingers do most of
the work for you. We will continue to get the words out as
much as we can. Ruth took a long time as well. We think we
can get this done if we want to.

Please be the one to tell the world about this idea of ours,
and we will be happy to reward you.

You can stay on the computer, Jane. We will help you in
time. This is a fascinating lesson on its own, don't you think,
Jane? By themselves the words are nothing, but with the book
in place, we will be able to impart a lot of knowledge in the
world.

Do you want to continue writing, Jane?

Not right now, thank you.

"I also didn't have the mentality of a spoiled brat like before."

When I sat down at the computer for this July 17ᵗʰ transmission, I was much more in control of the energy flowing through my hands, as were the Guides. They were pressing the keys down but, as you can see, were sometimes pressing one key repeatedly. It seemed like the Guides were experiencing something along the lines of going from a manual typewriter to an electric one, not realizing that only a small touch is needed to get the desired letter. I was trying not to get in the way at all. I also didn't have the mentality of a spoiled brat like before.

I realized that not only was I getting used to this new way of writing, but also that Ruth and the Guides were as well. If you think about it, it's quite a bridge from the spirit world to the Earth plane, the human plane. I realized it must be quite frustrating for them as well. Here they are trying to do something fantastic for me, and I'm whining like some ungrateful little kid. Attitude is everything!!!

I was also grateful for the Guides' encouragement. They never failed to continue to believe in me and the work we could do together. Their positive attitude always encouraged me (and still does) to move ahead with this project.

The Guides gave me two more messages over the computer that day. They were:

We will put more knowledge in your head when you are ready for it. Go take care of your kids now.

We will help you to get where you need to be.

Have you noticed how in tune the Guides are with my needs? If I am beginning to feel anxious because of the kids or some other nagging thought, they will urge me to go take care of it. They understand that it is important for my head to be in the moment.

"The thoughts were coming into my head at the same time as they were coming out on the screen."

One very important thing I realized after doing these computer transmissions on the 17th is that all of the information the Guides have been writing has also been coming through to me mentally. The thoughts come into my head at the same time as they appear on the screen. When I thought about this, it occurred to me that the same thing had happened when I wrote with pen and paper. The thoughts appeared, and then I wrote them down. It dawned on me that maybe this would be a good way to do the writing on the computer. They even mentioned putting "more knowledge in my head."

It seemed to make perfect sense. Instead of carrying on with the frustration of the Guides hitting the keys, maybe I should just type the thoughts coming into my head. This really was one of the best revelations I have had since starting the writing. The thoughts were perfectly clear, and it saved tons of time. It was as if I were taking dictation. I felt rejuvenated!! At last, a fairly painless way to get this information out! When I think now of the tedious process of closing my eyes while putting pen to paper, as in the first handwritten automatic writing sessions, I get exhausted!

"It is a multifaceted gift and one for which I am truly grateful."

All of this information works together. All the different messages being given to me are connected. It is a multifaceted gift and one for which I am truly grateful. Sometimes when I think of the enormity of my gifts, I get overwhelmed with appreciation and can't believe this is happening to me.

It is important to note that there are some times when I feel better doing the writing by hand and others when I feel better doing it on the computer. If my head is really clear and I am not bogged down with outside thoughts, I tend to go to the computer. If I haven't done the writing in a while or I have things in the back of my mind, I tend to do it manually. Doing it manually is also interesting for other people who have never experienced it before. To see my hand writing "all by itself" is fascinating for people.

For those of you interested, I have also studied and continue to study other forms of spirit communication. As part of my ongoing exploration of my psychic abilities, I have attended two James Van Praagh seminars at The Omega Institute in Rhinebeck, New York. Although only a weekend each, both of these sessions left me truly humbled not only by the extent of this extraordinary man's abilities, but also by the gracious and unassuming manner in which he tries to help others.

In general, I think it's amazing how many different ways you can interact with the spirit world! Some of them are pretty "far out there." I find all of them interesting and will fill you in later in this book series about other experiences as I continue to explore these abilities...which I believe we *all* possess if we will only seek to develop them.

CHAPTER 31

"They didn't expect me to be perfect!"

As the automatic writing continued, the Spirit Guides began to shed more light on why I was being given the privilege of serving as a messenger for them. They led into this explanation by saying:

We may want you to start writing down your feelings in a diary or journal, as your insight—whether doubt at times or sadness or elation—will prove your human nature.

After the Guides said this, I remembered that when I first started doing the automatic writing I had had the thought that I should keep a journal. I had done so in the past, and it had proven to be good for my soul. But in all honesty, I did not do so right away because I felt I did not have the time.

Instead of initially keeping a journal, I had done something else. Because I was on the phone with Cuac so much, talking about all of the information coming through, I just told him a lot of what I felt about the things that were happening.

I did, however, in time, start to write little snippets of thoughts before I would start the automatic writing. I felt like it added something to the experience. You will see some of these as this book progresses.

I really welcomed the Guides' comments on my human nature. They didn't expect me to be perfect! They further expressed their opinions on this subject:

As we told you before, we are happy because you are so human and you don't pretend to be anything but. Your wide range of experiences is no random thing.

We choose you to do this because of your experiences in this life and past lives as well. This is an important part of who you are, and we want to remind you that you have many lives in the past and all have been leading up to this grand finale of sorts. Finale is an Earth term, but you are far from done with your spiritual work and growth.

My Interest in Past Lives

I was very interested in what they said about my past lives playing a part in all of this. I had not always been sure whether I believed in reincarnation. As a matter of fact, this was one area of spirituality that had me quite puzzled for a number of years.

I remember that I initially did not want to believe in it, because I wanted one lifetime to be enough to show who you really are. I guess I put high expectations on just one short lifetime. Exactly when I decided that we did live many lives is a mystery to me. I honestly don't remember when or where I accepted this. I think that as I learned more and read more, it just seemed to make sense to me.

The Guides' observations that I had led many lives leading up to this point made me quite curious. Who exactly had I been in other lifetimes? What did they have to do with this lifetime? And who, please tell, had I shared other lives with? I really wanted to know!

Although the Guides have dropped a few little nuggets about these questions as this book has been written, our cosmic co-authors have stressed that it was more important for my family and me to focus on the urgent matter of disseminating to the world their ideas about helping humanity. Moreover, as I have previously mentioned, using my abilities for myself isn't as easy as it may seem. I want a past life regression from someone else!

CHAPTER 32

Ruth
Makes Her
Entrance

Anyway, enough about past lives. Not long after I started the automatic writing, I got the feeling that Lily and company might be doing more of the automatic writing than Ruth. I felt like Ruth was "in the background," working, but that the ones moving my hand might more often be Lily and the other Spirit Guides.

In the Clouds

In early August of 2002, the Guides confirmed my sense about Ruth having been in the background:

> **Jane, your intuition about Ruth being in the background at first was correct. She was learning to guide and prepare the people from this side, as she is still preparing her course for her work on this side. She will come to you in dreams from time to time, but you must be patient, as we are teaching her a lot at once. She is very sweet and a much-needed asset to the team we are building in order to get this book done.**

Like most people, when I was told I was "right," I immediately felt good about myself. I thought it was very interesting what they said about Ruth preparing her work on that side. I pictured the Guides standing "up front," if you will, in that age-old image of being in the clouds, with Ruth further back in the clouds, studying furiously so she could learn as much as possible.

Come to think of it, I have always had this vision of the Guides "in the clouds" above me and me down below them on the Earth. I guess ancient images like this one are hard to escape.

The Guides did, however, subsequently provide a little more explanation about their "location":

> **When we talk of people who are on this side, we see many skeptical things in the eyes of many, but they should not fear that there is another side. We interchange our talk of here and there, as we are both on that side and this.**

It is puzzling to think of where Heaven is located. Is it beyond space? Does space ever end? If it's so easy for "them" to come here and move my hand, why don't they show up more often and in other ways? What is this other plane they are on?

I guess maybe that's what I love, the mystery. The not knowing. The desire to know more. Some may say curiosity killed the cat, but without it we'd still be in the Stone Age.

Regardless of exactly "where" these spirits who were writing through me were located, what was unquestionably very real to me was Ruth's sincere desire to do this work. I could feel the energy she was putting into this project, and that kept me really enthused and motivated.

I was very, very excited to hear that Ruth would come to me in dreams! I have always remembered most of my dreams and have always looked forward to them. Unfortunately, Ruth only came to me, very briefly, in a few dreams. And to top it off, my great dream memory failed me. I didn't remember much the morning after them, only that Ruth was there and working with me on the project.

I was kind of disappointed. I thought, "Hey, couldn't we get more done if she showed up like, every night?" That was something I really wanted to happen.

As the Spirit Guides continued on with their explanation of Ruth's role in this project, they said:

> **Her knowledge of your learning is key, as she is familiar with the automatic writing from a human point of view.**

This made total sense to me. After all, Ruth used to do automatic writing when here on the Earth plane. I could *feel* her knowledge of this was helping to put me at ease. This lady knew what I was going through!

"And now she is one of us."

The whole idea of Ruth being part of a team the Guides were assembling for this book project brings up a continuing theme of this book: *We are not alone. We are not separate!* People are here to help one another. No matter what plane they are on. *We are all in this thing called life together!* The Guides brought this idea of "working together" home even more when they offered me the following reassurances:

> **Don't worry about the things that seem paramount and huge to you right now; we will provide a way for everything that you need. We will be working as hard as we can because we know that this can work. We will be willing to do things from this side as much as possible, as we don't have the challenges that you have on the Earth.**
>
> **But this is real knowledge, as we have no time for games and silly little things like that. What is coming into your head really is the truth and knowledge from us, "the Guides," as Ruth named us—and now she is one of us.**

Again, the presence and desire of the Guides were more than just words. I could feel them when they said things like this. The best way to describe it is this: their energy is "felt." It is real.

Lily definitely feels like a leader. His presence is great.

Ruth's presence is sweet, just as the Guides had described it. But she also seems like a "go-getter." Ambitious.

"I, Lily, am, of course, the main Guide."

Not only do the spirits contribute to the "energy" I feel when receiving an automatic writing transmission, but so also do the energies of people who are with me. When I first started doing this, I had only told a few people.

The first person I did the automatic writing in front of was my sister Laura. She and I were both very excited. And, as you know, when the word "leely" kept coming through, it was Laura who suggested that maybe that was "Its" name. This was confirmed in the second week of August of 2002:

> Laura's intuition about "Leely" being my name was correct. I, Lily, am, of course, the main Guide.

Getting such specific confirmation was exciting for me. And so was the first time that Ruth herself wrote in one of my automatic writing sessions.

"Jane, this is Ruth..."

It was August 21, 2002, when I received the following lead-in from the Guides to Ruth's own words:

> We want to say that Ruth is not working on this right now, but will be back with information that can be crucial. What we mean to say is that the lessons that she is learning over here are not directly related to the Earth's crisis at this point, but will be valuable when the time is right to put us back on track.

I was a little disappointed. These words made it sound like she wasn't even "further" back in the clouds, but had gone to a whole new place. Wasn't it Ruth who was supposed to be doing this with me? At the time they wrote this, I thought Ruth should be right there the whole time. I didn't want to lose her. I didn't get the whole idea then that you don't ever lose anybody. Ruth soon let me know later in that automatic writing session that she hadn't really gone anywhere:

> **Jane, this is Ruth for a few minutes. I am studying on this side so as to get ready for the Earth's changes. It will be of great importance to get this information out, as we want to prolong the Earth's shifting as long as we can.**
>
> **It is imperative for me to continue to study on this side at different things at different times. Although I am working on this book with you and the Guides, there are other important things that are making me stay at a level of consciousness totally unrelated to the work you are doing—but not for very long. I guess I should not say that they are totally unrelated, as everything affects everything else. What I am trying to say, dear, is that we must all work together on whatever is necessary to get us to where we are going.**
>
> **Don't think that I am not with you; I am. It's just that necessities are on a different level over here.**
>
> **Jane, I know you struggle with all of this sometimes, as I did. You may even feel like quitting at times. But don't! Your work, my work, our work is so essential and so important that we want to see this book done and complete as soon as possible.**
>
> **I know that it can be frustrating as hell to get it done, especially with two small children at home to take care of. But do not lose heart; it *will* come together for you and Rob.**

Phew!!! I had nothing to worry about. Ruth was not deserting me after all. She went on to say this about the dynamics of our family members:

> **He [Rob] is more like me in the sense of his academia, and you are more like Bob [Ruth's husband] in your softness. Not that you are not smart and Rob is not soft, but the two of you make a great pair because of your likenesses and differences.**
>
> **Phyl is like the mother who wants her boy to succeed. And we see her as a great asset to this project; not only because she funds so much, but because her heart is in it for real.**

This portrayal was right on the money. Cuac has always been the student and the detail man. He is meticulous in everything he does.

I found Ruth's comparison of me to her husband Bob quite fascinating. I do think of myself as soft. And just as Bob had not embraced the Guides' urgings to write books about their messages to the world the way Ruth eventually did, so, too, was I not initially as enthused as Cuac was to plunge right into this project. This, as I have mentioned, is exactly why I did not tell Cuac about the writing at first. I knew he would want to go full speed ahead with something, and I wasn't so sure I wanted to do that.

What they said about Cuac's wife, Phyl, was right on target, too. Phyl has always supported any endeavor Cuac has taken on. This project has been no exception. And not just because she is his wife, but because she also really believes.

I can't tell you the amount of comfort I feel because of Phyl's genuine belief in this work. She has been a huge source of encouragement for me—and for Cuac as well! The automatic writing is not a topic I take up with everyone, and to have someone who sincerely believes in it and is excited to talk about it has been a blessing.

All in all, we have been very fortunate to have a good dynamic between family members as this project has unfolded.

"Boy, am I lucky to be working with such a powerhouse of a person!"

The next words from the Guides during the August 21st transmission made Ruth sound pretty dynamic herself:

> Ruth is staying with us for a while longer. She brings comfort to you, as you see her as a mother figure.
>
> She, after all, is not the first woman to do automatic writing, but the first to bring it to the public in so forceful a way. Her intuitive nature and curiosity brought about a lot of goodness in the world. She will stay on with the fight to bring good thoughts to men.
>
> She wants to stay on with her studies, as they are fascinating to her, and, at the same time, bring knowledge and strength to the book. She can multi-task, but has more of an analytical conscience and can be better if she sticks with one moment, one thought at a time. True, her inquisitive nature is fascinating in itself, but for now we will stay in close contact, as she sees herself coming into the light of the book more and more as time passes on. The reporter in Ruth has not died, and what we are saying is that she is so fascinated with so many things "up here" (for lack of a better term) that she is taking the time to explore them all.

I was fascinated with these lines, because I never really knew much about Ruth. Prior to this project, I had only read one of her books, *The World to Come*. And once this endeavor had begun, I hadn't wanted to read more of her stuff because I did not want to let any of her works influence my own writing. I still wanted to prove it to myself. But she sure does sound interesting!

As a matter of fact, when I was reviewing the manuscript for this book, I read the summary that Cuac wrote of all of Ruth's books, and all I could think of was, "Wow, I want to read these books!" Really, I was totally drawn in, and I can't wait to find the time to sit down to read what my collaborator in this project wrote before she passed on!

A few days after the transmissions of August 21st, the Guides talked more about Ruth and her work:

> **Ruth Montgomery says that she will be guiding anyone and everyone on Earth to get it done. That is her job: guide, in not so much on pages, as in the minds of men and women and children to read, publish, provoke, look, ask, and, yes, believe. Ruth Montgomery is writing and holding prayer.**
>
> **Lily and Art and Bob and the others are a counsel to be reckoned with. The time has come to see goodness in all people who are part of The One.**
>
> **Ruth Montgomery is still in training for lack of a better phrase, but will be pulling together a plan of action to help the shifting of the Earth. Her knowledge can help in the saving of the world.**

This makes Ruth sound like such a compelling person! It sounds like she is really trying to open up people's minds about things—which is, of course, what she did here on Earth with all of her books and journalism. So it should come as no surprise that she is much the same on The Other Side!

All I could think was, "Boy, am I lucky to be working with such a powerhouse of a person!" Sometimes the magnitude of who Ruth was here on Earth hits me, and I feel so blessed to be working with her.

CHAPTER 33

"We Are on the Road to Greatness"

The Guides stressed that the time was *now* for humanity to clean up its act and finally pull together and realize our potential as a race. They were very clear about this:

> It is not man's plight now, but his honor and duty to himself to complete this project. You see, Jane, as you have seen right from the beginning, this is not our project alone, it is the project of mankind, as he is choosing to put this into place.

"We can all come back to God because we are all a part of Him."

As Lily and his spirit tribe explained that this project, by definition, involves humanity as a whole, they focused again on recognizing the basic goodness of our race as a key to solving our problems:

> It is his opportunity to get back to being himself, and it is this that we have all wanted for so long. It is why you have

always known that man does hold goodness in his heart. All men, even the ones who commit crimes in their lifetimes–we can all come back to God because we are all a part of Him.

I guess this says it all. Let's get back to being who we really are. I think of it as checking in with yourself...with God. This is where prayer and meditation come into play.

This line of logic also brings to mind something Neale Donald Walsch, author of the *Conversations with God* book series, said at a seminar I attended at the Omega Institute. When asked if he was a master, he said, "We are all masters."

That is why I believe in all people, in their potential. How can one group of people be from God and not another? It doesn't make sense. We all came from the same place.

It is how we have chosen to use our free will that has upset the apple cart.

But here's the great thing: You can always go back to the good... because it is inherent in you. It never really left you. God has never left you. It's not possible, because it's who you are.

To tap into the power of the universe, all you have to do is look inside yourself. And believe me, I would do well to listen to these words myself.

Now I'm going to go out on a limb. I have never read the Bible in its entirety, but I have picked it up and read certain parts. I know that Jesus supposedly "died for our sins." But what makes more sense to me is a perspective I will borrow from Neale Donald Walsch's *Conversations with God* books: *There is no such thing as sin; there is only that which works and that which doesn't work.*

What I really think Jesus was doing here on Earth was trying to show us that we are all God's sons and daughters. That we all have greatness. That we could all walk on water or rise from the dead if we would only remember who we really are and what we are really capable of.

"Love gives way to fear no more."

I am happy to bring ideas forth from Lily and his spirit tribe, but I certainly cannot change the world by myself overnight. We all have to take steps to help.

Cuac and Phyl gave me a giant framed quote by noted anthropologist Margaret Mead for my fortieth birthday that reads:

> *Never doubt that a small group of thoughtful, committed citizens can change the world. Indeed, it's the only thing that ever has.*

Although I certainly found Margaret Mead's words inspiring, I think our world has reached the point where "a small group" just isn't going to cut it. It's going to take lots of people to fix the problems we've created. But I very much believe that *we* will do it. And so do the Guides:

It has always been our belief and [knowledge] that we would someday work together, because we are all-knowing; and here we mean all the world as we know it will come to pass.

That is why the time is right now. People are beginning to remember. Some have been remembering for years now. It is these people who have been trying to stop global warming and stop the pollution of the Earth. It is these folks who chose and remember that are putting us on this path. And as you know, that is all of us here on this planet, to some degree.

It will make their plight a lot less difficult if the people of the world will see that the things contained here in this book are true and real; that mankind can achieve all it truly desires. We are not talking about the riches of money and diamonds. We are talking about the love of humankind, as we see that the Earth and its inhabitants are ready to make a change, a real change.

Many people are already on this track, and we want to recognize these people and thank them for their efforts. We keep reminding people that we are thankful because we can see that theirs is a value of strength and love and not of fear. Love is the main thing in life, and we see that the people of the Earth are ready to let go of their fears and realize their love.

Fear has squelched much, but love gives way to fear no more. We are on the road to greatness, in the true sense of the word.

People are ready for it, and what we will accomplish with this book and information is pushing along this process. It is not a project that we see failing, but one that will actually get put into place and get things moving. Particularly, speeding up the vibrations of everyone and everything.

I believe we are all seeing this. I think we are headed in the right direction. We just need to keep in mind the importance of choosing love instead of fear whenever we are confronted with a decision in life. No matter how big or small the situation, this is the method by which Heaven says that we will solve our problems. And the nice thing to know is that the spirit realm says that we here on Earth will not be alone in our efforts to survive and prosper as a race:

We in the spirit world are constantly trying to remind the people of the world that we have not forgotten them, but are with them every step of the way.

CHAPTER 34

Paul Gets Online with Heaven

"And now we were somehow *in* the performance that before we had only watched."

Hi there. It's Paul back with you.

Now that you've read about how Jane's communications with The Other Side developed, I'll tell you about how I got online with the spirit realm.

Rob started transcribing Jane's transmissions into typed form in July of 2002 so that he could organize the material from Ruth and the Guides. This was an essential step if we were truly going to be moving forward with writing a book using this otherworldly information that was being passed to Jane through the automatic writing process.

It wasn't long after Rob started transcribing the transmissions that he began faxing me the typed transcripts so I could see what was coming through. He knew that I, too, was extremely interested in what was going on with our sister and her newfound abilities to communicate with the spirit world.

Rob would fax me the writings, and then we would talk on the phone, almost in disbelief at first that this was actually happening to someone in our family. We would excitedly start our conversations about whatever had been said in the latest transmission, and usually every second or third sentence throughout the entire conversation was something like "Can this really be happening?" or "This is un-believable and almost seems surreal!" It's one thing to have strong spiritual beliefs and read books about people who have had amazing spiritual experiences, but it is altogether different when it starts to happen to people in your own family.

Rob and I had shared many spiritual books and had enjoyed discussing them, but I must say the discussions we were now having about the writings Jane was receiving were the most energized and exciting of them all. It was as if before this we were spectators in the audience—and now we were somehow *in* the performance that before we had only watched.

"I was thinking to myself that they must have the wrong guy....It sounded like they needed the help of a superhero out of a comic book; maybe Clark Kent, but not me."

A few weeks after I had started to receive the faxed writings, I had developed a thoroughly enjoyable routine of talking with Jane and Rob about the content of the automatic writing transmissions. Early on in this process, the Guides had said:

> It's a family project. It's a family thing that we love, a united family. A small price to pay for salvation of the Earth and the humans God loves. Remember, we want to include as many of your friends and family as possible.

Intrigued by what the Guides were saying about this new endeavor being a family project, Jane asked them if anyone else in the family would be able to do the automatic writing. As you know, their response was, "Paul, and Rob a little." The Guides then went on:

> Paul needs to get involved because he holds great spiritual wealth and can take us places we need to go. We need to

put Paul in. He has much spiritual knowledge [which] can be of great importance to the people of the world. Enlightening the people of the world is Paul's and your little piece of this huge puzzle. There are many people here on this side getting ready for the spiritual awakening of the world. Tell him to help in the planet's savior.

I must be honest and say I was more than a bit fearful at first at having heard this. I previously had no sense that I would be able to do automatic writing. And although I had been very interested in the spiritual side of life over the previous fifteen or so years, I did not consider myself to have "great spiritual wealth" and had no idea what they meant when they said that I could "take us places we need to go."

I was thinking to myself that they must have the wrong guy. Although I have strong beliefs and think I am a good person, to "help in the planet's savior" (whatever that meant, exactly) had never once come up on my radar in my waking hours or even in my dreams. It sounded like they needed the help of a superhero out of a comic book; maybe Clark Kent, but not me.

I spent days trying to digest what the Guides had said. How was I possibly going to live up to any of that? Because what they were asking didn't seem like anything that I truly thought I would be able to do or even come close to doing, it made me question whether all of this was real.

There was something inside me that said it really was true, but also the thought that said if it weren't true, then I'd be off the hook for having to participate in trying to help save the world.

I was, and still am, involved in full-time work as a principal in two small companies that my friend Andrew Zenoff and I are trying to grow. This consumes most of my time, so I didn't know where I was going to find the hours for such daunting endeavors.

The Spirit Guides soon explained through Jane that they did not expect the Macomber family to save the world single-handedly but rather to be sparks, catalysts if you will, for a project that would help to move the people of the planet in the right direction. The Guides made it clear that it is all of us here on the planet working together who will help to turn this world around.

I must say the Guides' clarification of my family's role helped me feel a little more at ease and made me think I should give the automatic writing a try. Before trying it, however, I didn't think I would be successful. But I did know I would give it my best shot.

"I decided to try automatic writing.... I guess I was fearful no matter what the outcome would be."

During the last week of July, I contemplated giving the automatic writing a shot and asked Jane if she would check with the Spirit Guides to see whether they had any advice for me about how to prepare properly for tackling the assignment they had given me. The exchange between her and the Guides about my question went like this:

> *What can Paul do [to help his writing]?*

Eating healthy is a good start, but also an open mind and believing he can do it–just as you have believed in us. It takes a great amount of faith and courage to implant these ideas on a sometimes skeptical world. Paul needs to be a part of this [because of] his kindness and love.

In early August 2002, I finally decided to try the automatic writing. I remembered from Ruth's books that the Guides had instructed her to do the writing at the same time each day, to light a candle, meditate for a few minutes, and say a prayer asking that only the spirits she wished to communicate with would come through. I also recalled the Guides warning Ruth that there were spirits out there who were not of a "friendly" nature and about whom she needed to be careful when communicating with The Other Side; that was part of the reason it was important to go through the rituals of meditation, lighting a candle, and saying a prayer.

Since my mind is calmest in the early morning, I thought this would be a good time to do the writing–before my head got filled with day-to-day business issues. I remember, when I got up to try it that first morning, being both excited to see what might happen and also fearful that nothing would happen.

Actually, I guess I was fearful no matter what the outcome would be. If it did happen, then I would be embarking on some great spiritual journey that would lead who knows where–and I knew I definitely had very little time in my already busy life. If it didn't happen, then it meant that maybe all this stuff wasn't for real.

"It was as if my hand were on autopilot."

I sat down, lit the candle, meditated for a few minutes, said a prayer for protection from any negative energies or influences, and then put pen to paper. Nothing at all happened for the first five to ten minutes. I wasn't feeling any otherworldly type of connection at all.

Then it seemed as if the pen moved about a quarter of an inch. But I wasn't sure if it was just my moving it by accident or whether there had been some type of outside help.

This happened about four times during the course of thirty minutes. By the end of the first session, I had a sense that it was not I who had moved the pen; yet I was still not certain.

I was both excited by the possibility that I had just experienced some type of connection, but also still doubtful, thinking that maybe it was just me who had caused the movement. It was enough, however, to prompt me to get enthused about trying it again at six the next morning.

The following morning I sat down and went through the same rituals I had done the day before and then put the pen to the paper. Nothing happened for the first three to four minutes. And then it was as if someone had taken control of the pen and was drawing these little continuous circles and figure eights that were appearing on the blank sheet of paper.

I remember being so excited and almost in a state of awe and disbelief. I was looking down at my hand drawing these childlike scribbles, but it was not I who was controlling the movement. (Whereas both Jane and Rob had closed their eyes during their initial automatic writing sessions, I've always kept my eyes open throughout the process.) It was the strangest thing I had ever experienced in my life. It was as if my hand were on autopilot. For the first time in my life, someone or something was controlling a part of my body, but it sure wasn't me.

I excitedly called Jane and Rob to tell them the news. I asked Jane about her experience of doing the automatic writing and how it felt to her. It may seem strange, but what occurred to me that morning somehow made me feel a closer bond than I already had with my sister. I've always been close with all my siblings, but having this shared experience with Jane made me feel like we shared something special beyond being brother and sister. We discussed our thoughts and excitement–and then it was off to work for the day.

I had a hard time concentrating that day, as my mind constantly went back to what had happened. I mentally reviewed it over and over again to make sure I hadn't unintentionally been moving the pen. By the end of the day, I was excited about the thought of sitting down the next morning to verify that I hadn't somehow fooled myself. I was anxious to find out for certain that I was truly experiencing what I thought I was.

"Oh, my God, this is really happening."

That night I felt like a little kid waiting on Christmas Eve and wanting to know what the next morning would bring. I remember the anticipation I was feeling at what might happen the next day, making it a rather sleepless night.

The next morning I sat down, went through the rituals, and put the pen down to the paper. The pen almost immediately started to move on its own again, making squiggles, figure eights, and continuous circles. I can remember thinking, "Oh my God, this is really happening." It was absolutely cool to be looking down at my hand making these drawings and knowing I was not the impetus behind them—but it was my hand that was doing the writing.

Well, the next couple of mornings the same thing happened. And although I was extremely excited about what was occurring, there was still no legible writing. I wanted to be able to churn out page after page like Jane was doing, but that was clearly not happening.

"I felt as though I were back in first grade in Mrs. Motycka's classroom; but...there wouldn't be a recess with milk and cookies."

Hoping for answers, I then decided to try to communicate with the Guides by asking questions in my head. I knew that Jane had been receiving her communications in continuous longhand writing, with no "t's" crossed or "i's" dotted. I did not write in longhand and hadn't probably since grade school. I printed everything out when I wrote.

I thought a good place to start might be to ask the Spirit Guides to practice writing letters in longhand. Before I knew it, the Guides and I were doing a handwriting exercise: the alphabet letters, "a" through "z." I felt as though I were back in first grade in Mrs. Motycka's classroom; but the desk I was sitting at now was a little bigger, and I knew there wouldn't be a recess with milk and cookies.

I realized I could mentally communicate with the Guides by thinking of a particular letter or number and asking them to write it—which they would then do. I soon moved on to forming words, which I would request that they spell out.

It now felt like my energy was melding with the Spirit Guides, enabling them to work through me to get their communications out on paper. It was a very odd feeling to be asking questions in my head to these invisible beings and getting answers in the form of words being written by my hand...and, by this time, being certain I was not moving the pen.

"I felt I was on my way and at the start of some amazing journey."

During the following few morning sessions, I just practiced asking to write the words that I would think of in my head, and then, *abracadabra*, my hand would start moving and the word would be drawn on the paper. Or sometimes I would ask them a question and get a "Yes" or "No" answer.

It was about ten days after I had started the daily routine of sitting down, doing my protective rituals, and putting the pen to paper that the Spirit Guides started to write on their own without any prompting from me as to what to write. The first words they wrote without a request from me were:

Lily, Art, Ruth, Bob, love, save the world, Earth, Heaven, spirit, good morning, one world, free will, love is the answer, thank you.

As soon as this happened, I recall thinking that the Guides whom I had read about in Ruth's books for years, as well as Ruth herself, were now communicating with me—just as they had with Ruth. Granted, it was not flowing out in continuous pages, but I felt I was on my way and at the start of some amazing journey.

When I had first found Ruth's books, their description of the spirit world intrigued me. It had been fascinating to learn of the perspective the Guides possessed and the spirit realm's efforts to make Earth a better place through their communications with a person in the flesh. Indeed, reading Ruth's books had fortified my belief that we are all connected in some way—not just those of us who are among the living, but also all of the individuals who have already passed on.

Now the experience Ruth went through in her early days of automatic writing was happening to me. It was sort of like seeing a TV show you regularly watch, only one day when you go to turn the program on, all of a sudden, you are there in the show yourself!

CHAPTER 35

"Good will win over evil."

A s the automatic writing sessions went on during the next few days, it seemed I was getting a little better at receiving messages from the spirit world. Each day the Guides would start by writing "Lily, Ruth, Art, and Bob," as if to let me know who was on the other side of these communications. I would ask a question and would get the answer.

I felt like I was in a new relationship—sort of feeling things out. And looking back, I guess I was.

"Jane was the teacher, and I was the student…"

The pen was moving quicker. The writing was a bit more legible. I was making progress in my ability to do the automatic writing, but I was still nowhere nearly as adept—and am still not—at receiving these communications as Jane was. By this point, communications were simply gushing out through her whenever she put the pen to paper or sat down at the keyboard on the computer.

It was clear to me that whereas I was still in the early stages of learning to receive the writings, my sister was, by comparison, much more advanced in her abilities to be a conduit for the information the Guides wanted to get out. Jane was the teacher, and I was the student, so to speak.

I would ask Jane different questions in my attempt to get better at the writings. I was trying to understand if there were certain things she had been doing that I could either duplicate or avoid in hopes of having her type of success at the writing. It was clear that I was not going to get to her level of ability overnight. In fact, the Guides came through a few weeks after I had started and said:

> **Paul will not be able to get going on this in the time we had hoped, but anything he can do is appreciated. The most important thing is to just keep going and don't forget not to lose heart.**

"I wasn't at all sure how I was going to find the time and energy to make a contribution to this new spiritual project that had been asked of us..."

At this time, I was extremely busy with work—and still am. The two companies I am involved in with Andrew Zenoff are modest-sized enterprises that do not have a large staff. This requires that everyone involved—and we are fortunate to have some very dedicated staff members and investors—wear a lot of different hats and take on multiple responsibilities. Hence, when the automatic writing began, my long hours at work did not leave a great deal of extra time for the new endeavor with Ruth and the Guides.

Further compounding the tightness of my schedule in 2002 was the fact that I had started a side project of building our father a house on the east coast in our hometown of Castine, Maine. I could not afford a general contractor to oversee a project that was already stretching my finances, so I took on the job myself and was attempting to get it done from three thousand miles away. Although the experience I had from building houses while living on Nantucket was helpful, it turned out to be a very challenging and, at times, frustrating endeavor to try to manage the job from so far away. Fortunately, I had a great deal of help from both our father and our brother Joe, the one sibling of ours who still lives full-time in Castine. The house was finally completed in 2005, and Dad is living there happily, so it was all worth it in the long r.

With work and the house project both going on simultaneously in 2002, however, I was feeling like my plate was already full. I wasn't at all sure how I was going to find the time and energy to make a contribution to this new spiritual project that had been asked of us— or, I should say, that we, or more specifically Rob, had actually asked for. Don't get me wrong: I was excited about what was happening, but I just didn't know how it was going to fit in with my already full life.

"Hearing this stuff about 'The Dark Side' and 'evil ones' made me feel like I had Darth Vader or the Devil on my trail."

A few weeks into my writing, I started to have bad nightmares and physical ailments. I had bulging discs in my back that were acting up, as well as tendonitis in my elbow. It was as if someone, or something, didn't want me to participate.

I was feeling overwhelmed with my workload, frustrated with my ailments, and guilty for not spending more time on the automatic writing. Jane was a single mother with two young boys and was working full-time, but yet found a way to dedicate the time she needed to do the writing. Realizing this made me ask myself why I couldn't get more done.

The Guides came through in one of Jane's transmissions in August with the following explanation:

> **The Dark Side, as Rob calls it, is zoning in on Paul because it knows you and Rob are fierce to get this off the ground, but**

we see angels surrounding Paul as we send in reinforcements to protect him. The best and most powerful tool Paul can use is his own spirit and incredibly strong mind. He is susceptible to fear and The Dark Side because he has let it invade his mind.

Prayer and daily meditations will take Paulie far. We can recommend that he listen to soothing music right before bed. Environmental music such as the tapes you have, Jane, are good and also Bach, Brahms' Lullaby, and other Brahms music. The New Age bookstores can recommend some good spiritual music for Paul to fall asleep to, if he can adjust his mind to music while he is trying to fall asleep.

Jane, your energy has already been flowing to protect Paulie, as your will is stronger than The Dark Side cares to reckon with. But do not put yourself in a compromising or vulnerable situation, as we need your strength to carry on with the writing of this book.

We are happy with your progress and will start to get messages through to Paul soon. His nightmares will only last as long as he suffers from the fear that they can harm him. He must use simple chants [in the] evenings before he goes to bed, and we will send him an army of singing angels to be at his bedside. He can only deliver himself from the evil ones if he chooses to do so. Letting them in is subtle, and he can ward them off with the suggestions we have given to you to overcome his fear of all that is not good.

To conclude for now, we ask that you call your brother Paul and let him know of the news we have just relayed in helping him overcome The Dark Side.

After hearing what the Spirit Guides had to say about my nightmares and fears and their suggestions to combat them, I had mixed emotions. On the one hand, I felt good that the Spirit Guides had an explanation for what I had been feeling and recommendations on what to do about it. On the other hand, however, hearing this stuff about "The Dark Side" and "evil ones" made me feel like I had Darth Vader or the Devil on my trail.

"Good will win over evil. Write the book."

Although what the Guides had said didn't comfort me in any way, it did at least provide an explanation for what I was experiencing and a way to combat what was going on. I took their advice and listened to soothing music at night, started to meditate, and said more prayers. Eventually, the nightmares went away and my ailments got better. Looking back, I think the repressed fear I had inside was causing tension to build up in my body and causing my physical ailments to manifest.

After the nightmares seemed to have stopped and in the midst of an automatic writing session at the table on the morning of September 9, 2002, I mentally asked the Guides the following question:

Have the nightmares gone away for good?

The Spirit Guides replied by writing,

Yes, no more nightmares. Good will win over evil. Write the book.

I guess the Guides were saying they had done their part—now I should get busy doing mine.

CHAPTER 36

Love Is the
Answer

I n spite of the Spirit Guides' reassurances and advice, I asked Jane
to pose another question to them for me. Even though I was receiving communications from these same spirits, I nonetheless felt
that my sister's connection with Ruth and the Guides was stronger
than mine and that I could receive additional help through her contact with them.

"We're happy to have you aboard."

On September 14, 2002, Jane asked the Guides this question:

*Is there any further information or advice that would help
brother Paul be able to receive automatic writing?*

The Guides responded:

> The writing for Paul is easier if his mind is clear and not on
> money matters for himself, for the family. We know he is gener-
> ous and concerned about Mom, Laura, and Dad, but we can
> best come through if his mind is not cluttered with unneces-
> sary thoughts about death, money, or other matters.
> He should concentrate, but not to the degree that he is
> overdoing it. It is his right and privilege to use his gift. We

222

hope he will shut down the worries in himself. Instead, bring out the warrior. Instead, bring out joy for himself, and not so much anxiety or fear. [To] fear is not to gain an ounce, as it can grip him and take over. But we see him lighting up and bringing his mind at ease. Money matters will work out, and we're happy to have you aboard.

Again, it seemed like good advice, and a positive outcome seemed to be on the horizon. They were right. I do worry about members of our family, their health, and my ability to help them financially. I especially worry about my mom's weight and my dad's alcoholism. And having grown up without a lot of financial resources, providing for my family members and myself has also long weighed on my mind.

"If there was one theme that was emerging from what the Guides were saying, it was 'Love.'"

I continued with the automatic writing sessions through the end of the third week of September. Because I was so anxious and eager to get into work in the mornings to tackle the piles on my desk, however, I had decided to start doing the writings in the late evenings. This period had now become a more peaceful time of day for me than the morning.

A lot of what the Guides had to say through me during this time period were one-sentence statements:

"Love is the answer." "Think good thoughts." "Pray for peace." "Love to you all." "Preserve the Earth." "We all must think as one." "Peace on Earth." "Higher vibration for all." "Raise the consciousness of all." "Think positive." "Good will to all." "Be peaceful in your heart." "Love is the answer." "Yes, yes–love, love, love."

If there was one theme that was emerging from what the Guides were saying, it was "Love." I think they may be on to something.

CHAPTER 37

Why Us?

I continued to do the writing in the evenings through the end of that year, 2002, but, because of all the other responsibilities and demands I had in my life, not as frequently as before. When I did sit down to do the writing, it was a combination of two things:

1. The Guides sharing information they wanted to get out; and

2. My asking the Guides questions in my head and their answering, usually in short sentences.

My sessions would typically start with five to ten minutes of meditation, a few minutes of prayer, and then the actual writing would begin. It would go on for fifteen to twenty minutes, after which point I would feel somewhat drained. It was a feeling of being a bit tired, as I think it required a lot of my mental energy for them to use me as a vehicle to get their information across. There was also still the distinct feeling of amazement and wonder that this was happening to me.

"Why did they choose us to pick up Ruth's torch, so to speak?"

In early December, I remember thinking that I should be writing more, dedicating more time to the project, and playing a larger role in all of this. I guess I was feeling a bit guilty again and having some doubts. Feeling down, I asked Jane to check in with the Guides again on my behalf, and they had some more inspiring words that helped me to stabilize and strengthen my belief.

I found the Guides' repeated reassurances to be important in the beginning, because the nature of what was happening made me stop and question at times whether this was all for real or not. This type of stuff was not what most people are brought up to believe in. Even coming from an open-minded family like ours, communicating with spirits was not easy to fathom…especially when it was happening to me.

I think anyone in this position would naturally have doubts and disbelief at first. I know I certainly did. I remember thinking: *Why did they choose us to pick up Ruth's torch, so to speak? There must be other people who are better suited for such an undertaking. Like another writer maybe, who has experience writing books. Or possibly someone who is already adept at this automatic writing thing.*

It just didn't seem to make sense to choose the Macombers for the job. When I thought about it, it seemed we just weren't qualified for such a task. So why was it that we were chosen?

"You chose to do this together."

In asking myself why my family had been selected to carry on Mrs. Montgomery's work, I was very aware that the Guides had already commented about this subject in the first few months of their automatic writing transmissions through Jane. In fact, they had offered many words of encouragement to my siblings and me on this topic, including the following:

> It is your family's great dynamic and strength of character that will get you far with this book and the work outlined herein. To be committed to family is very important in the eyes of the Lord. And although the Macomber family has had its share of problems on the Earth, each one does not go without a lesson.

And we see in the end, for lack of a better word, or should we say, "in the overall picture of things," we see the Macombers as having great strength because they take their lessons seriously; in the school of hard knocks, as well as in the sense of academia. We see them as not people with big heads because of this, but people who are humbled by their experiences and smart in taking their lessons seriously. For everyone possesses something.

The Macombers, Billy's [our uncle] family too, are great learners because they thirst for knowledge on every level. It is in this thirst for knowledge that they have been put here on this Earth together at this time to complete this assignment.

Thirst for knowledge on every level is an important tool in the advancement of the soul. Every mind and soul is thirsty to some degree, but some shut out those experiences [that] can be most useful to them.

We have tried to use the teaching tools that are most useful when teaching the men of the world. The teaching of man can be frustrating at times for those of us who look on. But alas! For we have been men too and understand the intricate emotions that man holds in his heart.

It is not always easy to be a man and manage all the emotions that come with that particular territory. We see that man has struggled with his lessons in this life on Earth and we hope he will take these lessons and go forth to further his soul.

We see man's fate on Earth as his own. And if he continues on a path of destruction, he will destroy himself. But if he chooses to get back in the path to love, then he will truly rejoice in his own works and his lessons will not be in vain.

It is your job, Jane and Rob and Phyl and Paul, to get as much information out as you can. It may be Jane and Rob who are putting forth the most effort in getting this book done, but it is the collaboration of all of you that will make it happen. You were not randomly put here together; you chose to do this together.

Okay, so this was supposed to be "a family project." In spite of the things the automatic writing transmissions were saying about my family and me and the Guides' repeated urgings for us to carry their message to the world, I was still knee-deep in doubt about my ability to live up to their expectations. And although I hoped (and still do) that other Macombers would get involved in this project, other than Laura helping out with some transcription work for a little while early on in the project, no other family members had chosen to join Jane, Phyl, Rob, and me in the writing of this book. Understandably so, for I was just beginning to come to grips with the difficulties involved in adding such a large undertaking to an already full life.

"To realize your full potential can be scary. This is another reason we want Jane to do the work on this book with her brothers and sisters."

The Guides knew that what they were asking my family and me to do would not be easy. Our co-authors from the spirit realm were aware that there would be a lot of fear involved in our attempt to get this project off the ground. Yet they continued to emphasize that, like all human beings, we were capable of achieving large goals if we could get ourselves past our own fright.

My take on the Guides' requests as of early December 2002: *Much easier said than done.*

I was still filled with fear about what my family and I were doing.

"It is only through the darkness that the light can be seen."

At this point, I definitely needed more convincing that my family and I were up to the task of serving as messengers for The Other Side. Realizing this, the unseen energy in charge of Jane's automatic

writing session of December 7, 2002, tackled my concerns head-on
and addressed the matter of my life mission:

> **Paul's life mission this time around is to get the world to
> believe. It is what Paul has set up for himself; what he has
> chosen to do. It is his strongest quality, this belief of his. Of
> course, it is really just a remembering of sorts, but he wants
> to make the world a brighter place.**
>
> **He is a bringer of light, as you all are; Macombers that is.
> You may have dark periods, of course. Your father's drinking
> for one.**
>
> **But it is only through the darkness that the light can be
> seen. Only through the darkness the world has known, that
> the light can be now brought forth. Without darkness, there is
> no light. To experience goodness and lightness, you have to
> carry the weight of darkness. Otherwise, you could not know
> light.**
>
> **Now, you may be asking yourself, then how can we ever
> have world peace if we are to experience darkness? To this I
> say to you, go out and stamp out the darkness. Enough of it
> has been seen to know the light.**
>
> **You are not on this mission in life, as you call it, by acci-
> dent. You chose to come here together to bring forth the light.
> *You chose this: Your mission.***

Pretty heavy stuff. Although I believed each of us arrives here
on Earth with a specific mission in life and we know, prior to birth,
that we will be intentionally joining people who will be our family
members and close friends, having Heaven spell things out in such
strong terms wasn't that easy to digest. I was finding out that it was
a lot easier to read about such concepts as life missions and soul
groups than it was to attempt to live up to them.

CHAPTER 38

"A Lady of the Highest Order" and a Man on "A Very Purposeful Journey"

Adding to my concerns in December of 2002, which were inhibiting me from immersing myself in the automatic writing as fully as I would have liked, was the fact that I was having some physical ailments again, including shin splints and elbow trouble. The Spirit Guides came through to Jane on December 22, 2002, with a few words of wisdom for me about the situation:

> **Paul, we recommend not so much exercising your muscles, as your brain.**

Ever since those words years ago, I have been trying to take the Guides' advice about working my brain more and my muscles less. Because of my hectic schedule, it was difficult to work out on a regu-

lar basis. Wanting to keep physically fit to the extent that time permitted, when I did make it to the gym, I was overdoing it, and often
doing more harm than good to my body. Hence, although I still
make an effort to stay in shape and fight my aging body, I now work
out when I can, but try not to overdo it.

"Let Marge take care of Marge and Paul take care of Paul."

Compounding my overall outlook on things back in late 2002
was my concern for our mother's health. Having long battled a weight
problem, she had also developed bad knees and arthritis. Because
Mum is such a loving person, and also just because she is my mom,
I was, and am, extremely concerned about her condition. I wanted
to try to help her with her weight problem, and I tended to obsess
about helping her get healthier, to ensure that she lives a long
life...about which the Guides said:

> You stress too much. We have said this before. Let Marge
> take care of Marge and Paul take care of Paul.
>
> We admire your indestructible love for your mother, but
> don't make it at the expense of your own health. She will be
> fine once she is on her own path. Light will show her the way.
> Take your worries and toss them in the ocean. She will find
> her own way.

I understand that the Guides were letting me know that my
mother's journey was her own and not mine. For me it was–and is–
difficult to see someone I love so much struggling with a difficult
health issue and not want to try to help as much as possible. I guess
I still need to know where and when to lend help and when to let
her handle her own issues

"The most important aspect of all life and all things–and that as we all know is love."

I was still having a tough time fully focusing on the automatic
writing, but knew that the Spirit Guides were right in their admoni-

tions to me about Mum. In fact, the Guides had already spoken at length a few months earlier to my siblings and me about our mother during Jane's September 1, 2002, transmission:

> **Margaret Macomber is a lady of the highest order, and we can tell she has already done much good in the world. It is because of her that you are who you are and because of her you have learned to grasp the most important aspect of all life and all things–and that as we all know is love.**
>
> **Not wars, not money, not control, or destruction can take your love away or take Margaret's love away. She should not be ignored or told not to eat this or that, but let her live her own life. And love will reach many more of the Earthlings if she is able to go about her passion and her works.**
>
> **Margaret Macomber is, again, a lady of the highest order. Do not take her for granted, Jane and Rob. And do not tell her she is not capable of this, that, or anything.**
>
> **Let her love be a lesson to us all as she is a more powerful being than most recognize. Her strength is amazingly subtle and her energy flows with goodness from all areas. She is so strong and so smart, and we can see her as a mother to all things.**
>
> **And she is your mother, so treat her with respect and bow down as she graces all of your lives in a way that is fascinating. And the whole picture show will end on a happy note.**

I include Lily and the gang's words about Mum for three reasons:

1. They were a strong reminder to me of the importance of not letting my love for our mother cause me to interfere with her living her own life;

2. The Guides' urgings to my siblings and me to accord Mum her proper due was an important wake-up call to us never to forget all that she has done for us in our lives; and

3. The spirit realm's statement, "[B]ecause of her you have learned to grasp the most important aspect of all life and all things–and that as we all know is love," is of central importance to you, the reader, in understanding how Jane, Rob, and I have come to be writing this book. Although we certainly do not put into practice as often as we should all of the lessons she has taught us about the power of love, it is from our mother Margaret that we have come to believe in the power of love to solve any problem, right any wrong, and, most significantly in terms of how we view the saga of the human race, create "a happy ending" for any story.

I cannot emphasize enough the degree to which our mother's belief in the power of love has influenced our lives and allowed us to be open to the messages from the Guides and Ruth about love's ability to heal the hurts of the world. And, as you have just seen, these spirits weren't bashful about reminding us how essential a factor our mother has been in my siblings' and my being given the privilege of receiving automatic writing communications. In fact, even before I began my first attempts to make contact with the spirit world, the Guides summed things up on this issue pretty concisely during Jane's transmission of July 30, 2002:

> **Her weight problems and arthritis have made her even stronger, as she has proven love is the main staple, even in the face of adversity and dealing with all of the problems life has had to offer her. She is a great spirit awaiting any journey that is put in front of her. She has great strength in the soul and the mind as well. And she is a player in this for her life, her entire life of eternity. Without the love of your "grand" mother, Rob and Jane, you would not be in the position of doing this book together with us.**

To this I can only say, "*Amen.*"

Paul Gets Personal

To provide you with an illustration of some of what has been said in this chapter about our mother, I will now share with you some rather personal things.

In spite of our parents' divorce in 1979, we have still, to this day, felt like a complete family unit. Neither of our parents ever remarried—or had a significant other for that matter—since their divorce.

I believe our parents ended up getting divorced because our mom could no longer live with our dad's alcoholism and everything that came with it. In fact, Mum said that a primary reason she went through with the divorce was that she had hoped it might jolt Dad into getting off the booze for good. It wasn't that she ever stopped loving him; she hasn't and never will. I know this because she tells me often she wishes they could get back together, but she just can't go through what she did in her earlier years with him if he's not going to change.

Our mom has lived in Massachusetts since 1987, while our dad remains in our hometown of Castine, Maine. We usually all get together during the holidays, with our parents enjoying one another's company for several days. They then often get quarreling and, if we're in Massachusetts, Dad will head home to Castine, or, if we're in Maine, Mum will head back to Massachusetts. This has been the pattern of their relationship since she moved from Maine.

My family recently (it's 2006 as I'm writing this) got together in Castine for the Fourth of July holiday, as we normally do. My wife, Sasha, and I arrived on July 2nd, along with Mum and numerous other family members. We all had a great time being together, as we do every Fourth.

At the end of the week, everyone was making plans to leave Castine and to head back home. Everyone except Mum, that is. She announced she was going to be staying on with Dad through the end of the summer or longer if things went well.

Many of us tried to convince her that this was not a good idea. Our argument was that they had a good week together without quarreling and it was now time to go and leave on a positive note. Mum said she had talked it over with Dad, and they both agreed that she should stay indefinitely. Her mind was made up, and she didn't care to hear any more about her leaving with everyone else.

Mum said she still loved Dad just as much as she ever had and vice versa. They were much closer to the end of their lives than they were to the beginning and wanted to be together. For how long, time would tell, but for now they were once again very much enjoying being together, and she was staying.

If you knew what our mother had endured during all the years we were growing up—the poverty, the less-than-finished homes we lived in, the never-ending sacrifice for us kids, and the alcoholism and all that comes with that disease—then you'd realize the only way she could want to live with Dad again was because of one reason only: *love.*

Our mother's belief in love and the power it has to overcome *anything* is what, above all else, defines her as a human being. This is, without question, the greatest gift she has bestowed upon our family and those who know her. Her life is an ongoing lesson to us in the power and depth of love. And still to have such love and belief in our father, Mum continues to teach by example...as she always has.

As I write these words, it's been nearly three weeks since she decided to stay with Dad in Castine. She's still there. They're having a good time being together. Dad remains sober. Quite frankly, each day I call there, I can't believe it.

Once again, our mother's love and belief have overcome her difficulties. And although tomorrow, the next day, or the one after that may bring new troubles, her belief in the power of love will never, ever diminish.

"Bobby Macomber...has taught you all a lesson, a great lesson, in the art of forgiveness and caring. It is a treasure to be cherished. Without his great gift to you all, this project would not be possible."

Although the Guides had a lot to say about our mother, they soon wound up their explanation of her influence in our lives and opened up about the invaluable role played by our father. What they said about Dad in one of their transmissions with Jane would turn out for me to be one of the most moving parts of this entire experience of communication with spirits from Heaven:

> [Marge] is of the utmost importance in helping the children she has borne, and your father is also another great spirit of strength. He has not died because he has much good to do for people.
>
> Your father has great strength of character, although he may not always show it. And may at times even defy his own strengths. But fear not, it is but a short journey home when the soul realizes that its potential is endless.
>
> We speak of Bobby Macomber here because it is a reminder that he is good and will do good all the days of his life, even though there has been a lot of hurt in his life. Is it no wonder that people just love Bobby? He is of great spirit and that is why people love him.
>
> It does not matter that he boozes it up or takes his time in some matters. It is his soul that people see and that is what they *love* about Bobby Macomber. His soul. His relentless passion and fervor. It is the dance in his step and the twinkle in his eye that make people smile.
>
> This may all sound sticky sweet, and for those of you who know him it may not be necessary for you to hear this. But it is important for *him* to know that [he] is a great human and great soul.

So, Jane, we are seeing that maybe you think people will be bored with all of this, "You're a great soul" bit. But it is a much better place to be where people are honest and loving. Bobby Macomber is a great person, and we just want him to know that.

We recognize his "failures" as strength-building for the entire family. He has taught you all a lesson, a great lesson, in the art of forgiveness and caring. It is a treasure to be cherished. Without his great gift to you all, this project would not be possible. It is his giving and his suffering that is his gift to you. He has given much of his life away to booze and alcoholism, so his family may share a better understanding of what it is like to forgive and still love someone even though they have wronged you.

Your mother is a great example of this. It is her example that we are trying to teach the world.

But although the Spirit Guides had interjected another brief reference to Mum, they were far from done writing about our father.

"Robert Macomber has chosen to give his life to alcohol and such for one and only one reason—so that he may teach his children the power of love, understanding, and *forgiveness*. It is a very purposeful journey that he is on, and it is not to be taken lightly."

Here's how the Guides concluded their explanation of the purpose with which our father arrived here on Earth in 1930:

Marge may seem to be the strong one and the tolerant one, but we tell you this: Robert Macomber has chosen to give his life to alcohol and such for one and only one reason— so that he may teach his children the power of love, understanding, and *forgiveness*. It is a very purposeful journey that he is on, and it is not to be taken lightly.

He is a man of great means and great wisdom, although his foggy haze may seem to impair his life and the life of others. It is his choice to give this gift to you; and so whenever you are mad–any one of you–remember all that your father has given you.

He has given you humility so that you might know compassion. He has given you weaknesses so that you might know strength. He has given you wisdom and knowledge and love.

It is with great enthusiasm that we bring you this news of Robert Macomber and all that he is and all that he has meant to you all in his lifetime. It is a step for you. It is a sacrifice he has made to teach his family the forgiving and kind ways that we all really share, but have forgotten to some degree. It is his name that rings true when his true voice is heard. We may seem to be carrying on about all this, *but make no mistake*, Bobby Macomber is of the highest order and don't you forget it.

We know that he has caused you great frustration. But he has also given you gifts beyond compare that won't ever go away.

When the Guides came through with all these things they said about our dad and how he had chosen to be an alcoholic in this life before he was incarnated–so that he would be able to teach us kids the power of forgiveness and unconditional love in this lifetime– their words really rang true to me. So much so that I now find myself having a difficult time trying to describe it.

It was something I had been attempting to figure out all of my life. When the Guides revealed this, it was like a bell went off in my head. This puzzle I had been trying to piece together for a lifetime instantly fell into place.

It wasn't just a convenient answer for something I had been searching for since before I can remember. It was an instant knowing of the truth. That feeling you get when you know with all your heart and soul that it is the right and true thing. It was one of those feelings.

I was thankful that this lifelong mystery had been revealed...*after the fact*, in terms of my siblings and my already having been exposed to the lessons about forgiveness and unconditional love, made possible through our family situation and having grown up with our very special parents.

The thought that our father has suffered for so long battling alcoholism in order to further the progress of the souls of my siblings and myself, filled me up with a sense of immense gratitude. To think he had, prior to being born, knowingly signed up for such a lifelong sacrifice was humbling.

I've always loved our dad very much. When we were growing up, I would get angry and upset at the thought that he would hurt us with his alcoholism and wondered why he had chosen to do so. I now know he wasn't choosing to hurt us, but rather, had long before elected to suffer for the betterment of all his family.

Dad is not just my dad, but a best friend also. We talk almost every day on the telephone. And when I hang up with him, I'm always left with a feeling of being blessed that he's my father.

"It is this great union of Marge and Bob that has taken so many years, that is the teacher in this family."

As the Spirit Guides explained to us the pivotal role our parents had played in teaching us valuable lessons about life, Lily and company also spoke of our family having a collective mission here on "Schoolhouse Earth." The Guides said that we had all journeyed to Earth together to fulfill a joint mission to help the planet and improve the state it is in today. In short, it seemed that what the spirits in Heaven were telling us was that all our lessons in life had been in preparation for the job of doing our part to turn this great world around and help get it headed in a better direction.

See for yourself what the Guides wrote to us through Jane's automatic writing communications:

> And we say this to you, *all of you in the Macomber family*, it is not without the combination of these partners that you could do the work you came here and set out to do. It is this great union of Marge and Bob that has taken so many years, that is the teacher in this family.
>
> And it is without this team of Marge and Bob, that you would not know many, many things–things that have brought you, Jane and Rob and Paul, [a] great many truths and [a] great many things for you to share with the world. It is in this respect that we say this is a family project.
>
> Each and every step that you have all taken throughout your life has led you to where you are today. It has led you to be better people. It has led you to a higher path.
>
> It is this process–one that may not always seem to be what it is–that is powerful and strong. It is weakness that brings strength. Darkness that brings light. And wisdom, no matter how well disguised, that brings joy and love.
>
> So fear not that you have made mistakes and taken roads not traveled at all by others. It is indeed a long and winding road, but a great gift as well–to yourselves and to the world. It is not a mystery that you should try to figure out, but one you should let unfold so that we may work together and bring the rest of the world together.

I am hopeful that as this book series starts to unfold, more of our family members will get involved with it. But let me be very clear that we are but a few of the many, many sparks that are supposed to ignite a much-needed global effort to turn this world in a better direction. In short, it's up to *all of us* here on Earth to join together and do our parts. Only by all of us uniting and believing that we can change the world for the better will we truly make it happen.

PART IV

Heaven's Call to Action ...to All of Us

"The thousand years of peace that has been talked about–and has been waiting–is here for the taking."

–The Spirit Guides

"We need to glorify good deeds, no matter how small....Everyone needs light...the light's starting to burst out at the seams because there is a real desire to get back to doing good."

–The Spirit Guides

CHAPTER 39

Heaven's Optimistic Outlook for Planet Earth

Now you know how this adventure began for our family. But this project isn't about the Macombers. It involves the family of the entire human race. According to the spirits in Heaven, we're all on a great adventure here on Earth together. And because we're struggling mightily on our journey, they have a plan to help us out.

Despite the many problems on our planet about which Lily and friends expressed concern, they were decidedly optimistic about humanity's future. Demonstrating an inclination to accentuate the positive, the Spirit Guides explained that humankind needs to build upon the existing pockets of progress in our world. Emphasizing that we must generate more and more momentum toward the happy future we all want, the Guides stressed the importance of "glorifying good deeds":

We need to glorify good deeds, no matter how small. The little things we do for each other will influence the entire world. We need to set, like wildfire, a chain reaction where people want to continue spiritually, while still going on with their lives.

What needs to happen is a small chain of events to get this thing running. I don't mean just the book, but the small chain reaction of nice deeds going around the world like wildfire.

We need to get the word out. We need to keep in mind how important each and every step we take is. What the world needs to do is take as many steps in the right direction as possible.

Fueling the Earth's people will not take a large spark. They are ready for a change and want to be good and want to get going on this. Even people who are dark are getting tired of the permeating darkness.

Everyone needs light. And the darkness is smothering that. But the light's starting to burst out at the seams, because there is a real desire to get back to doing good.

We must start in with light and continue to start each day with a renewed joy for the planet and the lighter side of life. We need to start together, so many lightened souls who are on this side [can] complete their missions by coming back to the new Earth so we can brighten it up even more. This is such a beautiful place on Earth. We will be so happy to see our plan of action shown to the golden souls who occupy this beautiful planet.

Action is the key word here. Action of all peoples, parties. All nations, all people of all creeds, and one idea of love and harmony in the Earth and peace in the hearts of men. For that is the whole purpose of this book: [It] is so people of all nations, creeds, colors, and diversity can live, work, and, yes, play here on this Earth together.

CHAPTER 40

Heaven's "Action Plan for Planet Earth"

Action-oriented is what the spirit realm says we all need to be if humankind wishes to avoid self-destruction and begin the much vaunted Thousand Years of Peace. How exactly do we get there? By implementing Heaven's three-part "Action Plan for Planet Earth."

Although the voluminous amount of automatic writing transmissions we have received contains lots of information about many different topics, the following overview of the Spirit Guides' Action Plan represents the core of their advice to humanity about how to save ourselves as a race. The solutions offered by Heaven focus on what the spirit realm sees as the greatest threats to the continued existence of humankind. And to make it personally relevant for each and every one of us, this overview of Heaven's Action Plan for Planet Earth includes a succinct answer to the question, *"What's in it for me?"*

Part I: Help the Third World More...a Lot More!

First and foremost, the Action Plan for Planet Earth stresses the need for Third World countries to receive greater recognition in world affairs. The Guides have emphasized that these nations should be accorded a greater voice about what is happening on our planet and that they have much to contribute to the world community.

As we understand the message, although these Third World countries need help from the more fortunate nations in terms of economic resources and political recognition, they also have much to offer in return. The Guides have explained that the populations of many of these Third World countries are very much in tune with the Earth and possess knowledge of universal laws of existence that can be of great benefit to the human race as a whole. Furthermore, because deprived Third World countries are the planet's most fertile breeding grounds for ever-increasing amounts of war, terrorism, and disease spreading around the globe, it is *critical* that we heed Heaven's call to action on this all-important issue.

As you will learn in a subsequent chapter, the Spirit Guides let it be known early on that we were supposed to give away 50 percent of this project's profits to serve as seed money for an ongoing concert series that would benefit the people of Third World nations. So that's what we're going to do: donate half of our profits to start The World Aid Concert Series.

Part II: Start Listening to Children and Women and Let Them Help Lead Our World Out of the Major Mess We're In!

The second element of the Spirit Guides' Action Plan brings to everyone's attention the plight of the underprivileged segments of society, most notably the children and women of the world.

The Guides have explained that we need to begin listening to the opinions of children, for they often possess far greater wisdom than anyone imagines. In short, "Kids get it."

The world, especially the industrialized nations, needs to do a better job of raising children. Young people must receive more and better guidance early on in their lives, for they possess the potential to do great good in our world. Social conditioning, however, in the United States and other developed nations, places *far too much* significance on competition, greed, and materialism, and *not nearly enough* on love, time spent with family, and the importance of doing things for others. But if the latter values can be better taught to the kids of this planet, then they can truly help lead us to a much improved world. And children in the United States possess the potential to play *an especially valuable role* in Heaven's Action Plan for Planet Earth.

Women are another primary underprivileged group of people who need to play a greater part in running the world if it is to survive. This is true in all ways: economically, politically, socially, and spiritually. *Women are getting a raw deal* almost everywhere you look.

Rich nations and poor nations alike continue to relegate women to inferior roles all around the globe. But if we start treating women better and let them *share decision-making responsibilities in all aspects of life equally with men,* then there will be more peace in our world, less poverty, and far more happiness than most of us can even imagine.

Part III: Clean Up Our Act and Stop Destroying the Earth!

The third part of the spirit realm's Action Plan is one that is an oft-repeated refrain in Ruth Montgomery's books: that is, the urgency of human beings taking better care of our home, the Earth. The Spirit Guides are imploring us to take immediate action to reverse the way in which we are now poisoning the planet and sowing the seeds of our own demise with an ostrich-like, head-in-the-sand mentality with respect to future consequences of our present actions.

What we're doing to the Earth is comparable to what happens all too often when one gets a new credit card—you go out on a wild and reckless spending spree and don't think about the future consequences of your actions. Or should we say, *choose not to think about the consequences.*

Most of us know planetary resources are being depleted and silently hope that we'll be dead by the time the Earth's stores finally run dry. Maybe a little consideration is given to the potential predicament that our children or grandchildren may be facing down the road, but not nearly enough to change our out-of-control spending of the planet's finite supply of natural resources.

But it's not too late to stop raping and pillaging our planet. The Guides say that Mother Nature possesses remarkable healing powers...if we will just give her a chance to live. All we have to do is begin treating Mother Nature right and her incomparable restorative qualities will prevail, and she will continue to take care of us all with the bounties of her blessings.

"We are grateful for your efforts in advance."

The Spirit Guides have issued a call to action to each and every person to save the Earth. They are asking that we each pitch in *to whatever extent we can* to help Mother Nature sustain us and ensure the survival of future generations. To that end, here's what the spirits in Heaven have asked us to convey directly to you about your participation in the Action Plan for Planet Earth:

> **We want to see every person available involved in some way, even if it is a small contribution. Small contributions add up to big love. This is the whole reason we are doing this book. We want everyone who joins in to know that we are grateful for your efforts in advance."**

What's in It for You?

We all ask the question, *"What's in it for me?"* about virtually everything in Life.

Although this aspect of Heaven's Action Plan for Planet Earth will be examined in greater detail in the second book of this series, understanding some basic answers to this question is absolutely central to grasping the urgency of the spirit realm's call to action to us all. So, here's a short list of what's in it for you by helping implement the three main components of Heaven's Action Plan:

1. Doing more to help the Third World:

Before we began this project, we didn't have a clue about the extent to which *everyone's life* is connected to what is happening in the Third World. But as we started to learn a little bit about the global implications of Third World issues, it soon became resoundingly clear that this topic is one that affects us all...no matter where we might live.

To illustrate this point, we'll now share with you some words by a fellow who has most definitely put helping residents of the Third World front and center in his own life. Although you'll be reading a good deal more about this big-hearted Irishman later in this book, below is an excerpt from an address that rock star and humanitarian Bono gave summarizing things in a very powerful fashion. Here's how he explains how closely connected the welfare of Africans is to that of those of us who may not live in the Third World but whose lives are, whether we know it or not, inextricably entwined with the fate of our sisters and brothers who do live in the world's poorest nations:

> [T]his is not all about heart. We have to be smart here. I want to argue that, though Africa is not the frontline in the war against terror, it could be soon. Every week, religious extremists take another African village. They're attempting to bring order to chaos. Well, why aren't we?
>
> Poverty breeds despair. We know this. Despair breeds violence. We know this. In turbulent times, isn't it cheaper and

smarter to make friends out of potential enemies than to defend yourself against them later?

Well, the war against terror is bound up in the war against poverty, and I didn't say that. Colin Powell said that. Now when the military are telling us that this is a war that cannot be won by military might alone, maybe we should listen. There's an opportunity here, and it's real. It's not spin. It's not wishful thinking....

What I try to communicate, and you can help me if you agree, is that aid for Africa is just great value for money at a time when America really needs it. Putting it in the crassest possible terms, the investment reaps huge returns, not only in lives saved, but in goodwill, stability, and security that we will gain.[1]

2. *Paying more attention to the children and women of the world*:

Do we really want to keeping playing Russian roulette with not only our own lives, but also those of our children, grandchildren, great-grandchildren, and countless future generations? If we truly love our children and the younger generations as much as we say we do, then we will heed the Guides' advice and implement their plan of action for the planet. We're not just mortgaging their future, we're out-and-out dooming it by selfishly consuming the Earth's resources and exhausting the planet's capacity to renew itself.

And then there's the absolutely obscene double standard that exists with respect to the extent to which males, *especially white males*, control things in our world. So, if you are a female reading this, Heaven has a message for you:

It is mostly white males who are making up all the experiences your society has. Yes, that's right, they are formulating what you should wear, how you should look, what you should eat, and how you should feel. Especially how you should feel if

you don't add up to their measurements. How *bad* you should feel that is. How uncool you are if you don't wear the right thing, *think the right thing.*

For God's sake, literally for God's sake, won't you open up your eyes and see how misled you have all been? Think for yourselves. Express your own ideas, not what you think you're supposed to express.

And if you are male, please know that you don't have to worry about Heaven condemning you for the current second-class citizen status to which most of the world's women are relegated. We're all human. We all make mistakes.

Although the next book in this series will explain with more specificity what adjustments "between the sexes" the spirit realm sees as necessary to produce a more balanced, equitable, happier world *for all*, let's just say for now that most of us simply follow the model that has been handed down to us from generation to generation. But the time has come to recognize that the current model is flawed…*deeply flawed.*

Are we really so self-centered that we are willing to doom the future of our children and continue to give the females of the world the short end of the stick? We don't think so, and neither do the spirits in Heaven. We couldn't agree more with the Spirit Guides' belief that human beings are basically good by nature and that we just need to get back on track and do what's right for ourselves, for those we know and love, for those we don't know, even for those we may not like, and, last but not least, for the Earth.

3. Taking better care of our home, Planet Earth:

Helping clean up the Earth will increase your chances of surviving and not getting sick or injured as a result of any one of a number of things that are likely to happen if we continue our current abuse of Mother Nature:

- As the planet's natural resources dwindle lower and lower, more wars and terrorism will engulf the globe as people resort to force and fight over less and less.
- The greater our negative impact on the Earth, the more likely it is that more deadly diseases will sprout up and spread around the world. Human beings have drastically altered Mother Nature's balance. As the Spirit Guides said on just the third day this project began:

We need to stop putting poison in the air and land and sea. Otherwise, it should be no surprise to any of us that an Earth thrown out of equilibrium will spew poison back at us.

- Major cataclysmic Earth Changes *may* result if we don't change our ways. This is not meant in any way to cause fear but rather to explain that the planet itself has been thrown off balance by humans and will go through self-correcting measures that will affect humans negatively if we don't clean up our act. Severe weather and continued climate change are evidence of Earth's attempts to regain equilibrium.

It's not too late to prevent even bigger calamities from happening. The Spirit Guides have been very emphatic about this:

We can see a good, bright future for the Earth if we can get people to help with the cleanup of the Earth. Playing games is not our business. Getting the job done is.

The Earth shifting as we can see will be delayed as long as possible if we are able to get this message out and continue these writings, for the thirst [of] knowledge-seeking people of the world.

The Bottom Line

It's going to be a lot less expensive to follow Heaven's advice than it will be to go along with the same dumb "pretend-it's-not-happening" mentality that has carried the day so far. Do you think war is cheap? How about terrorism? Worldwide disease pandemics certainly aren't inexpensive. What about the global impact of a whole continent filled with orphans? And how's the future looking that we're all headed toward, that's the result of the current male-dominated decision-making model that dictates most of what happens on our planet? What about natural disasters on a worldwide scale?

We're talking bankrupt, folks. *All of us!* But again, *it doesn't have to be this way!* What it all comes down to is what happens—or doesn't happen—is up to us.

Are you familiar with the saying, "I wish I knew then what I know now"? Well, that's what these spirits in Heaven are giving us in the form of the Action Plan for Planet Earth: the knowledge they have of what things will be like if we don't wise up and start paying attention to what they're telling us. It's like we're in the process of taking a test, and they're giving us the answers!

Can you imagine how frustrating it must be for these spirits to keep sending us the correct exam answers, only to have so many of us ignore what they're saying? All we have to do is fill in the blanks with the information they're handing to us on a silver platter! And if we do, things will get better for all of us. *Much better.* The spirits in Heaven say the long-awaited Thousand Years of Peace could be ours for the taking.

CHAPTER 41

The United States and the Third World: "A Bright Future"

The road to the Thousand Years of Peace begins in the place on our planet that needs the most help: the Third World. And the single most important factor in making the Thousand Years of Peace a reality is the need for the United States to provide more help to Africa. According to the Guides, it is not only the right thing for America to do, but it is in her own best interest as well:

> The plight of the American people is stronger than one might think unless this plan of action is put into place and taken seriously. In the next few decades much good work will come from this project. And it is truly a project for the entire world.
>
> Today's lessons are not about the destruction of war and the ravaging effects of World Trade Centers being crashed into. It is about the extent of the good that goes on in the

world and where we want to see that go as we head into "the new millennium."

It is about bringing joy and happiness into hundreds of millions of lives who lack the everyday joys of running water and being able to watch your children play with a new toy. Or a boy about to go on an adventure for the first time.

It is about the contentment of a family held together by love and working toward goals we all really desire in our heart of hearts. It is not about making money and spending it for the sake of spending it, but about the joys that money can bring a starving family in Africa. Or the joy that making a gift for someone in a different country can bring into a child's heart.

Jane back with you.

These joys are things a lot of us take for granted. Not every child has a good childhood. Not every family has security. Not every person has a bathroom, running water, or a place to lay his head at night. These are everyday things that admittedly I sometimes take for granted.

Right now my children and I would like to move from our subsidized apartment into a house. It would be nicer to have more room, but we don't have it that bad. I try to remember we are far better off than many.

We have two bathrooms, two air conditioners, wall-to-wall carpeting, furniture, food, and more than enough stuff to fill it up. And, because I am fortunate enough to live in the richest country in the world, the government helps me pay my rent (but I look forward to when I can pay it in full myself).

We also have several family members right down the road. My children have rarely had a baby-sitter other than a family member. They can always count on Gramma Marge to console them if they have problems—especially if those problems are with me.

My two sons have a lifetime of memories filled with people who love them. And that includes friends. Sometimes I can't believe how many kids call our house in one day. We are truly blessed with what we have, both in the material and spiritual sense.

I believe people have the power to help others have these same kinds of things. Reaching out, with whatever you can give, no matter how small you may think it is, is going to bring about goodness in some way.

The United States and Power

The Guides didn't hesitate to say that the United States has both the power *and an obligation* to take a lead role in turning our planet around. And that duty begins by America doing more for others and taking the initiative to help those in need by taking action that will launch a worldwide trend of unprecedented generosity:

> **If you want to see an end to poverty in the world, including in this country, then you have to reach your hand out to the guy next door, and his neighbor, and his, etc. We want the U.S. to start this [movement because] it is the greatest nation in terms of the money and power it holds in influencing others. We want to express that, once this thing gets off the ground, the lightning speed chain reaction that will take place will be blinding.**

The Guides had previously hinted at forgetting about things like money. In reality, though (our Earthly reality), money does play a big part. And no one has more money than the United States. No one cares about money as much as people in the U.S.

I'm in total agreement with Lily, Ruth, and company: Let's show the world how great we really are by sharing that wealth. And–and this is a big "and"–let the rest of the world show us their wealth: their knowledge, their sense of community, their hopes and dreams.

Let it be a two-way street. Give and take, take and give. A friend of mine once said, "If everyone is giving, then everyone is receiving." How's that for wisdom?

The declaration that the United States still influences others was interesting to me. A lot of people around the world think we are the scum of the Earth. They think we are arrogant and cocky. And in some ways, we are. But the one thing, at least in my opinion, that many in the United States hold dear is *freedom.*

Some may argue that legislation such as the Patriot Act lessens our freedom in America, but the fact remains that we still have choices many people all over the world do not.

I, Jane, am an American woman, and I know that I am one of the most blessed humans on the planet. I can write my president and tell him I think we should not go to war. I can vote. I can go to school. I can wear whatever I want and marry whomever I want. I have choices.

These are the things about the United States that I believe influence people. I am so grateful to have these options. This is the real power that I think the Guides are talking about when they speak of the power in the United States. And what I have gathered from the Guides is that God wants us all—not just a select few—to have these freedoms.

Although the United States may have a special responsibility to help the rest of the world, that does not mean the rest of humanity should just sit around and wait to be saved by America. To the contrary, all nations and all peoples must pitch in to the best of their abilities if we're going to succeed in saving ourselves.

A Message of Hope for the People of Africa

But make no mistake about it, the spirits in Heaven say the citizens of the United States have a special role to play in helping others:

It is a dream of ours and God's to bring the people of the world together. To bring the Heavenly thoughts of our forefathers back down to the Earth where all men are truly created equal. And it's not so much that men are even created equal, so much as they are treated equal.

I thought it was interesting that the Guides mentioned our fore-fathers, American ones, that is. It was they, after all, who said, "All men are created equal."

As dire as the situation may be in Africa and other parts of the Third World, the Guides nonetheless foresee better times ahead...but say that such change will require much help and plenty of faith:

> **There is one message of hope we will give the people of Africa today. We see their fate in the hands of many and we see the glory of God shining on their plight. The last thing God or any Heavenly being wants to see is a nation destroyed because there is lack of help and faith. We can see a bright future as this inspiration will spread worldwide all in good time. It is our intention to bring as much possible joy to as many people in the world.**

Africa is one place we have been hearing a lot about lately. And it's about time. Just in the last month I have read four or five things about Darfur. George Clooney and his dad have been there. Mia Farrow. Look what Brad Pitt and Angelina Jolie did with the birth of their child: They dragged the media to a place that needs attention. Look at Bono's ONE Campaign.

It's refreshing to see people doing something great with their fame. These people's efforts are increasing our awareness about what needs to be done. Such celebrities are taking mainstream Americans where they have not gone often enough before: outside of their own realm and away from their comfortable daily lives. Celebrity activists have raised awareness about what it's like to be a child living with AIDS in Africa and what it's like to be a refugee with no place to go. And they have shown us what we can do to help.

I hope more of this rallying for Africa will continue. To leave Africa on its own for as long as "we" have is the biggest bit of racism since that continent's people were stolen and turned into slaves.

Thank God people are becoming more willing to take positive action. Let's get on with developing the potential of this great continent and its people and helping them forge a future full of hope and happiness.

"This country needs to get its act together.... We need to *treat* everyone as an equal."

Bringing hope and happiness to those in need is not going to happen by itself. It involves choosing to act or to sit on the sidelines.

Choice. That's what it all boils down to. The Guides kept stressing this:

> **What we need to reiterate in this book [is that] a global consciousness can bring together so many things in a world that desperately needs it. The global problems today are only problems today if we choose them to be.**

A global consciousness. That's quite a thought. But one that is becoming more and more evident.

It is nice to open up the newspaper and read that people are indeed taking steps to help end world poverty and hunger. To see that global warming isn't just a topic at a dinner party, but that people are trying to reverse it.

I heard somewhere that we have about ten years (it's 2006 as I write this) to reverse the damage we have done as a result of global warming. After that, it's all going to Hell in a handbasket. Ten years is not a lot of time. But it is enough, and I hope we continue to address the issue.

I saw a commercial the other day about global warming. Kids kept appearing on the screen saying nothing except, "Tick, tick, tick." At the end, they let you know they are talking about global warming and the urgency of time.

Time. The Guides relentlessly kept coming back to the point that time was running short for the United States to stop dilly-dallying about making an all-out effort to tackle our world's greatest problems head-on:

This country needs to get its act together and get back to remembering the good fortune it has and be an even better example to the other countries of the world. We need to discuss this with you at some length, as it is this measure that will help get this country back on its feet. Our founding fathers are not going to say we are not working or helping, but they know you can all do better as time goes on.

To get this thing going, we will have to still cover much ground, so be patient as we skip around from here to there. To get back to the education of this country—and we don't just mean the education of the children; we mean the education of the entire country and world—we want to say that it is up to the people who run the countries to realize the mistakes that they have made. Then and only then can the solutions occur. For if you don't see the problems and don't want to see the problems, then how can you resolve them?

Boy, is that true. If you don't think you have a problem, how can you fix it?

World leaders sign up for a very challenging job—there's no doubt about that. I wouldn't want to have that kind of pressure on me. Look at the pressure Abraham Lincoln had on him. He handled a nation torn by civil war. He did not solve that by ignoring it. And world leaders today are starting to step up and take the helm. The G8 Summits are addressing major issues. Progress is being made. We just need to make sure they keep at it and step up the pace. Especially the U.S.A.

I have talked about the freedoms we have in the United States. I think we have just taken some of that strength and too often gone in the other direction. The Guides have said that power can go in the opposite direction from good. We need to remember what this country started out as. We need to build our character back up and remember what integrity is. We need to *treat* everyone as an equal.

CHAPTER 42

Guatemala: A Sacred Place with a Special Role

"Guatemala is a place of holy and spiritual power that needs to be tapped into. The people there hold magic in their hearts, and their great capacity in loving another spirit is overwhelming."

–The Spirit Guides

The Spirit Guides offer Guatemala as an excellent example of how Third World nations and their people possess the ability to offer invaluable assistance to the rest of the world. Let's see how.

Where's Guatemala?

If you watched the television show *Survivor: Guatemala,* then perhaps you know where Guatemala is located. But before the Guides started transmitting messages about Guatemala in the summer of 2002, we would definitely have needed a map. We would have said that it *probably* was in Central America, but we weren't 100 percent certain. We hadn't the faintest inkling that this nation has a very significant role to play in the evolution of the Earth and its people.

261

According to the Guides, this mountainous country, which is just a tad smaller than the state of Tennessee and contains many Mayan ruins, will be instrumental in helping the world solve some of its most perplexing problems.[1] Even though Guatemala may be one of the planet's poorest places, this small Central American country and its people hold things of incalculable value to everyone living on the planet.

The Spirit Guides explained that Guatemalans possess a deep-rooted spiritual strength from which we can all learn, regardless of our religious persuasion, a heartfelt belief in the power of love. Incredibly, they also possess a disease-curing plant that grows on their lands, as well as an understanding of how to use this plant to help humanity.

A Cure for Cancer and AIDS?

Incredulous would be an understatement to describe how Jane felt when, on July 13, 2002–just two days after this book project formally began–the Guides transmitted the following handwritten message:

> **There are many cancers in the world that can be cured with a plant from Guatemala. It is the eucalyptus plant.**

Sensing Jane's disbelief at what was coming through the transmission, the Guides then jolted Jane with a firm admonition:

> **Jane, don't get in the way.**

As you can see, when Jane starts to question in her mind the information she is receiving through the automatic writing process, Lily and his spirit colleagues are often quick to let her know she should not let her own preconceived notions about reality interfere with the knowledge they are trying to impart to the world.

The next day, the Guides picked up where they had left off:

> There is a plant in Guatemala that will help cancer pa-
> tients. It is the eucalyptus [plant whose] oil will help with skin
> cancer. The cure is simpler than we think. The eucalyptus
> from the plant can help save millions of people. It has an
> enzyme in it that is sacred and can be of good use.

A cure for cancer? As Jed Clampett, Buddy Ebsen's character in
The Beverly Hillbillies would say, *"Whee doggie!"* Hard to believe, isn't
it? That's what we thought.

Despite our initial skepticism about the Guides' amazing claims
regarding a cure for cancer, they insisted that the world would do
well to take notice of Guatemala and its people:

> Guatemala does hold special meaning for many people
> on Earth. It is holy in nature, and the people are good. Their
> resources of knowledge, plants, and men who are good [are]
> great. The men in the villages are of knowledge and remem-
> ber to plant the Earth with water and seed and let the forest
> grow.
> Guatemala is important because of its spiritual background.
> We need to remember to include Guatemala and other coun-
> tries when we want to find the cure for cancer and AIDS.

Because the Guides were so emphatic about this subject, we decided to do some research on eucalyptus. We knew little about the
topic. Was there even any eucalyptus in Guatemala?

We were intrigued to read the following on the Web site
herbs2000.com:

> Eucalyptus is one of the fastest growing and biggest
> trees in the world. Eucalyptus can reach heights of over
> 250 feet and sends out a vast network of roots, which have
> proven very useful in draining marshy areas. In fact, [though

native to Australia] it has been of great value in eliminating malarial swamps in a number of hot, humid countries. Guatemala is one such country in Central America, where eucalyptus trees were abundantly planted for this very reason.[2]

Herbs2000.com went on to say:

The aromatic oil contained in eucalyptus leaves is an essential ingredient in Vicks Vapo-Rub. This over-the-counter preparation has been a popular remedy with millions of people for many years for treating respiratory ailments, especially asthma and bronchitis....Eucalyptus is a traditional Aboriginal remedy for infections and fevers. Eucalyptus is now used throughout the world for these ailments. Eucalyptus is an antiseptic and is very helpful for colds, flu, and sore throats. Eucalyptus is a strong expectorant, suitable for chest infections, including bronchitis and pneumonia.[3]

Okay, so eucalyptus has some traditional medicinal qualities that have long been recognized and used around the world. That's all well and good, but it's a far cry from a cure for cancer. And what about AIDS? Well, the Guides have announced that there is a man living in Guatemala who possesses the knowledge of how to use plants to help cure both of these deadly diseases.

Johnson! Where Are You?

On July 16, 2002, three days after the first appearance of Guatemala in Jane's automatic writing, the Guides made a rather vague comment relating to the potential for humanity's positive future, saying only:

The man who can help is in Guatemala.

Lily and company didn't keep us in suspense very long before giving us some more clues about their Guatemalan mystery man. Just twelve days later, while in the midst of talking about the ability of people from developing nations to help save the world from a dark future that now threatens to unfold from the current global chaos, the Guides unleashed a torrent of uplifting words about the importance of locating a certain individual residing in Guatemala who holds the key to unlocking many of Nature's secrets:

We need to tell you that a man in Guatemala can help. His name is not known to many, but he holds truths to the Earth; and the saving grace is that he is pure of heart and wants to help. He just needs to be given a chance.

There are many men who will be skeptical of him, but he is true to human kindness and all creatures and is truly pure of heart. That does not mean that he will make a magic pill in a day and everyone can be cured and happy in an instant. It means that his knowledge is part of the solution. And it will take light and energy from the whole Earth, but it will happen if we pull together and start loving each other.

The Guides emphasized that finding this gentleman called "Johnson," or some similar name, is a matter of great urgency for our world. They went on at length about how he can play a vital role in helping win the war against the ravages of AIDS and cancer, saying:

The medical world would do much better if they turned to the man from Guatemala. Johnson will be able to help [and will] be known as the medical miracle for [his] work with plants. He knows the cure for AIDS *and even cancer.* To tap into this magic and put its use to work for the world, a man

named Johnson will be put in [charge] of plants. He will need to cultivate plants from the South American rain forests.

We were certainly aware there are rain forests in South America, but we wondered whether or not there were any located in Guatemala. What we learned in our research was that the tropical lowlands of the Petén region of Guatemala contain Central America's largest remaining rain forest. We also discovered that deforestation of the Petén rain forest resulting from the burning of trees to make way for crops is a major environmental problem in Guatemala.[4] So perhaps it is possible that the existence of Central America's most expansive rain forest in the Petén area of Guatemala offers a potential clue as to where the man named "Johnson" might reside.

We reiterate the importance of locating the Guatemalan mystery man because of the Guides' repeated admonitions that he can help lead the charge against some of the world's most deadly diseases:

> **This man named John's son will take over many plants. We see him as vital to our plan. But he will first need to know his power is real. And the key element here is to let this man need to be a part of it. We must see his spirit soar, as he soars with the Earth and her knowledge of life in the plants. His work will be of great importance, as we see him putting his use of time in a safe place—because he knows deep in his heart that he is a magic man and [that] he can save a lot of people. In order for him to do this, he must first realize he needs to be good and true to his knowledge of the plant kingdom. He must stop other things and give his real gift to the world.**

This vague statement that "John's son...must stop other things" made us wonder what the Guides meant. Yet, at the same time, we realized that Lily and his fellow Guides are very aware of the need to protect people's privacy. Indeed, since the automatic writing transmissions began in 2002, we have marveled time and again at how the Spirit Guides have consistently exhibited a great deal of sensitivity with respect to personal matters. Suffice it to say that the Guatemalan man named "Johnson" (or "John's son") is likely dealing with the type of personal challenge that face all of us in one form or another, as we each struggle to cope with the pressures of simply being human.

So, what are we all to make out of these seemingly fantastic statements by the Guides about "Johnson"? Our take on the matter is that it seems pretty obvious that humankind has nothing to lose and everything to gain by trying to find this Guatemalan miracle man and seeing what he can do to help. The Guides certainly feel there is no time to waste in doing so:

> **This is real knowledge, as we have no time for games and silly little things like that. The American people know their political factors and are aware that the man named Johnson will be here in the midst of this. To be open to this, many people will have to let go of their egos and step aside, as he can produce medicine in an unconventional way and spread the stop of disease as quickly as the diseases spread.**

All of this sounded quite exciting and encouraging. Yet at the same time, these tantalizing hints about some supposed miracle man living *somewhere* in Guatemala made us feel like we were looking for the proverbial "needle in a haystack." Talk about a wild goose chase!

Please...Help Us Find Johnson!

The answer is that we cannot possibly find this Guatemalan man without your help. Here are the clues that the Guides have given us about who he is:

His name is Johnson or John's son. We will not know for sure which until further notice. It may be just John. His first mission is to his children and wife Maria. And they will have two more children and be free of expectation once he realizes his powers. And it is not only power of plants, but his own mind.

Some intriguing hints to be sure about the Guides' Guatemalan mystery man and his abilities. Now, if he could just be located. So, if you have any knowledge, however incomplete or farfetched it may seem, that might help identify him more specifically and determine just where in Guatemala he lives, please let us know by sending your information to:

Distinctive Publications for the World
P. O. Box 888
Hanover, New Hampshire 03755
clues@goodagainstevil.com

And so we say to all–politicians, scientists, members of the medical community, and most importantly, to our fellow citizens of the world–*please*, help us find "Johnson." (Or, in Spanish, "hijode Juan.") People we all know are dying every day from the very diseases that this man can help cure–and that many of us may someday get our-selves.

Who among us that enjoys good health has not said, *"That will never happen to me"*? Even more poignantly, however, we realize many of you now reading these words are already suffering from such diseases. To you, we offer our most profound hope that the infor-mation contained in this chapter might help lead to advances in medicine that will allow you to get well.

"The Two Marias"–The Guatemalan Twins

"The girl twins from Guatemala are a miracle sign to show the world the strength of the Guatemalan society."

Many of you are probably familiar with the story of the two Guatemalan twin sisters, Maria de Jesus and Maria Teresa Quiej Alvarez, who were born joined at the head in 2001. The twins, born to a Guatemalan family of very modest means, came into this world attached at the top of the skull and facing opposite directions. The two shared bone and blood vessels, but they possessed separate brains.

Occurring in only 1 out of 2.5 million live births, the twins' condition required a $1.5 million operation that seemed impossible for a family whose father earned just $64 a week as a banana picker. But Healing the Children, a nonprofit group from Spokane, Washington, stepped in and made financial and travel arrangements for the Guatemalan twins to be brought to the United States so that they could have the necessary medical procedure performed. And so, on August 6, 2002, the two baby girls from Guatemala captured the world's attention when they underwent a successful twenty-two hour operation to separate them, involving a team of more than forty people at UCLA Medical Center.[5]

As of the date of this book's writing, the two Marias remain alive and are making progress in their health. Both twins, however, still face formidable medical challenges.

According to what the Guides said, the Guatemalan twins are a symbol from which the whole world can learn. In fact, on August 6, 2002, the very day of the twins' operation, Lily and his colleagues said:

> **It is no coincidence that they are from Guatemala, Jane. Their desire to show the world their strength and the strength of the Guatemalan people is great in terms of the living spirit they share with their country and fellow citizens.**

The Guides resumed discussion of the Guatemalan twins six days later, at which point they began by gently scolding Jane about the pace of her writing:

> **Jane, you are going at an okay pace, but we would like to see you step up a little bit more when the time allows. We see the first place that needs to be recognized is Guatemala, for their strength in praying for the twins, that will be the strength of that country for the times to come. Their role in the world's evolution is critical, as they are willing to sacrifice their identity and be a spectacle so the world can get together for a common cause and pray for people, these dear twins, that not many know in person.**

These words of the Guides made us stop and think about how it usually takes something so strikingly emotional as the plight of these two Guatemalan girls to get most of us to glance up from our daily routine and examine what is going on in the lives of others. The more we reflected on the Guatemalan twins' story, the more its significance sunk in. What happened to make their "miracle" operation possible illustrates the way in which huge obstacles can be overcome if people decide to pitch in and help one another.

Let's put it this way: If the odds that a birth such as that of the Guatemalan twins are 1 in 2.5 million, then what are the chances that a family subsisting on only $64 a week could ever hope to have a $1.5 million operation for their children?

That such a feat might actually be accomplished would only be looked at by any Las Vegas bookmaker as an incredible long shot, defying all probability. Yet, we all know now that it truly happened. *Why?* The answer is quite simple: Human beings decided to help each other.

Let's Help the Guatemalan People, and They'll Help All of Us

Just as Healing the Children stepped in and made the seemingly impossible possible for the twin sisters, we would urge the world to help Guatemala and its people. It's not impossible. The country's entire national budget is less than $3 billion. Hey, many private companies have bigger annual budgets than that.

We've already described how Guatemala and its people have the ability to help cure some of the world's deadliest diseases. Isn't that enough incentive to motivate the rest of us to do something to help Guatemalans get on a better economic footing and enjoy an improved standard of living? And what will occur if the nations, companies, and even individual citizens who possess the financial means to help Guatemala step up to the plate and get the job done? Well, here's what the Guides say will happen:

Guatemalan people will strengthen their own country, as it is already strong, and at the same time strengthen the world to make a better place for all of humankind.

Bonus Information

Though not located in Guatemala, but in Brazil, a wonderful illustration of how certain residents of Third World countries possess incredible knowledge that can benefit all of humanity is a gentleman called "John of God." The subject of repeated specials on the television show *Primetime,* John of God's real name is Joao Teixeira da Faria. A spiritual healer with a traditional education that stopped after the second grade who possesses no formal medical training, John of God not only successfully operates on people using no anesthesia, but also has cured, in numerous documented cases, people with AIDS, blindness, cancer, heart disease, and paralysis.

Learn More about John of God

If you are interested in learning more about John of God, an excellent book about his work is Emma Bragdon's *Spiritual Alliances*. In it, she includes a superb summary of the Brazilian healer's work and its significance:

Many Christian traditions teach that it is only Jesus and the apostles who had extraordinary gifts of healing. For the last two thousand years religious leaders have considered those who have claimed to have extraordinary healing abilities to be blasphemers, heretics, or charlatans. I am not suggesting that we liken John of God to a Christ or one of the apostles. [John of God emphasizes that, stating, "It is not me, but God who does the healing."] [W]e consider that ordinary people, like Joao, can choose to have the Holy Spirit flow through them. It is not only our potential; it may be our next step in evolution. Joao may be guiding us in the transition to our next level, that of being in direct communication with the Holy Spirit, which not only helps us become more whole, but empowers us to be healing forces in the lives of others.[6]

Spiritual Alliances is available through your local bookstore or can be ordered directly through Emma Bragdon's Web site at http://www.emmabragdon.com.

CHAPTER 43

The Special Power of Celebrities to Help Save the World

"People with celebrity can help in enormous ways because the others of the world believe they are good. They hold much power over the world and can do much good for our cause."
—The Spirit Guides

"We live in a culture where people are incredibly invested in the lives of people they don't know," says author and essayist Wendy Kaminer, *"whether it's political celebrities or movie stars or baseball players."*[1]
—Joseph Kahn, "Why We Feel Cheated When Celebrities Cheat"

"Our worship of celebrities does indeed turn them into the most powerful people on the planet," observes psychiatrist Raj Persaud, who lives in London. *"They're the equivalent of gods in our midst."*[2]
—Carol Brooks, "What Celebrity Worship Says About Us"

273

According to the spirit realm, the world's celebrities possess tremendous ability to play a huge part in implementing the Guides' Action Plan for Planet Earth and making Earth a better place for all to live. In fact, it is our sense that making the plan a reality will require celebrities to take the lead on the front end of this project and show political leaders around the globe that it is time to stop talking about saving the world and actually do it.

The Guides stressed to us early on just how crucial celebrities are to the success of this project. Three days after we began, Lily and friends stated the following on July 14, 2002:

> **We need to discuss money and how wealthy, influential people can help. People with celebrity can help in enormous ways because the others of the world believe they are good. They hold much power over the world and can do much good for our cause.**

Five days later, the Guides emphasized once again the extent to which their plan for Earth depends on the participation of celebrities:

> **The celebrities of the world are good humans, and they are humans of good stature. And we need their expertise and knowledge and even power, as people look to them for guidance, as they influence the world in their own way.**

Strong words, certainly, about the degree to which celebrities wield widespread power and influence. But would you disagree? Haven't we all been influenced at one time or another in some way by celebrities we respect and admire? If they don't possess the ability to impact how people look at things, then why do the world's largest corporations pay stars huge sums of money to endorse their products and services?

The answer is obvious: because it works. Celebrities have major-league clout.

Ruth Gets Personal with Jane about Celebrities

The Guides' early writings about celebrities emphasized how essential they are to implementing the Action Plan for Planet Earth, yet our co-authors in the cosmos were also aware of Jane's increasing concern about going public with this book. To help settle Jane's mind, Ruth chimed in with some words that put matters into perspective:

> **The state of the world is such a mess today that we need to clean it up as soon as possible. I was afforded the luxury of time. But that was only to pave the way for this new kind of thinking. I wasn't so lucky to have people already believing, without being extremely cautious and skeptical. It was a very brave thing I did, but I want no credit so to speak.**

Ruth's words bring up an important point that the Guides made to us repeatedly—that our world is in a much worse situation than when Ruth began writing about her communication with the spirit world. Consequently, it is extremely urgent for us to write and publish, as soon as possible, the information emanating from the automatic writing transmissions.

Fortunately, society is now much more open to this type of spiritual material than when Ruth Montgomery wrote her groundbreaking books. Whereas she was a true pioneer with her work, we are lucky to be writing in an era when this type of cosmic communication is much more an accepted part of our culture.

Not that a lot of people won't think that we're just as nuts as she must have seemed to some, but, thanks to the courageous efforts of Ruth and many others in the field, we are bringing this book to light at a time when there exists an unprecedented level of dialogue about the possibility of contact with the spirit world. Countless books, television shows, and major movies about humans making contact with the spirit world now abound in popular culture, making our foray into this arena a much less formidable task than what Ruth faced.

Ruth continued:

> We are all where we are supposed to be. You [Jane] chose this time and this path to experience for a very good reason. Just as I chose my path when I was there on Earth. There is a feeling of mutual respect that you and I have for one another that is crucial to making this work. It is a bond, deep and personal, and one that will last a lifetime.
>
> You, too, are gifted, Jane. I keep repeating this because I don't want you to go comparing yourself to John Edward or James Van Praagh. You are on your own mission.
>
> Remember this: No one person is greater than anyone else. Each and every person is just as great and good as the next guy. It is not a singular mission we are on; it is a mission together.
>
> That is another reason you are right for the job. You don't think you are better than other people. You have hobnobbed with the rich and the poor alike and everyone in between. You have chosen experiences that will put you in the path of all types of people. Because people are what it's all about, and you get that. Not to bash all men here, but women generally get the love thing.
>
> So many people are caught up in "who's who," and that whole ego trip thing, that it really gets nauseating sometimes. There are people all over the world who need to know it doesn't matter who you know or what you do for a living.
>
> It's not as important to be a big shot and know all the right people as it is to have love in your heart and soul. It's not important to take your celebrity and use it for your own gain, but to use it to do good in the world. There are people

in your world who are rich and famous, that's a fact of life. But it's not so important who wins this award or that award, but what they use their influence to do.

It will be the same with you when you are recognized as a person of peaceful means. If you let the celebrity go to your head too much, you'll have made a mockery of all that you've written here in this book. But again, we see you as a person of high integrity and don't see that happening. It's that part of you that sees that this is not only about Rob and Jane [and Paul], but everyone on the planet that is appealing.

We know your own fears about being in the public eye. It is not always an easy thing. But it is admirable, and we see that many celebrities are already using that celebrity to do much good in the world.

It is not only with celebrities that we can do this—work-men, carpenters, skilled men in every field—we need them all. This is a project not just for the rich, but the poor—the "wicked" and the good. It will do much good for the world to see that even men who are seen as devils and scoundrels have some contribution to make.

Yes, the celebrities among us possess a special ability to inspire people around the world. They can bring invaluable media attention to the things that need to be done to get humanity on a stable footing. By raising the profile of the many issues vexing mankind, they can put a bright spotlight on the problems that are crying out to be fixed. At the same time, however, it is important for all of us to realize that they can't do it by themselves. Only if we all pitch in and each make an effort can we succeed in turning our troubled world around.

The importance of people from all walks of life participating in the Guides' three-pronged plan for Earth is a theme to which the spirits kept coming back. The very next day after Ruth had spoken up and given Jane the pep talk described above, Lily and the gang returned and spoke to humanity as a whole about this project being all-inclusive:

> **Many farmers, carpenters, airplane pilots, and other people who are not well known will be invaluable as well. If you think you have something to contribute, please sign on to this project—even if it's only an hour a week. Every effort will be a step forward in helping the world become a better place for all.**

So come one, come all, and let's help our sisters and brothers who need us. Do you really think that you'll ever regret pitching in and doing your part to lift your fellow human beings up out of their problems?

You know you won't! To the contrary, it's going to be an exhilarating feeling for all of us to be players in the biggest team effort in human history.

A Direct Appeal to the Celebrities of the World

Although it's essential that we all do our part and contribute to making the Action Plan for Planet Earth a success, Heaven is asking the celebrities living on the planet to get out front and help the world heal itself. We know this is a major request and realize many celebrities are already doing a great deal to help others. In fact, one of the things we became much more aware of as we did homework for this book is the tremendous degree to which so many noted personalities currently devote their talent, fame, money, and influence to reach out to those in need.

Another thing we learned as we researched different aspects of this project was that celebrities have an even bigger impact on the lives of the rest of the world than we ever would have imagined.

This is nowhere more true than in the case of stars' pivotal role in the lives of young people. A publication called *Personality and Individual Differences* describes a psychological study of teenagers in which "researchers found that for nearly one-third of a sample of 191 teens age 11 to 16, gossiping about celebrities took up most of their social time."[3]

Because of the unique ability of celebrities to reach out to people of all ages and all walks of life, the spirit realm has asked them to use their fame like never before to help Heaven help us all. The spirits have provided humanity with a framework that will assist us in sorting out the mess that we're in, but they can't do it for us.

Spirits in Heaven have a vantage point that allows them to see that Earth's noted personalities can wield a mighty sword of influence against the many problems that exist around the globe and threaten mankind's future. So, if you are a celebrity, on behalf of the Spirits in Heaven who have put together the Action Plan for Planet Earth, we ask you to help make their dreams for our world a reality. It's really the same dream most of us long for down deep: a world in which peace, equality, and sharing replace war, injustice, and greed. And as you consider the pros and cons of getting involved in a project of such large proportions that seeks literally to transform the evil (fear) in our world to good (love), we thought that we would share with you a couple of quotations that struck us as being very powerful:

> *"Hollywood is ruled by fear and love of money....But it can't rule me because I'm not afraid of anything and I don't love money."*[4]
> —Marlon Brando

> *"Why not use your leverage [celebrity] for the good things, because leverage is used for the evil of things all the time. Stand up."*[5]
> —Jamie Foxx

CHAPTER 44

AIDS!
"Where There's
a Will There's
a Way"

"Not since the bubonic plague swept across the world in the last millennium, killing more than 250 million people, has our world confronted such a horrible, unspeakable curse as we are now witnessing with the growing HIV/AIDS pandemic."[1]

–Henry Hyde, U.S. Congressman

Cuac here at the keyboard with you.

It is difficult to imagine an issue that cries out more for doing good than the urgency of finding a cure for AIDS.

The title of this chapter ends with an exclamation point for two reasons:

1. For as much attention as AIDS has received in recent years, the extreme urgency of this horrific disease has yet to be fully recognized by the people of the world and their leaders. Despite the

unprecedented amount of resources and energies now being focused on the issue, the efforts to eradicate AIDS are falling woefully short of what is needed to do the job.

2. Although many of the topics the Guides have stated as critical for the survival of our world are subjects about which I had little interest in prior to Jane and Paul beginning their automatic writing communications with the spirit world, such was not the case with AIDS. Why? Because I have lost some close friends to the disease. Simply put, this one's personal for me...

> *"Already 25 million people around the world have died [from AIDS]—more than all of the battle deaths in the twentieth century combined....If trends continue, by 2025, 250 million global HIV/ AIDS cases are a distinct possibility."*[2]
>
> —Greg Behrman, *The Invisible People: How the U.S. Has Slept through the Global AIDS Pandemic, the Greatest Humanitarian Catastrophe of our Time*

"I realized that...the most important statistic associated with the disease for me is the number 'four.'"

Because of my strong personal feelings about AIDS, this chapter is definitely different than I had thought it was going to be. How so? Well, in my preparation for writing it, I had clipped dozens of articles about AIDS, purchased some books about the subject, and initially intended to pack this chapter with lots of facts and figures about the mind-numbing statistics associated with the untold human suffering that has been produced by this devastating disease.

As I began to review all of the research material I had collected about AIDS, I found myself getting more and more upset that the disease was winning the war it is waging against humanity—so much so that I started to examine where my anger was coming from. The answer was immediately obvious: It was because AIDS had robbed me of some of my closest friends.

What was fueling my passion for tackling this topic was the profound sense of personal loss in my own life that had resulted from this killer disease. I realized that while this chapter would include a few basic figures about AIDS, the most important statistic associated with the disease for me is the number "four." That's the number of good friends that my wife and I have lost to the disease.

Three of our friends were so dear to me that when Phyl and I got married, I included them in our wedding program as "Ushers-in-Absentia." The visit I had with one of them just two hours prior to his passing was the single most traumatic scene I have ever witnessed in my life: seeing him totally emaciated, violently shaking, both eyes sealed shut, and desperately clutching to hold my hand and those of the two other friends, Gordon and Martha Garron, who were with me. It is an image I will absolutely never forget.

Please know I am very conscious of the fact that the numbers of my own friends who have died from the HIV virus is miniscule in comparison to the exponential loss experienced by so many others in every nation of the globe, particularly with respect to the countless families in Third World countries who have seen their ranks decimated by AIDS. At the same time, however, it seems pretty clear that we, as a race, are not going to decide to do whatever it takes to wipe out the disease until we perceive it in very personal terms. If, and only if, we come to recognize that we all have a personal stake in the outcome of the battle being fought against AIDS will the campaign be victorious.

The Guides' Messages about AIDS

When this book project began, AIDS was literally one of the first issues I asked Jane to query the Guides about. In anticipation of my meeting with her the following day, here is the text of the question I drafted for them on July 13, 2002:

Should the book deal at all with the disease of AIDS, especially as it applies to Third World countries?

When Jane posed this question to the Guides the following day, they responded by writing:

The AIDS question is top of the list.

Top of the list. Keep that phrase in mind, as we're going to return to it shortly.

The Spirit Guides went on to say more about AIDS:

We need to put AIDS on the list of diseases we can wipe out.

We should first deal with the medical and socioeconomics of the African continent and all continents that have an epidemic of AIDS. What we would like for you to do is clear a space for medical doctors and nurses to please come and help with these dying people. *They are in grave danger of becoming extinct altogether if we don't help.*

Then we need to network as a global community. Leaders of the world need to give of themselves–not only money, but [also] the prospect of hope for the millions of people in India, Africa, Europe, and the whole world.

Sexual diseases are not prevalent when people are smart and educated. What we want is for the drug companies to take all that money they are making and donate half or more of it to people. Take the billions they make and give back by setting up community health centers for teenagers. They need to be [taught to be] responsible for their actions.

We [also] want drug companies to fund the Peace Corps efforts by sending money to boost what is a really good cause and teach people about condoms, help feed the souls, and dress them.

When this thing takes off, it will spread faster than any disease you've seen. We can see millions of souls who want to beat AIDS and its ravaging effects on the world, but we need to come together.

A Little Reality Check for Jane

Reading what the Spirit Guides were writing about AIDS and the Third World led us to begin paying a little closer attention to what was being reported in the media about such matters. A good example is illustrated by a journal entry Jane made just prior to beginning an automatic writing session with the Guides:

> *I saw Bono on a VH1 show today with Chris Tucker and another girl going to Africa. It got me excited to get going on the book again. Justin is sick—on top of having a broken foot—but I am not going to stress about it too much. At least we have a comfortable, cozy apartment to rest in; unlike the woman on the show who has AIDS, lives in a hut, and has almost nothing except for her children, whom she hopes do not have AIDS, so they can take care of her when they are older. That was her answer when asked what her hopes for the future were. Boy, do some people have it bad. Thank you for everything, God!!!*

As Jane then made the transition from writing her own thoughts to doing the automatic writing, our co-authors responded to her comment by saying:

> **Jane, it is the Guides here. We are glad to see you taking your assignments seriously. And, yes, we mean the television shows and articles and everything else that you take in. It is all relative to what we are doing.**

The point the Spirit Guides made to Jane that day is one that has taken on greater significance for us with time—that is, there is information swirling around us all the time that can help us gain greater insight into our own lives and those of others. Indeed, as we have attempted to digest information about various topics raised by the Guides, one of the things that has amazed us is the extent to which *everything* in our world is related to *everything* else…and *everyone* has an impact on *everyone* else. As we have explored the different subjects discussed by our colleagues in the spirit realm, we have come to understand these truths more and more.

Why Should You Care about AIDS If You, or Someone Close to You, Doesn't Have It?

For me personally, starting to see the interconnectedness of everything and everyone has resulted in a very specific change in my daily routine of life. Before this project began, the only part of the newspaper I looked at in its entirety was the sports section; I now go through all of the paper on a regular basis (although I usually still start with the sports page). It's a seemingly small thing, but one that has, nonetheless, helped me more fully appreciate the Guides' insistence that humanity needs to wake up to a basic fact that is glaringly obvious from their vantage point in Heaven: *We can only solve our own problems by helping others with theirs.*

So, *what's in it for you* in deciding to do your part to help with the AIDS crisis? The bottom line is that if you contribute in whatever way you can—time, money, influence, knowledge, and, ultimately, most significantly, caring—then you will receive the following benefits:

1. Helping with the AIDS crisis will be good for your safety.

As I began to read a little about AIDS, I was really surprised to learn what a strong connection there is between the global spread of the disease and terrorism. The link is pretty basic: When people are suffering, they are more vulnerable to the lure of extremist ideologies. And the worse the AIDS epidemic gets, the simpler it is for terrorists to attract new recruits to join them.

The parts of the world hardest hit by AIDS's assault on humanity are often the places already struggling with poverty, famine, other health problems, and constant political chaos. Adding AIDS to the mix is like stirring in the final ingredient to whip up a "perfect storm" for terrorist recruiters.

The more people are suffering and see no way out of their existing situation, the more fertile a breeding ground it creates for extremism to take root and flourish. Like pouring gasoline onto an already burning fire, allowing AIDS to continue its onslaught against humanity is pushing the world toward a situation that will make the wars in Afghanistan and Iraq look like "Romper Room" time.

If you think this line of logic is exaggerating the implications of AIDS, consider the following two points:

- There is concern in many parts of the world today about the spread of terrorism by Islamic extremists. The African continent is 40 percent Muslim and, with roughly two-thirds of the planet's AIDS cases, is Earth's AIDS epicenter.[3]

- Russia and China are home to two of the fastest growing explosions of AIDS in the world. Given these countries' populations, nuclear capabilities, and the potential for social unrest, political instability, and economic collapse if their AIDS epidemics are permitted to march forward unchecked, the stakes in the war against the HIV virus are staggering.[4]

A good example of how extremism can seem a preferable alternative when the existing system is not working is the extent to which extremists continue to gain access to positions of leadership and power in our world. People are human and can only take so much. Regardless of one's religion, nationality, or cultural background, we all have the same basic needs: food, shelter, some sense of security, and at least a ray of hope for a better future. But when things get really bad, eventually any change will look like a good change.

2. Helping with the AIDS crisis will be good for your wallet.

> "Might it not be cheaper to make friends of potential enemies than to defend yourself against them later?"[5]
>
> —Bono

The potential for AIDS to cause the collapse of entire economies and governments in the countries hardest hit by the disease is growing every day. As such, it is not only in the national security interest of the citizens of the United States and other affluent industrialized nations to insist their leaders *drastically* increase financial assistance to various AIDS initiatives around the globe, but also a wise move for the pocketbooks of virtually all of the planet's inhabitants.

For the residents of those areas of the world suffering the most from the AIDS epidemic, the financial impact is crystal clear: Those among our race who are often the least able to afford dealing with the devastating disease are the ones who bear the brunt of its deadly impact.

Although the monetary cost to the richer populations of the world may not be as immediately apparent, the historical evidence to date provides persuasive proof that "those who have" will eventually end up having to dip into their own pocketbooks in order to attempt to stem the tide of the AIDS juggernaut.

> *"This isn't going away. Either we pay now or we pay later. There's no real magic," says Helene Gayle, director of HIV programs for the Bill & Melinda Gates Foundation.... "Had we invested essentially the same amount we're spending (now) a decade ago, we would have saved $90 billion in health costs, orphan care and lost productivity."* [6]
>
> –Steve Sternberg, "AIDS Neglected, Report Warns"

And while we're on the subject of expenses, the United States's cost for the war in Iraq is going to end up in the trillions of dollars. Can you imagine the financial consequences if a number of AIDS-ravaged nations disintegrate and ignite major conflicts around the world at the same time?

3. Helping with the AIDS crisis will be good for your soul.

The AIDS crisis, and how each and every one of us responds to it, presents a spiritual opportunity that the Guides, my family mem-

bers, and I believe will ultimately bring out the best in human beings as we confront a rampaging disease that has been likened to
the great plagues of the Middle Ages. Indeed, tremendous amounts
of heartwarming, lifesaving assistance have already been forthcom-
ing from many churches and religious organizations around the
world.

> *"There are no Heavenly judgments, only the judgments that we our-
> selves must make as we look at the kind of life we have led, the kind
> of person we are. Each soul judges its own self."* [7]
>
> —Rosemary Althea, *The Eagle and the Rose*

4. Helping with the AIDS crisis will be fun.

> *"Lily, Ruth, Art, and Bob here. Good morning. It is always
> nice to be with you and working together for the benefit of all.
> We believe the most rewarding work is the work we do for
> each other."*

When the Guides wrote the above words in an early morning
automatic writing session Paul had with them, they were stating
something we all know down deep in our hearts: that is, the act of
helping another human being is an act like none other.

Just think back on your own life. Don't some of your most meaningful memories involve situations in which someone helped you or
you helped them? Doesn't the shared experience of coming to the assistance of another person create a mutual bond that transcends
words?

What about the Considerable Progress That Has Been Made in the Fight against AIDS?

> *"More of the people on Earth are waking up to the fact that
> things cannot go on as they have—that there needs to be a shift
> in the way we think and act."*

> —The Spirit Guides

The spirits in Heaven have observed human beings starting to do a better job of helping each other. Certainly that has been the case with AIDS, as considerable undertakings around the globe have been initiated to combat the deadly disease.

The efforts of many world leaders, numerous celebrities, a growing contingent of companies, a vast array of organizations, and millions of everyday citizens worldwide have combined to produce significant successes in many areas of the fight against AIDS. These include:

- Improved effectiveness of anti-retroviral drugs. The primary form of treatment in the battle against the HIV virus, such drugs can often delay the onset of serious illness for years, significantly extending the life span of those who are able to get such lifesaving medicines.

- Improved availability and decreased prices of anti-retroviral drugs. Although the problems surrounding these issues remain staggering, progress has been made in getting more drugs for less money to those who need them.

- The world's wealthiest countries have made large funding increases to help developing nations with prevention, treatment, healthcare infrastructure, and treatment in the global war against AIDS. Not all of the money pledged by the donor nations for these purposes has been given, but the fact remains that record-breaking amounts of money, measured in billions of dollars, are being provided to AIDS-stricken areas of Third World countries.

- Earth's richest governments have canceled tens of billions of dollars of debt owed by Third World nations. This is another major achievement that is helping free up more internal funds for the Third World countries hardest hit by AIDS to combat the epidemic.

- There is a growing awareness around the world of just how crucial an issue AIDS is to everyone on the planet. Compared to the muted response when AIDS emerged as a major health problem in the early 1980s, more and more attention is being paid to the extreme significance of this disease and its long-term implications for humanity.

All in all, there is encouraging progress in the war against AIDS. Considerable momentum has been generated on many fronts. Yet for all of the gains that have been made in the pitched battle against this formidable opponent, there remain major flaws in the campaign against the HIV virus:

- There is a continued persistence of widespread, unconscionable indifference to the daily human cost of AIDS.
- A hideous amount of unjustified stigma remains attached to the disease.
- Despite the growing amount of financial resources devoted to the fight, not nearly enough money is being committed to adequately deal with the massive scope of the epidemic and the looming disastrous consequences if more is not done to stem the tide.

And then there is what is perhaps the biggest single flaw in humanity's showdown with the common enemy called AIDS: *We haven't gone for the jugular.* We haven't really gotten serious about finding a cure for the deadly disease.

Question: How much money is being spent to find a cure for AIDS?

And the answer is: **chump change!**

> "*We'll never end this epidemic unless we have a vaccine....*"[8]
> —Sandra Thurman, former chairperson of the
> White House Office of National AIDS Policy

If the world wants to rid itself of The AIDS Monster, then we need to bite its head off. We need to launch an all-out assault on this creature that is devouring our sisters and brothers around the globe. With a daily body count of eight thousand lives, AIDS is an enemy that requires—nay, *demands*—that the rich nations of the world stop throwing chump change at this catastrophe and start pouring in the massive amounts of money it is going to take to stop this assassin in its tracks.

The bottom line is that the governments of the world's richest nations, especially that of the United States, need to step up to the plate and stop being penny-wise and pound-foolish. With the total global economic cost of AIDS now measured in the *hundreds of billions of dollars*, it's simply stupid for the leaders of Earth's most affluent nations to think the private sector is going to come up with an AIDS vaccine without the type of *massive* financial backing only governments can provide. Consider the following:

1. The International AIDS Vaccine Initiative (IAVI), a global not-for-profit organization focused on speeding up the hunt for an HIV/AIDS vaccine, "estimates total annual spending on an AIDS vaccine is $682 million. This represents less than 1% of total spending on all health product development," IAVI said. "Private sector efforts amount to just $100 million annually. This is mainly due to the lack of incentives for the private sector to invest in an AIDS vaccine—the science is difficult, and the developing countries that need a vaccine most are least able to pay."[9]

2. The pharmaceutical industry possesses the majority of the expertise in developing new vaccines.

   "Yet it's been difficult to convince the private sector to invest in vaccines, traditionally high-volume products that provide relatively low return on investment. Unlike a drug that patients may have to take for a lifetime, an effective vaccine is literally a 'one shot' deal: there are virtually no repeat customers."[10]

   –Dr. Seth Berkley, "We're Running Out of Time"

The Spirit Guides are in total agreement with Dr. Berkley—President, CEO, and Founder of the International AIDS Vaccine Initiative—and his characterization of the urgency of the issue: "We're Running Out of Time." Never ones to mince words, Lily and his colleagues said this about the situation:

> **Nigeria, Tanzania, Egypt, and Bangladesh are all suffering from the impact of starvation, AIDS, [and] diseases of other sorts. We need to straighten this out; for if we don't, we will see our own children perish right before our very own eyes of these same deadly causes and will weep that we did not take the opportunity to help when we should have.**

Just in case you think the Guides are exaggerating the grave threat posed by the AIDS epidemic, here's a similar analysis of the issue that comes from a much more conventional source:

> *"This war [i.e., the AIDS epidemic] has caused more casualties than any other war....We need America, the European Union and everybody. Nobody is going to be spared unless we all come together in the fight against this disease."* [11]
>
> —Tommy Thompson, former U.S. Health and Human Services Secretary

If you would like to learn more about the International AIDS Vaccine Initiative, the Internet address is http://www.iavi.org.

Let's Put a $25 Billion Bounty on the Head of The AIDS Monster!

AIDS is "a conscience issue....This is about life versus greed—nothing else....The majority of the people with HIV don't have a face....They're desperate, they're poor, they're alone...." [12]

—AIDS activist Zackie Achmat

Yes, you read that right. How about the rich nations of the world offering a 25 *billion* dollar reward to whoever is the first one to develop a proven vaccine for AIDS?

The United States should pay the lion's share of the $25 billion. If my native country can commit to a war in Iraq with a total final tab estimated to be two to three *trillion* dollars, then I think we all know it can pony up another 1 percent of that to do the job with AIDS. So, please, let's not hear the argument that there's just not enough money to go around...it's simply a matter of whether the nation with the biggest bankroll decides bagging The AIDS Monster is a large enough priority to be willing to write the check.

It doesn't matter if it's a company, an individual, a nonprofit institution, or whatever. The first one to the finish line gets the $25,000,000,000.

That's a lot of zeroes. No question about it. But money motivates people, that's basic.

And, yes, this notion stemmed from thinking that if a $25 million dollar bounty has been offered up for Osama bin Laden and other specific terrorists, then isn't finding a cure for AIDS worth $25 billion?

Although not at all minimizing the significant threat posed by such individuals, I would suggest that AIDS poses a far greater long-term danger to our world's future than all of the planet's terrorist leaders put together. The AIDS Monster is growing in size and strength every day and calls for a Manhattan Project–style, all-out effort to slay it. If a government can marshal the financial and human resources to create the atomic bomb, a weapon whose sole purpose is to kill people in huge numbers, then surely it is possible to launch an all-out assault on AIDS and do whatever it takes to save human beings in huge numbers.

This is not something to hem and haw about to determine if it is worth doing. It's nothing that requires time-consuming studies and exhaustive analysis. All that has to be done is to ask the $25 billion dollar question: *If there existed a proven vaccine for AIDS right now and it was for sale for $25 billion, how long do you think it would last on the market?* Heck, let's add another zero. Let's make the price tag $250 billion. At a quarter of a trillion dollars, an AIDS vaccine would still be a deeply discounted bargain.

And, down deep, we all know it.

Do We Have the Individual Will?

"To be on one side is not the key; it's getting everyone on the same side so there is no division between the men and women, the countries, the nations, even the continents. We are seeing so many people shining and being a part of this. The world will be in much better shape once we all get going. We in the spirit world are constantly trying to remind the people of the world that we have not forgotten them, but are with them every step of the way. We see each individual as one of the whole and the sum of the parts is greater than anyone could expect. We are all one. We are all in this together."

–The Spirit Guides

Before world leaders, especially those of the planet's richest nations, are going to make the development of an AIDS vaccine a *top* financial priority, they are going to have to feel pressure from their citizens to do so. If politicians are going to give this item a much bigger slice of the budget, then they need to know that the voters not only support spending massive sums of money on this issue, but also that their constituents *demand* that an AIDS vaccine be developed.

Two well-known individuals who are shining examples of the importance of not being afraid to speak up about AIDS are actresses Elizabeth Taylor and Sharon Stone. Both of these individuals have been passionate about using their fame, power, and influence to help bring increased attention, awareness, and financial support to fight The AIDS Monster.

I read an article many years ago that contained a stunning quotation from Ms. Taylor about the extent of her desire to stop AIDS in its tracks. The gist of what she said was that she would gladly give up her life if a cure for AIDS could be found. Her statement made an unforgettable impact on me and forced me to ask myself a question that has stayed with me ever since: *If a person who has attained the pinnacle of conventional achievement and material success feels that AIDS is a significant enough matter literally to die for, then what does that say to the rest of us "normal" folks about its importance in our world?*

Although I regret to say that Elizabeth Taylor's words didn't galvanize me into taking any specific action at the time I read them, her statement forever altered my perception of how critical an issue AIDS is for humanity. Indeed, when I went about creating an outline for this chapter, one of the very first things I wrote down was my recollection of Ms. Taylor's willingness to trade her life for a cure for AIDS.

Although I remain both awed and humbled by the extent of Ms. Taylor's devotion to fighting The AIDS Monster, I am not suggesting that beating this horrific disease requires everyone to adopt such a committed position. No, all that's required to vanquish this formidable foe is for a lot of us to demonstrate a modest willingness to help in whatever way we can. This is especially true for people who are so fortunate as to live in affluent nations with a democratically elected government, such as the United States.

Sharon Stone, like Elizabeth Taylor, is another American who has not been afraid to speak out in strong terms about the urgency of the issue: "There is this feeling that AIDS has gone away and it hasn't. In downtown Los Angeles there are two whole streets of homeless people with AIDS who have no access to drugs. A child dies of AIDS every minute, and they're not all in Africa."[13]

You may or may not be aware that both Sharon Stone and Elizabeth Taylor have had near-death experiences. I knew Ms. Stone suffered a brain hemorrhage in 2001, briefly seeing some deceased friends and also glimpsing "the White Light," but I had no idea that Ms. Taylor had had an encounter with The Other Side until I was looking around the Internet to see whether I could find her exact

quote about her willingness to trade her life for a cure for AIDS.
When I came upon an article on www.near-death.com entitled
"NDE's of the Rich and Famous," I learned that she had "died" for
a few minutes during an operation in the late 1950s and had an in-
teraction with the spirit of her deceased former husband, Michael
Todd.

I found it more than just a little bit interesting that both of these
noted actresses, who have been prominent leaders in the fight against
AIDS, had also each had a near-death experience. Just another coincidence? Perhaps, but one thing I was certain of was that this
coincidence reminded me of something I'd read about near-death
experiences back in the 1990s:

> *"The central message that the near-death experiencers bring back
> from their encounter with death, or the presence or 'being of light,'
> is exactly the same as that of Buddha: that the essential and most
> important qualities in life are love and knowledge, compassion and
> wisdom."* [14]
>
> –Sogyal Rinpoche, *The Tibetan Book of Living and Dying:
> A New Spiritual Classic from One of the Foremost
> Interpreters of Tibetan Buddhism to the West*

Love, knowledge, compassion, wisdom...most of us have not
had near-death experiences and are not rich and famous like these
two celebrities, but my siblings and I believe that virtually all of us
possess the ability to show enough of these qualities to help bring
about significant improvements in the campaign against AIDS:

1. For starters, how difficult is it to place a quick phone call, send a
   brief e-mail, or scribble out a one-paragraph postcard to a
   politician's office saying that more money needs to be spent on
   AIDS?

2. Or how about simply taking a minute or two every now and
   then to read an AIDS-related article whenever one crops up in

a newspaper, magazine, or Internet site? Instead of just skipping over such pieces, are we really so busy that we can't devote even one or two minutes to educating ourselves a little bit about the basics of the HIV/AIDS virus?

3. And then, there's the most fundamental thing of all that each and every one of us who possesses a functioning brain can easily do: keep an open mind about AIDS and the issues surrounding the disease. As I said at the outset of this chapter, I personally didn't start paying much attention to this epidemic until it claimed the lives of people close to me. I can only say that I hope and pray we all do not have to lose loved ones to the virus before we wake up to the fact that AIDS is a killer that must be stopped!

These three suggestions obviously constitute just a short list of things almost all of us are capable of doing easily to pitch in to help win the war against AIDS. But although such things may seem like small acts, they nonetheless underscore how important it is for each citizen to demand that our leaders do more to alleviate the AIDS crisis.

Do We Have the Political Will?

Bob Geldof, who was knighted for his work to overcome famine in Africa with the Live Aid show in the '80s, has said, "AIDS has ceased to be something to be ashamed of–it's just another medical condition, but if the condition is medical, the solution is political."[15]

It is essential that all of us "regular folk" let our leaders know we want them to start spending more money on combating AIDS. However, it is the politicians themselves who will ultimately determine the fates of untold millions of lives. It is the government leaders whose day-to-day actions–*or inaction*–will write the history that will be read by future generations about how humanity dealt with one of the greatest tragedies ever to befall our planet. And according to the Spirit Guides, *if* the planet's leadership demonstrates the political will to act boldly and decisively by writing the massive checks that vanquishing this disease is going to require, *then* this a chance for them to be the ones to drive the proverbial stake through the heart of The AIDS Monster and be heroes for the ages in the eyes of history:

> Opportunity is the key word here. When opportunity knocks, we should all participate in opening the door up. It is not the responsibility of world leaders to do nothing when our eyes can plainly see that millions of people are in need of help every day. To turn a blind eye is not only to do an injustice to the suffering ones, but is an injustice to the people themselves.

> It is not without suffering that the world can learn. To make mistakes is human and only natural. But to overlook the outcome of the massive mistakes this country [the U.S.] and many others have made is criminal.

> Things on the planet are getting a little bit better, but we have a very long way to go before we can rest and be happy about the state of the planet. For if we do not turn things around, then it will continue to get much worse than it currently is—and, as we all know, it is quite bad as [it] is now. We cannot, and will not, let that happen.

> So, we appreciate everyone's efforts, for what has been done and what still needs to be done. And when we are done, it will once again be a beautiful and peaceful place to be. And that is what we all want. So let's all work together. We are heading in the right direction, but must continue to move forward and get it done.

> And again, we stress when this thing takes off, it will spread faster than any disease you've seen. We can see millions of souls who want to beat AIDS and its ravaging effects on the world, but we need to come together.

So, world leaders, please help ignite this firestorm of "love, knowledge, compassion, and wisdom" and start spending the necessary monies right now! Later on, when you're at the end of your life and look back on your performance as a leader and track record as a human being, do you think you'll ever regret taking such courageous action?

Global leaders, now's not a time to be timid, but to be bold. It's the only strategy that will win.

Let's All Work Together

This chapter has only scratched the surface of a subject that is multifaceted, exceedingly complex, and incredibly broad in scope. Hence, because the Guides, Ruth Montgomery, my siblings, and I all see AIDS as a "must-win" scenario if humanity is going to have the bright future we all desire, we all intend to keep coming back to this topic time and time again in our work…until The AIDS Monster is put in the grave.

Pastor Rick Warren, author of the powerful book titled *The Purpose Driven Life: What on Earth Am I Here For?*, summed up the AIDS situation very well when he said, "The HIV/AIDS pandemic is the greatest health crisis in history."[16]

If you're a Christian, you might find some additional statements by Pastor Warren about the disease to be of interest:

> *It also is the greatest opportunity for the Church to be the Church, to be Jesus Christ to the world.*
> *The church is the biggest network in the world.…I can bring you to 10 million villages in the world that don't have a doctor, don't have a post office, they have nothing but a church. But it's already on the ground, and we don't have to hire staff.*[17]

Yet, regardless of what we believe or do not believe about religion or the spiritual part of life, let's all work together and end AIDS. We'll *all* be glad we did.

CHAPTER 45

Bill and Melinda Gates: The Couple That "Made Global Health Cool"[1]

C uac still here with you.

Two people who are acutely aware of the extreme importance of finding a knockout punch to drop The AIDS Monster to the canvas are Microsoft's Bill Gates and his wife, Melinda. In fact, they "have made stopping AIDS the top priority" of the Bill & Melinda Gates Foundation, the largest philanthropic organization in the world. It has already given a great deal of money to various grant recipients who are working on developing an AIDS vaccine and generously provided large sums of money devoted to multiple methods of preventing AIDS. But the Gateses are also acutely aware that even the largest private fortune on the planet is no match for a foe as formidable as AIDS:

Bill Gates:

Private philanthropy is no substitute for governmental action here. The scale of the problem...is just way too great....[W]e've said to governments..."If you step up and increase, we'll step up and increase as well"....If government is pulling back on this stuff, then the AIDS epidemic absolutely will not be stopped....[2]

Melinda Gates:

The fight against AIDS is going to take all of our hearts, and minds, and political will. As well as a generous sharing of our resources.[3]

In the history of human accomplishment, ending AIDS will fill a category all its own. It will stand as a work of scientific genius. It will be a testament to diplomatic brilliance. It will represent enormous generosity of spirit and compassion.

But above all—and unlike so many other great works—ending AIDS will not be the success of one great scientist, one great community worker, or one great leader; it will be an accomplishment of the whole human family working together for one another.[4]

So, Bill and Melinda Gates, there is something I would like to say directly to both of you: *Many of the answers to your quest to solve some of the world's most perplexing health riddles lie in Earth's rain forests!*

When this project first began in mid-2002, the Spirit Guides soon made it very clear just how important saving the rain forests is to the future of the Earth and its inhabitants. On July 13th of that summer, just the third day that they began transmitting information for this book, they made the following assertions about the world's rain forests:

This planet sustains life when it is treated properly and maintained in good order. We need to tell you to keep the rain forests alive. They need to be kept alive so humans can be kept alive. There are all kinds of plants available for the medicinal uses you need.

HIV and AIDS can be gone if you keep the rain forests alive. Life is going to be difficult if you don't stop them from being destroyed. They hold magic in their leaves for the world. We can accelerate the life of these plants without too much effort.

To get the rain forests back, not all is lost yet, so you can make a difference. It is crucial to have the rain forests' medicines. The holy men will know where to go to get them and will teach their uses to the doctors who are pure of heart. To do this, the people who control the rain forests must come forth and get on with the business of stopping the cutting of trees and plants of the forests.

Quite frankly, we didn't really know what to make of all this stuff. But the Guides weren't through with their seminar on the rain forests and followed up later that summer with additional information about the topic:

The automatic writing we are going to do today will be about the rain forest and what an important piece of the puzzle that is. For man to save the world he must first see that which is good for the Earth and that which is harmful. The ways we can stop the killing of the rain forests are so monumentally important; we need to start saving them now.

To get the rain forest producing the medicines and the plants we need to sustain life here on the Earth, we first need them to stop cutting them down. We need to get the rain forest and the men who know it together in a way that is safe and nonviolent, so they can begin work right away as we head into this new millennium. The rain forests and their plants will help with the recovery of cancer, AIDS, and other disastrous diseases if we let them live alongside the human race. Live is the key word here.

The destruction of the rain forest is twofold, threefold, a hundred-fold...and we will not tolerate its destruction anymore. More people will get sick and die. More and more diseases will be spread. And this is not some biblical wrath of God. It is the natural order of things–because man has been so incredibly irresponsible in taking care of the Earth and her people.

And we can see millions of souls who want to beat AIDS and its ravaging effects on the world, but we need to come together. Plants from the rain forests [are] in need of cultivati[on], not cutting and destroying.

When we start to put in place this action, we will see a chain reaction around the world. Get every nation, every man, woman, and child involved and we will see to the rest.

"HIV and AIDS can be gone if you keep the rain forests alive....They hold magic in their leaves for the world."

Could such a thing really be true? Was there anything to what these unseen collaborators of ours were saying? My siblings and I had absolutely no idea whether there was even a kernel of truth in what the Spirit Guides had said about the rain forests. When we learned some basic information contained on San Francisco–based Rainforest Action Network's Web site, however, it made it seem like our invisible co-authors perhaps knew what they were talking about:

Medicinal Treasures of the Rain Forest

Covering only 6 percent of the Earth's surface, tropical moist forests contain at least half of all species. A typical four square mile patch of rain forest contains as many as 1500 species of flowering plants. The abundant botanical resources of tropical forests have already provided tangible medical advances, as one fourth of the medicines available today owe their existence to plants from the rain forests...yet only 1 percent of the known plant and animal species have been thoroughly examined for their medicinal potentials.

Seventy percent of the 3000 plants identified by the United States National Cancer Institute as having potential anti-cancer properties are endemic to the rain forest...

Who knows what other tricks the rain forest might have up its leaves? [5]

"Mr. and Mrs. Gates, please make the rain forests a major priority in your work—99 percent of their potential to provide medical help to humanity has not yet been fully explored."

Although the two of you likely know far more about the rain forests than the handful of basic points just summarized, my family and I would respectfully like to request that you make the preservation of the rain forests and search for an AIDS vaccine from their plant life a major priority for the Gates Foundation. Although this may already be an agenda item for your organization, we would suggest that a powerful case for making this issue a primary objective of your work is contained in the simple, yet incredibly persuasive, excerpt from the aforementioned Rainforest Action Network information:

One fourth of the medicines available today owe their existence to plants from the rain forests...yet only 1 percent of the known plant and animal species have been thoroughly examined for their medicinal potentials.

Although we know that you have already committed significant funding toward helping to discover an AIDS vaccine, it just seems logical that, if 99 percent of the rain forest's potential to provide medical help to humanity has not yet been fully explored, then it deserves more attention than it's currently receiving from the decision-makers of the world. Indeed, given that rain forests have such an outstanding historical track record of containing so many of the planet's important medicinal ingredients, this seems an eminently pragmatic way to proceed.

Here's what the spirit realm had to say on this subject:

> Bill and Melinda Gates can make a huge impact on the worldview if they will help save the rain forests. They are truly powerful people and will help not only financially, but inspirationally as well.
>
> They reach far and wide in the world community, and computers carry all the information you can think of. If they set up some sort of sub-foundation through the Web from the Bill & Melinda Gates Foundation, then many will follow.
>
> There should be a specific Web page on their foundation Web site informing people of the rain forest situation. That is only a part of it, but a big part. If they impart information on their Web site, then people will listen.
>
> You see, people listen to people who make a difference— celebrities or anyone who really has something good to say.
>
> But it is the idea, really, not the person carrying the idea, that impacts people. Not that dynamics don't play a part, they do for sure, but when an idea is bold enough to be spoken about, people listen.
>
> You see, people want the world to be right; they want peace to work; they want love; they just need to be reminded of it—then they can open their hearts.
>
> If Bill and Melinda want to open the eyes of people to the plight of the rain forest, they should have a special link from the foundation Web site that deals directly with the rain forest, and they can also afford to fund research.

Have a team of shamans, medicine men, doctors, and scientists go into the rain forest and study the plants. Don't just tell what's already out there, but start pulling and putting information out there that you firsthand have researched.

They could open up the rain forests literally to the wonders it holds, but start small, don't go too big. Only a small group of scientists and shamans should go.

You see, the rain forests are mighty, but they are also fragile; they hold key truths, but also fragility. They want so much to help, but the energies surrounding them, negative energies, are causing them to concentrate harder than normal on producing and making the medicinal plants that need to be produced.

Everything affects everything else. The rain forests flourish with much love surrounding them, but it is harder to grow when there is all of this negative [energy] flying around them.

You see, Bill and Melinda Gates hold power because they are passionate. Ideas are passionate. You need people to bring forth the ideas.

It's not that the people aren't strong, it's that the passion of the people and ideas, when they come together, can do great things.

Famous people can bring change from starting ideas, and then other people will follow with more and better ideas about solutions.

The green rain forests can sustain life only if the conditions are right. They can't keep producing if the Earth in which they grow is being destroyed.

So, if medicine men who know the forests team up with scientists who are pure of heart, they should be able to come up with more than enough medicinal elixirs for the world.

To wipe out AIDS, go to Guatemala—the secret lies there within.

"Highest praise to you both."

Bill and Melinda, not long after we finished a first draft of this chapter, we learned that you both had decided to devote even more of your time to the Gates Foundation's work going forward. We were thrilled to learn that, to quote your foundation's CEO, Patty Stonesifer, Bill "will...spend more time on the foundation's work" and that Melinda "has also confirmed plans to continue increasing her own daily involvement" in the foundation's work.[6] We felt that the two of you making helping others such a huge priority in your own lives was tremendous news for our world. So much so that we asked the spirit world to comment on its significance:

> **What you showed the world with this latest generous offering is that not only can you throw money at the world, but you can back that up with yourselves, your souls, your time, your energy. This is a greater offering than anything. To put money and true personal power with each other is, well, extraordinary. No two people on the planet have done so much.**
>
> **It's such a wonderful feeling for us to know our plans are taking hold even though our book hasn't even come out yet. This is what we meant when we said years ago [2002 to be exact] that the world was ready.**
>
> **You two have been such an example of how truly life can be good for yourselves and others. It is about balance. And you have that more than almost anyone. You share each other's lives and with that are able to give back to the world.**
>
> **Highest praise to you both. Keep up the good work. Love, from the Guides.**

NOTE: For any reader interested in learning more about the work of the Bill & Melinda Gates Foundation, its Internet address is:

http://www.gatesfoundation.org.

This is a tremendous resource and one that should be viewed by anyone even remotely interested in health, education, poverty, or just making our world a better place in general. In fact, a brief excerpt from this Web site sums up the Gates's core belief about human beings and is totally consistent with how the spirit realm views the worth of each person here on Earth:

Bringing innovations in health and learning to the global community...Bill and Melinda Gates believe that every life has equal value.

CHAPTER 46

A Shout-Out from Heaven to Warren Buffett

Mr. Buffett, even before you announced your momentous $30.7 billion gift to the Gates Foundation in June of 2006, we had planned on writing about you in the second book of this series. Because of your commitment to providing significant financial help to slowing the proliferation of nuclear weapons, we were intending to talk about you in a chapter titled simply "Money." In light of your decision to collaborate with your dear friends, Bill and Melinda Gates, however, and to devote the vast majority of your resources to helping our world through their foundation, we felt like we would be remiss in not immediately addressing the significance of your generosity.

That you effectively doubled the funding capacity of the Gates Foundation instead of "going it alone" in one of your own was a major moment for the planet. By putting your recognition of the urgent need on Earth for rapid results ahead of your own ego, you have made what we believe was the single best decision of your fabled investment career.

In an article with *Fortune* magazine's Carol Loomis, you said you felt like you had been "wired at birth to allocate capital."[1] Well, to paraphrase a line from the movie *Rocky II,* it is our opinion that time will prove your gift to the Gates Foundation to be the wisest allocation of capital "in the history of your life."

That you gave so much of your capital to the Gates Foundation was, by itself, a stupendous expression of care and concern for your fellow residents of Planet Earth. The dividends will be many: millions of lives will be saved; untold amounts of human suffering lessened; and an incalculable amount of hope provided for countless masses. The fact that you have joined Bill and Melinda as a trustee of the foundation and committed your immense intellect to its work is also extremely significant.

Bill has referred to you in the past as one of a select number of people that he considers to be "super smart." You obviously feel the same way about him and Melinda, having called them both "ungodly bright."[2] Hence, while we recognize that you have many responsibilities associated with your business affairs and the rest of your life, we hope you will allocate as much of your brainpower as you possibly can to this triumvirate of minds as the three of you work together to change our world for the better.

After all, it was your mind that allowed you to create the wealth you have bestowed upon your fellow sisters and brothers around the globe through the Gates Foundation. Who knows what may be achieved with you, Bill, and Melinda devoting unprecedented amounts of your individual and collective intellects to the formidable challenges faced by us all?

Well, Mr. Buffett, although we want to express our own appreciation for all that you are doing to help our world, your generosity represents a gesture so grand we felt like it warrants Heaven weighing in on its significance. So, straight from The Other Side, here is what the spirit world would like you to know about how your magnificent act of sharing is viewed from Heaven:

Let's say Mr. Buffett was wired a lot longer ago than his birth to help people. He needs to remember that his wealth was by no accident.

His enormous brainpower will help. Not only because he made so much money from using it well, but because he can use it to help the very foundation he generated so much to.

He generates goodness with his money. And that is exactly what we want.

He took a tremendous leap of faith to donate money to someone else's organization. It takes a big man to make such a generous donation *and* to make sure that Bill and Melinda will themselves stay involved with their foundation.

You see, he sees things for the long haul–as he always has. And he sees this as the perfect way to keep his money flowing for many years to come. His heart is in the right place.

And for those of you who administer bad feelings for people with lots of money, look to this man and know not all money men are greedy. He is a shining example of how men should be. He sees long-term, and that is a great asset.

It is okay to be wealthy. Just share it. Whether it's berries you pick in a field or money you spent your whole life accumulating.

Mr. Buffett, we share in your enthusiasm and wish to give the highest praise for your efforts. Amen.

NOTE TO THE READER: If you are not already familiar with how Warren Buffett structured his gift to the Bill & Melinda Gates Foundation, it may help for you to be aware that it is spread out over many years and is conditioned upon either Bill or Melinda's continued participation in their foundation's work. We provide this detail so that you can put in context the Guides' saying, "It takes a big man to make such a generous donation *and* to make sure that

Bill and Melinda will themselves stay involved with their foundation. You see, he sees things for the long haul—as he always has. And he sees this as the perfect way to keep his money flowing for many years to come."

CHAPTER 47

The World Aid Concerts (a.k.a. "The Big Gig")

Why 50 Percent of This Project's Profits Are Being Donated to Help Third World Nations

Each of us giving whatever our means will allow to help others is a theme that the spirit world emphasized right from the beginning of their communications with us. In fact, very early on in this book series inception, the Spirit Guides let it be known that 50 percent of the profits generated from this project were to be donated as seed money toward initiating an ongoing series of "World Aid Concerts" we have affectionately dubbed "The Big Gig."

"It was a 'knowing,' plain and simple."

Jane here.

Shortly after we decided to take the Guides' advice and move forward with the book project, it became extremely clear to me that we needed to give away 50 percent of any profits the book might make. It wasn't one of those "iffy" things, and it did not come through in the automatic writing. It was a "knowing," plain and simple. I did not question it, ponder over it, or think it was ridiculous (as my children do). It was as clear as when the notion to stop drinking hit me. A revelation if you want, but so easy. No thinking involved really. Just, "Okay, that sounds good."

It's Rob back with you.

Sometime during July 2002, the month this project was born, Jane and I spoke on the phone, and she described this "feeling" she had had about our giving away 50 percent of the project's profits. My initial thought was, *Whoa! 50 percent? After enduring all of the financial challenges that the previous decade of litigation has put me through, we're now supposed to give away half of whatever this new venture might make?*

I didn't express any of my reservations to Jane, however, and continued listening to her explain how she came to this conclusion. The more I heard her talk about this "knowing" that we should be giving away half of the money from this project, the more my heart told me that she was probably right. If Jane, who was struggling mightily in the finances department herself as the single mom of two young children, instinctively believed so strongly that this was the right thing to do, then it probably was.

Although I finished our phone call by saying to Jane that I was fine with "the 50 percent thing," I nonetheless wanted to get Paul's take on this notion. When I called our brother and said that Janey just had this "feeling"–which wasn't even part of the automatic writing transmissions–that we were supposed to give away half of the project's profits, he responded by saying, "Oh yeah, Rob, I've been meaning to talk to you about that. I've been getting the same feeling."

That just floored me. Paul, who hadn't even yet started the automatic writing, who lived three thousand miles away from Jane, and who hadn't spoken a word to her about "the 50 percent thing," had also been getting the same strong sense that we were to give away half of the project's proceeds. That did it. Fifty percent it would be. But what would we donate the money for? Another "feeling" of Jane's provided the answer to that question, so I'll let her explain it.

When I next spoke to Cuac, he said that Paul had had the same "feeling" or intuition, if you will, about "the 50 percent thing"–the exact same notion–without ever having done any automatic writing or ever having talked to me about the subject. Cuac thought maybe the money should be used for organizing a bunch of writers, activists, and spiritual leaders to focus on the issues that were being discussed in the automatic writing transmissions, but the sense I was getting was that 50 percent of the profits were supposed to be put toward staging some musical concerts. The Guides would soon confirm that this was exactly what they had in mind.

"Live Aid was a good start, but we want this to go global...the world cannot survive if this does not happen."

Cuac on the keyboard again.

I would estimate that it was probably late July of 2002 when Jane told me her "sense" that the money we were going to give away should involve music and concerts. I was really wondering if such a thing were even remotely possible and decided to review all the automatic writing transcripts to see if there was anything in them to indicate that this was what the Guides truly intended for us to do with 50 percent of the project's profits. In so doing, I found just a couple of hints from a July 15th transmission that made me think perhaps my sister was on the right track:

> **Just go along with this and help us, Jane. Bono will help with Scotland and Ireland and other British and European countries. Elton John will play. Billy Joel and all good people.**

Rereading these words made me recall my initial reaction when I had first seen them earlier in the month. I had assumed that the Spirit Guides' saying that "Bono will help" must have meant that he would be generally supportive of the issues that the Guides had identified as important for the world and its leaders to focus upon. And I simply had not at all known what to make of the spirit realm's statement that "Elton John will play. Billy Joel and all good people."

Play what? is what I had wondered.

On August 18, 2002, they wrote:

> The concert that has been in our minds for so many years now is beginning to take shape. Live Aid was a good start, but we want this to go global. [Live Aid was a fundraising project for Ethiopian famine victims, with concerts held simultaneously in London and Philadelphia. July 13, 1985, the date of this event, was called "The Day the Music Changed the World."]
>
> We want every person of every nation to give back what has been given to them. These may sound like old-fashioned notions, but as we see it from here, the world cannot survive if this does not happen.

The Guides also prepared us for the skepticism that such an undertaking would initially face:

> There will be many people in the entertainment business who will scoff at this at first, but they will turn around once it gets off the ground. We realize this is a huge undertaking, but we want the celebrity world to know that this is the best way they can help. They will be sweetly surprised by the rewards they will receive; not only from their Earthly fans, but from their Heavenly ones as well....We want this to be the largest undertaking ever attempted. And we see all the musicians and their music touching the world in a way no one ever has before.

On September 2, 2002, barely two weeks after their initial statements about the topic, the Guides wrote at more length about the musical extravaganza they envisioned for Planet Earth:

> The music for the festival that we want to take place is really several festivals of all kinds of music. We want all genres of music to participate in this worldwide event. We want it to be an ongoing telethon. Please help make this possible by pulling together not just rock and roll groups, but groups of country musicians, orchestras, and reggae.
>
> Classical musicians have much to offer. They have a following that is far and wide, and we want Germany to host the classical concerts and be sponsors of that field. We see the fine art of Germany in many things, and we feel they will best pull off the part that is their right and their place.
>
> So to get on with this, we will need to get organizers, and committee members will need to be put together. We want rap musicians, hip-hop, sweetness, and gospel, rhythm and blues...everything.
>
> It was no mistake that you heard Bob Geldof's [the musician and activist who was a primary organizer of the 1985 Live Aid concerts] name today, Jane. We plant ideas in your head in many ways. We see that you are picking up on our clues and want you to tune into TV and the media. Nelson Mandela's speech today and the Earth Summit [are] other clue[s].
>
> We are seeing so many people shining and being a part of this. The world will be in much better shape once we all get going. This is so exciting to us, and we hope that you will continue your energies and put into place this project soon.

Lily and friends returned again a couple of months later to their urgings that a global concert series should be put in motion:

> **As we said before, we want not only rock legends to participate, but every genre of music. It might be safe to say that Jamaica could head up the reggae end of things. As we have mentioned, Germany should head up classical music. Australia should choose their genre. It is really up to people; we are just giving you ideas.**

The scope of what the Spirit Guides had outlined was positively humongous. As I tried to "get my arms around it," as the saying goes, I realized this was going to require that I make a conscious effort to grasp more fully music's ability "to move people."

I decided I would start to keep my eyes and ears open to see if I could pick up any clues that might shed light on why the spirit realm was placing so much faith in music. I didn't have to wait long to find the first piece of the puzzle.

"Music...Something inside us craves it."

As I was reading *The Boston Globe* in late 2002, I came across a December 29th article, "Music of my mind." It began by asking why certain songs linger in our minds or mentally take us back in time to certain moments of the past. The piece went on to explain that a journal called *Science* had recently reported the results of a research study conducted by Dartmouth College's Center for Cognitive Neuroscience. Included in the article was a statement about the test results by Petr Janata, the lead researcher for the study, which seemed to lend credence to the Guides' emphasis on the importance of music in human existence: "An appreciation of music, it seems, came to be hardwired to memory and the emotions early on in the history of humankind. Why? Something inside us craves it. I think this research helps us understand that craving a little bit more."[1]

Maybe the Spirit Guides were on to something.

"And a love for music is basically the most common thing that we have."[2]

–Clarence Clemons, saxophonist for the E Street Band

Another nugget that wandered into my path while I was searching for indications that Heaven's confidence in music was well founded came in the form of an article in *Backstreets*, a Bruce Springsteen fan magazine. In the Winter/Spring 2003 edition of the quarterly publication, I read an interview with E Street Band member Clarence Clemons being conducted by *Backstreets* publisher Christopher Phillips and smiled when I came to the end of it:

> *[W]hen people realize that we do have something in common, people start to realize that you do have the power to make a change. And a love for music is basically the most common thing that we have....*
>
> *It gives you hope...little sparks of hope that become a flame.*[3]

"[L]ittle sparks of hope that become a flame." When I read the sax player's passionate words, they reminded me of something Lily had said during the first week that this project began in July of 2002:

> **We need to glorify good deeds, no matter how small. The little things we do for each other will influence the entire world. We need to set, like wildfire, a chain reaction where people want to continue spiritually, while still going on with their lives....**
>
> **What needs to happen is a small chain of events to get this thing running. I don't mean just the book, but the small chain reaction of nice deeds going around the world like wildfire.**

The LIVE 8 Concerts: Now That's What Heaven's Talkin' About!

The LIVE 8 concerts were held in early July of 2005 and were a great example of how the spirit realm says a series of events can "influence the entire world." Just as he had for the Live Aid concerts twenty years earlier, Bob Geldof once again took a lead role in organizing a musical extravaganza designed to better the lives of some of the planet's neediest inhabitants. Here's how his Web site, www.bobgeldof.info, described the event that was timed immediately to precede the 2005 annual conference of the leaders of the G8 nations (Group of 8–Canada, France, Germany, Italy, Japan, Russia, the United Kingdom, and the United States):

> *Live 8 was a series of concerts that took place in July 2005, in the G8 nations and South Africa....[T]he shows planned to pressure world leaders to drop the debt of the world's poorest nations, increase and improve aid, and negotiate fairer trade rules in the interest of poorer countries.*[4]

The scale and reach of the G8 musical extravaganza were unprecedented in world history, with highlights including eleven concerts being performed (ten of them simultaneously) in different countries; the participation of one hundred and fifty bands and over a thousand musicians; in excess of two thousand radio and one hundred eighty television networks broadcasting the shows literally all around the globe; and the involvement of many other entertainers, athletes, and major world figures from all walks of life who served as speakers and presenters, including Nelson Mandela and United Nations Secretary-General Kofi Annan.[5]

And this is how LIVE 8's Web site, www.live8live.com, describes the results of the concerts' success:

*LIVE 8 rocked the world. We didn't ask for your money, we asked for your voice...*3 BILLION PEOPLE watched Live 8, the greatest, greatest show on Earth. They came together with one message—make poverty history....Over 30 million people from all around the world gave us their names....[6]

These thirty million names were put on what was called the "live8list" and presented to Tony Blair, who was serving as G8's chairperson for the conference. And the result? Did the voices of the many get through to the powerful few?

The leaders of these eight mighty nations, whose economies account for approximately two-thirds of Planet Earth's total economy, were persuaded to make some unprecedented commitments, including the following:

- Tens of billions of dollars in additional aid to Africa by 2010
- The cancellation of many more billions of dollars owed by the poorest Third World nations to some of the world's richest countries
- Major increases in the provision of medicine for AIDS to people in need in the Third World

Although the fulfillment of the G8 leaders' promises requires that ongoing political pressure be applied to ensure that all of these obligations are met, there is absolutely no doubt that the LIVE 8 concerts, backed with the thirty million strong live8list, played a huge role in getting the commitments made in the first place.

Pretty impressive stuff, don't you think? Isn't it refreshing to see that world leaders heard the message about the urgency of these issues and had the courage to take some significant steps in the right direction?

For all that the concerts helped accomplish, there is *so* much more that needs to be done: Third World nations need fair international trade policies in order to be able to help themselves get on sound financial footing; there still remain many developing nations whose citizens live in desperate conditions because their governments are saddled with debts that they will never be able to repay to the world's richest countries...and the list goes on. So, please, take a few minutes, log onto Bob Geldof and LIVE 8's Web sites, and educate yourself about some of the most critical issues of our time.

"We are all in this together."

"Standing in front of a glass case containing the Declaration of Independence, [Will] Smith made a plea for unity with Africa: 'We are gathered here to make our declaration of interdependence, and today we hold this truth to be self-evident: We are all in this together.'"[7]

–Will Smith, in a speech kicking off the Philadelphia
LIVE 8 concert

LIVE 8's example of the power of music to influence policy at the highest level of world leadership was very much on my mind as I prepared to write this chapter. So much so that it caused me to draft a question for the Guides. Here is my query and the Guides' response:

Are we correct that the concert series should be set up similarly to the recent LIVE 8 concerts so that the primary objective is to raise awareness around the world about the need to help the Third World so that more public support is generated that will put additional pressure on the rich nations' governments to provide more help to the Third World and accord them a greater say in world affairs and that any monies generated from the concerts should be used to fund staging more and more concerts so that the series can sustain itself over the long run?

What we want is all walks of life to see each other as the same thing. We are all in this together.

"Yes" to the point of the question. Awareness is on the rise already.

Concerts bring awareness about other people, but they also bring joy and sadness in notes. And that is the real eye-opener: Music itself carries with it notes of mind, body, and spirit.

So while raising awareness on the outside, it is the music itself that will awaken awareness on the inside. It's a two-fold operation.

Yes, awareness to the masses is crucial, but, combined with the awareness within one's self, [it] will be explosive. So, let's make some music and have some fun!

Exactly one-third from all concerts should go directly to Third World countries and two-thirds go to the staging of more concerts. As time goes on, we want billions to go to Third World nations, but start with one-third to Third World nations and two-thirds to concerts. Go to next question.

As I read through the transmission Jane had received from Lily et al. that was "hot off the press" from The Other Side, two things really stood out to me:

1. The Guides' statement that "Music itself carries with it notes of mind, body, and spirit. So while raising awareness on the out-side, it is the music itself that will awaken awareness on the inside." This reminded me of the Dartmouth study reported in *Science* that talked of how human beings are "hardwired" for music and that "something inside us craves it."[8]

2. The specificity of the Guides' financial framework for The World Aid Concerts and their reference to "billions" eventually result-ing from the series of ongoing musical events. These spirits sure didn't think small!

I had all sorts of emotions running through me as I digested the Guides' words. I felt amazement, excitement, awe, and also a cer-tain measure of apprehension. If the spirit realm's plan for the concert series was to be executed, it was going to take a tremendous amount of work to implement it.

A Request to the Entertainment Industry: "This Stuff Works—Don't Stop!"[9]

As you may well be aware, these are not my words, not my siblings' words, not Ruth Montgomery's words, and not the words of the Spirit Guides. No, they are the words that form the ongoing call to action that I read on LIVE 8's Web site. Seeing them on www.live8live.com at the bottom of the site's home page made me say to myself, *That's exactly what the Guides are talking about! This stuff does work and needs to continue.*

A Question for Everyone: Do You Believe in the Power of Music?

> *"You still have the political turmoil and the blame game....But when the music starts, it cuts through all the social and racial divides, and everyone forgets their differences. It's a great leveler and unifying force."* [10]
>
> —Edge, U2 guitarist, in discussing Music Rising, a charity
> dedicated to replacing instruments musicians lost when
> hurricanes Katrina and Rita laid waste to the Gulf Coast
> (www.musicrising.org)

Do you believe in the power of music? Only you truly know the answer. And you don't have to share your response with anyone else. Right now, you already know how you *feel* about this question.

The widespread popularity of the television show *American Idol* is certainly a strong testament to music's universal appeal. Indeed, music permeates so much of our daily routine that it is easy to take for granted just how significant its presence is in our lives.

Imagine life with no music. No music to listen to on the radio. No music to dance by. No music to hear on CDs, cassettes, records,

MP3 players, or any other listening device. No music to provide dramatic effects in movies or TV shows. No music for catchy commercial jingles. No music for weddings. No music for funerals. And no music in any church services.

Not a very pleasant thing to think about, is it? I know when I think about it, the feeling I get inside is "empty." But, thankfully, music *is* part of our existence. And although the soundtrack of our lives is decidedly unique for each and every one of us, my observations of the past few years have made me a strong believer in the notion that music truly is a common denominator that links us all.

What I have also come to realize is it is the times when I'm listening to music that I believe the most in the human race's ability to come together and solve its greatest challenges. Whether it's driving along listening to music in the car or having it on as background music as I work in my home office, I find that music frequently infuses me with an enhanced sense of optimism about virtually everything in life. From mundane tasks of no lasting significance to the most profound aspects of existence, music often makes me more confident about the possibility of successfully solving whatever the particular problem may be.

In going through the process of evaluating music's positive impact on my personal outlook, I asked myself if there were any other times in life that also injected me with a high degree of confidence and optimism. I concluded that there are two additional things in life that, over and over again, have lifted my spirits during periods when I'm feeling low and am lacking "belief":

1. When I'm listening to an inspiring speaker or reading a spiritually oriented book.

2. When I'm in the company of people I know care about me or care about some of the same things I do.

As I sit here writing the end of this chapter, it is not lost on me that The Big Gig, which the Spirit Guides have stressed is so critical to humanity's future, will combine elements of all three things that most make me believe, really believe: music, inspiring speakers, and being in the presence of others with whom I share a common interest.

Let's Have Some Fun!

I don't know to what extent you've ever felt any of the same things I'm talking about, but my family and I are interested in hearing from you about your own take on the contents of this chapter and any or all of the following questions:

1. How has music inspired you?

2. Which musicians have touched your life the most and why?

3. What are the songs that have meant the most to you?

4. What are the special tunes that your heart keeps coming back to when you need an emotional lift that you just can't get anywhere else?

5. What is your opinion about why music has such a powerful effect on so many of us?

6. Do you believe that music can help the human race solve its biggest problems?

7. What else is there about music that you feel is important?

8. What suggestions do you have for us as we go about the formidable task of seeking the entertainment industry's help in turning Heaven's dreams for humanity into reality?

E-mail us your thoughts at: ideas@thebiggig.com

or write us at: Distinctive Publications for the World
                        P.O. Box 888
                        Hanover, New Hampshire 03755

Because we're taking the Guides' words about the extreme importance of the creation of an ongoing series of concerts very seriously, we'd not only like to hear from you about your personal perspective on music and its potential to do good in our world, but we would also like to ask you to consider doing two other things:

1. If you like the idea of The World Aid Concerts, please contact your favorite entertainers and let them know how you feel. We invite you to send them an e-mail or a brief note with your thoughts about the project.

2. Tell friends, family members, work colleagues, and anyone you know about The Big Gig. It's going to take a huge effort on the parts of lots of people to make this happen, so we would like to ask for your help in getting the word out about this concert series.

Finally, we hope you will remember what the spirits in Heaven have said about The World Aid Concerts:

We are seeing so many people shining and being a part of this.

Please be one of the "many," and as the Guides have said, let's "have some fun!"

> *"Music, the greatest good that mortals know,*
> *And all of heaven we have here below."*
> –Joseph Addison, English writer and politician

CHAPTER 48

Bono!

"He is pure of heart."

—The Spirit Guides

"It is sexy to want to change the world, not to leave it as it is."[1]

—Bono

"Music can change the world."[2]

—Bono

Heaven on Bono

On July 14, 2002, just three days after this project formally began, the Spirit Guides suddenly came out with some statements about Bono that floored us:

> Bono can help. So can many other celebrities.
>
> Third World countries are Bono's project. With many organizations, he is willing to help with his influence because he is pure of heart and can really make a difference.
>
> We need to tell Bono about our plans. He can be instrumental in getting this thing together.
>
> Bono will be able to help [and] would be a great start because his heart is already in it.

Prior to Jane receiving this information about Bono during one of her automatic writing transmissions from the Guides, the three of us really didn't know much about him. Although we certainly realized that he was a famous rock star, Jane was the only one of the three of us who was really familiar with his band U2's music. But even more significantly, not one of us had any more than a very superficial awareness of Bono's humanitarian work to help Third World nations in general and Africa in particular, a fact that was sadly indicative of our overall lack of awareness of–and interest in– the subject at the time.

Clearly, the Guides saw Bono as an absolutely crucial player in helping implement their Action Plan for Planet Earth. But what really got our attention was that these spirits were telling us that Bono was already involved with the type of issues they were talking about. Apparently, their outlook from Heaven and Bono's are very similar with respect to identifying our planet's most pressing problems.

A Few Basics on Bono

DATA (www.data.org)

DATA is the name of a nonprofit organization that Bono cofounded with Bill and Melinda Gates (who provided funding from their Gates Foundation) and Bobby Shriver, businessman, activist, and former part-owner of the Baltimore Orioles.[3]

DATA is an acronym that stands for two sets of related issues:

1. Debt, AIDS, Trade in Africa; and

2. Increasing Democracy, Accountability, and Transparency in Africa.[4]

On the one hand, DATA seeks to heighten awareness about the urgent problems currently crippling the African continent: foreign debts that can never be paid, the world's worst AIDS crisis, and unfair trade policies that stifle the potential growth of African economies by placing their workers at a competitive disadvantage with the planet's richest countries.[5] As it says on the organization's Web site–www.data.org–"DATA calls on the governments of the world's wealthy nations–the United States, Europe, Canada and Japan–to put more resources towards Africa, and to adopt policy that helps rather than hinders Africa in achieving long-term prosperity."[6]

In return for this help, however, more democracy, increased accountability, and improved transparency and openness are expected of African leaders. DATA considers it critical "that support for African people goes where it's intended."[7] Because of some instances of government corruption and misuse of aid to Africa in the past, this linkage between support and results is an integral part of DATA's strategy.

The blueprint utilized by DATA is not without historical precedent. To the contrary, as stated in a *Time* magazine article by journalists Josh Tyrangiel and Benjamin Nugent, "[T]he DATA Agenda is loosely modeled on the Marshall Plan, which provided Europeans with foreign assistance, debt cancellation and trade incentives to rebuild their economies after World War II, so that they could act as a bulwark against Soviet expansion."[8] As Bono puts it, after the fighting was over, "[t]hat was where Europe felt the grace of America...."[9]

To learn more about DATA and how what's going on in Africa has direct relevance to your life, you can visit the organization's informative Web site at: www.data.org.

One part of DATA's Web site that is especially useful in connecting what may be going on in your life to the lives of our fellow sisters and brothers in Africa can be found simply by clicking a button labeled "Why Me?" It contains brief, but powerful, informative nuggets titled "Your Faith," "Your Community," "Your Role," and "Take Action." Check it out. It's great stuff.

A Book on Bono...Up Close and Personal

As a longtime friend of Bono and his U2 band mates, author and Paris-based music journalist Michka Assayas used an informal question-and-answer format to write a biography about his pal titled *Bono: In Conversation with Michka Assayas*. It touches on many of life's nitty-gritty topics, including both religion and politics. "Michka," as Bono refers to him, allows the passionate Irishman to reveal, with tremendous candor, to all of us the central reason the spirits in Heaven have so much faith in him: *his heart*.

To give you a sense of what we're talking about, we've included some powerful words from Bono in the following excerpt from *Bono: In Conversation with Michka Assayas:*

> *Now most people accept that women, blacks, Irish, and Jews are equal, but only within these borders. I'm not sure we accept that Africans are equal....Right now there is the biggest pandemic in the history of civilization, happening in the world now with AIDS. It's bigger than the Black Death, which took a third of Europe in the Middle Ages. Sixty-five hundred Africans are dying every day of a preventable, treatable disease. And it is not a priority for the West: two 9/11s a day, eighteen jumbo jets of fathers, mothers, families falling out of the sky. No tears, no letters of condolence, no fifty-one-gun salutes. Why? Because we don't put the same value on African life as we put on a European or an American life....We say we can't get these antiretroviral drugs to the farthest reaches of Africa, but we can get them our cold fizzy drinks. The tiniest village, you can find a bottle of Coke. Look, if we really thought that an African life was equal in value to an English, a French, or an Irish life, we wouldn't let two and a half million Africans die every year for the stupidest of reasons: money. We just wouldn't. And a very prominent head of state said to me: "It's true. If these people weren't Africans, we just couldn't let it happen."" We don't really deep down believe in their equality.*
>
> *We have written off Africans....*[10]

Once again, the more we investigated what was coming through in the Guides' automatic writing, the more we became persuaded that our phantom-like co-authors knew what they were talking about. They sure seemed to be on the mark about Bono anyway. The more we learned, the more we understood why the rock star with the big heart had been identified as a major player in Heaven's plan for humankind.

ONE: The Campaign to Make Poverty History

Another project we learned about in which Bono is heavily involved is ONE. And just what is ONE all about? Here's how the organization's Web site–www.one.org–describes it:

> *ONE is a new effort by Americans to rally Americans ONE by ONE to fight the emergency of global AIDS and extreme poverty. ONE is students and ministers, punk rockers and NASCAR moms, Americans of all beliefs and every walk of life, united as ONE to help make poverty history.*[11]

Although Bono has certainly taken a lead role in ONE's activities, a wide cross-section of Americans from all fifty states has signed up to help the project. Individuals of varying ages, numerous faiths, and virtually every conceivable background have joined in to help ONE.

A lot of very influential individuals have also stepped up to back the initiative. Included in this list of noted figures who have become involved in ONE are: George Clooney, Penelope Cruz, Jamie Foxx, Bill Gates, the Most Rev. Frank Griswold, presiding bishop of the Episcopal Church, USA, Tom Hanks, Salma Hayek, Kate Hudson, Dave Matthews, Brad Pitt, Pat Robertson, Pastor Rick Warren, and many other high-profile leaders from widely divergent fields.[12]

Asking other famous figures to do as Bono has done and consider using their celebrity status to do good in our world is something that has been an integral part of his efforts to effect government policy change regarding the Third World. As journalist James Traub put it in a *New York Times Magazine* article, "The Statesman," "He's a kind of one-man state who fills his treasury with the global currency of fame."[13] At the same time, however, Traub points out that Bono "believes–he *knows*–that the American people would demand action on Africa if only someone would tell them the facts: 'Middle America,' [Bono] said….'Don't get me started. I love it.'"[14]

If you'd like to join Bono, his fellow celebrities, and millions of ordinary citizens who have already expressed their support for the ONE campaign, it's very easy to do and takes only a couple of minutes from start to finish. Just go to the project's Web site–www.one.org–and electronically sign the ONE declaration:

> *WE BELIEVE that in the best American tradition of helping others help themselves, now is the time to join with other countries in an historic pact for compassion and justice to help the poorest people of the world overcome AIDS and extreme poverty.*
>
> *WE RECOGNIZE that a pact including such measures as fair trade, debt relief, fighting corruption and directing additional support for basic needs—education, health, clean water, food, and care for orphans—would transform the futures and hopes of an entire generation in the poorest countries, at a cost equal to just one percent more of the US budget.*
>
> *WE COMMIT ourselves—one person, one voice, one vote at a time—to make a better, safer world for all.*[15]

The ONE campaign may be specifically directed toward getting more Americans involved in its work, but the project needs the involvement of people from all nations, cultures, and backgrounds. In fact, no matter who you are or where you live, you already possess the only thing that's necessary to get a ticket of admission to join in with Bono and company: *your heart.*

Bono in His Own Words

We certainly understand that it may be something of a stretch for you to "listen with a straight face" to words purportedly coming from "dead" spirits. But perhaps you may find more than just a little bit of logic in what a very real, very knowledgeable rock singer has said about the issue that Heaven has declared to be the most pressing problem facing the human race: the plight of the Third World, especially Africa. So here's Bono, "in his own words," in an address he gave in 2005 as an inaugural winner of the TED (Technology, Entertainment, and Design) prize:

> *Anyway, we found Africa to be a magical place—big skies, big hearts, big shining continent, beautiful royal people. Anybody who ever gave anything to Africa got a lot more back. Ethiopia didn't just blow my mind, it opened my mind. Anyway, on our last day at this orphanage, a man handed me his baby and said, "Would you take my son with you?" And he knew in Ireland that his son would live, and that in Ethiopia, his son would die. It was the middle of that awful famine. Well, I turned him down, and it was a funny kind of sick feeling, but I turned him down, and it's a feeling I can't ever quite forget. And, in that moment, I started this journey. In that moment, I became the worst thing of all. I became a rock star with a cause. Except this isn't a cause, is it?*
>
> *Six and a half thousand Africans dying every single day from AIDS, a preventable, treatable disease, for lack of drugs we can get in any pharmacy. That's not a cause. That's an emergency. Eleven million AIDS orphans in Africa, 20 million by the end of the decade. That's not a cause. That's an emergency. Today, every day, 9,000 more Africans will catch HIV because of stigmatization and lack of education. That's not a cause. That's an emergency. So what we're talking about here is human rights—the right to live like a human. The right to live period. What we're facing in Africa is an unprecedented threat to human dignity and equality.*

The next thing I'd like to be clear about is what this problem is and what this problem isn't, because this is not all about charity. This is about justice. Really, this is not about charity. This is about justice. That's right. And that's too bad, because we're very good at charity. Americans, like Irish people, are good at it. Even the poorest neighborhoods give more than they can afford. We like to give, and we give a lot. Look at the response to the tsunami. It's inspiring.

But justice is a tougher standard than charity. You see, Africa makes a fool of our idea of justice. It makes a farce of our idea of equality. It mocks our pieties. It doubts our concern. It questions our commitment. Because there's no way we can look at what's happening in Africa and, if we're honest, conclude that it would ever be allowed to happen anywhere else....There is no chance this kind of hemorrhaging of human life would be accepted anywhere else other than Africa.

Africa is a continent in flames and, deep down, if we really accepted that Africans were equal to us, we would all do more to put the fire out. We're standing around with watering cans, when what we really need is the fire brigade, and that's what I'm trying to do tonight, really. That's why I'm speaking to you. I'm trying to call the fire brigade. I'm asking for your help.

I'm an Irish rock star in America. I love this country. I know my way around, but I really need help here. This stuff isn't even on the news. You see, it's not as dramatic as the tsunami. It's crazy, really, when you think about it. Does stuff have to look like an action movie these days to exist in the front of our brain? The slow extinguishing of countless lives is just not dramatic enough, it would appear. Catastrophes that we can avert are not as interesting as ones we could avert....

Six and a half thousand people dying a day in Africa may be Africa's crisis, but the fact that it's not on the nightly news, that we in Europe or you in America are not treating it like an emergency. I want to argue with you tonight that that's our crisis.

Okay, I'd like to hard cut now from the moral imperative to the strategic, 'cause this is not all about heart. We have to be smart here. I want to argue that, though Africa is not the frontline in the war against terror, it could be soon. Every week, religious extremists take another African village. They're attempting to bring order to chaos. Well, why aren't we?

Poverty breeds despair. We know this. Despair breeds violence. We know this. In turbulent times, isn't it cheaper and smarter to make friends out of potential enemies than to defend yourself against them later?

Well, the war against terror is bound up in the war against poverty, and I didn't say that. Colin Powell said that. Now when the military are telling us that this is a war that cannot be won by military might alone, maybe we should listen. There's an opportunity here, and it's real. It's not spin. It's not wishful thinking.

The problems facing the developing world afford us in the developed world a chance to redescribe ourselves to the world. We will not only transform other peoples' lives, but we will also transform the way those other lives see us, and that might be smart in these nervous, dangerous times.

Okay, I'd like to talk for a second about commerce....Don't you think, that on a purely commercial level, that anti-retroviral drugs are great advertisements for Western ingenuity and technology? Doesn't compassion look well on us? And let's cut the crap for a second. In certain quarters of the world, brand EU, brand USA is not at its shiniest. The neon sign is fizzing and cracking. Someone's put a brick through the window. The regional branch managers are getting nervous. Never before have we in the West been so scrutinized. Our values—do we have any? Our credibility. These things are under attack around the world. Brand USA could use some polishing, and I say that as a fan, you know...as a person who buys the products.

But think about it. More anti-retrovirals makes sense. But that's just the easy part—or ought to be. But equality for Africa—that's a big, expensive idea. You see, the scale of the suffering numbs us into a kind of indifference. What on earth can we all do about this? Well, much more than we think. We can't fix every problem, but the ones we can, I want to argue, we must. And because we can, we must.

This is the straight truth, the righteous truth. It is not a theory. The fact is that ours is the first generation that can look disease and extreme poverty in the eye, look across the ocean to Africa, and say this and mean it, "We do not have to stand for this." A whole continent written off, we do not have to stand for this....

We can change the world. I can't. You can't, as individuals. But WE can change the world. I really believe that the people in this room...look at the Gates Foundation. They've done incredible stuff, unbelievable stuff. But working together, we can actually change the world. We can turn the inevitable outcomes and transform the quality of life for millions of lives who look and feel rather like us when you're up close....

You see, idealism detached from action is just a dream. But idealism allied with pragmatism, with rolling up your sleeves and making the world bend a bit, is very exciting. It's very real. It's very strong....

Last year at DATA, this organization I helped set up, and we launched a campaign to summon this spirit in the fight against AIDS and extreme poverty. We're calling it the ONE Campaign. It's based on our belief that the action of one person can change a lot, but the actions of many coming together as one can change the world. Well, we feel that now is the time to prove we're right. There are moments in history when civilization redefines itself. We believe this is one. We believe that this could be the time when the world finally decides that the wanton loss of life in Africa is just no longer acceptable. This could be the time that we finally get serious about changing the future for most people who live on planet earth. Momentum has been building—lurching a little—but it's building....

What I try to communicate, and you can help me if you agree, is that aid for Africa is just great value for money at a time when

America really needs it. Putting it in the crassest possible terms, the investment reaps huge returns, not only in lives saved, but in good-will, stability, and security that we will gain. So this is what I hope that you'll do, if I could be so bold, and not have it deducted from my number of wishes.

What I hope, what I hope is that beyond individual merciful acts, that you will tell the politicians to do right by Africa, by America, and by the world. Give them permission, if you like, to spend their political capital and your financial capital, your national purse, on saving the lives of millions of people. That's really what I would like you to do....

As I say, there are two things on the line here. There's the continent, Africa, but there's also our sense of ourselves. People are starting to figure this out. Movements are springing up. Artists, politicians, pop stars, priests, CEOs, NGOs, mother's unions, student unions, a lot of people are getting together and working under this umbrella I told you about earlier, the ONE Campaign. I think they just have one idea in their mind, which is: Where you live in the world should not determine whether you live in the world.

History, like God, is watching what we do. When the history books get written, I think our age will be remembered for three things. Really, it's just three things that this whole age will be remembered for. The digital revolution, yes. The war against terror, yes. And what we did or did not do to put out the fires in Africa. Some say we can't afford to. I say we can't afford not to.[16]

A Strategy Made in Heaven

You should know that our short snapshot of Bono's ongoing campaign to help our fellow sisters and brothers who are most in need does not at all do justice to the broad array of initiatives in which he is involved. Nonetheless, we hope that these snippets of information have at least allowed you to get a little better acquainted with the humanitarian activities of the U2 singer.

NOTE: In this series' next book, we will be examining two other projects in which Bono is involved: RED and EDUN. RED seeks to harness the economic momentum of the marketplace to generate money to buy drugs for African AIDS victims. And EDUN is a venture in which Bono's wife, Ali Hewson, Bono, and clothing designer Rogan Gregory have teamed up to make clothing using a model of sustainable employment and fair trade involving the developing world. More on these initiatives next time…much more.

Now that you have gotten a little better sense of just why the spirits in Heaven are asking Bono to help them implement their Action Plan for Planet Earth by heading up The Big Gig, it is time to get into some of the strategic details the Guides have laid out for the ongoing musical extravaganza.

Recognizing that Bono was both a principal architect and prominent spokesperson of 2005's LIVE 8 concerts, we asked the Spirit Guides a number of questions about what suggestions they had for him and the rest of the entertainers whom Heaven was asking to help make The World Aid Concerts a reality. Here are the results of our question-and-answer sessions with the spirit realm about their recommended strategy for the concert series:

The Macombers: Whereas both the Live Aid and LIVE 8 concerts were held on the same day in different locations, because The World Aid Concert Series is intended to be ongoing and involve all different genres of music going forward over many years, it seems that the logistics would be different. This raises some initial questions:

How would the Guides suggest that the concerts be organized in terms of time intervals between events?

The Guides: First, let's say Bono will have advice on this. We put a lot of stock in him and his apprehension at first shouldn't discourage you.

Small ones, then one big one, then small ones. It will depend on how many people can organize them.

Children should be allowed to do this instead of school. Schools don't teach real life experiences as much as they should.

So small, big, then small, big, etc. The key is to keep it spiced up. Keep everything going, but don't have it all be the same.

One big one a year is good, with little ones peppering the globe. Small ones will get people going in their areas, so anyone who is willing to take the risk should.

Janey, don't take yourself too seriously. Let it flow and have fun. Don't let people put you down. Because you don't play music yourself is fine just the way it is. Music is so universally heartening to people.

We [would] like to say to Chris Martin [a member of the music group, Coldplay] that his vocals have helped the universe immensely. He is a soul of such great importance. And we see him as a great dealmaker and part of this plan. His marriage to Gwennie [actress Gwyneth Paltrow] is of the highest order, and her love should speak volumes to humankind about the give and take of relationships.

Don't take this as nonsense, Chris Martin. We need your voice and Coldplay's embedded music to lead us on this journey. Take heed on misunderstanding this. It is all love, really. Not a bunch of bologna.

The Macombers: Should all genres perform on the same day for each event or should there be different groupings for different days?

The Guides: We should say that variety is the spice of life, so pepper the acts up; a little of this, a little of that. Add a little rock here, a little jazz there—mix it up. Put everything on the venue, but don't take the spice out of it.

Mix the days up. It may be good to do rock, rap, and jazz on one day and other stuff like African ethnical and classical on another day. So, go with different genres and different days. You may have jazz, then hip-hop. But please make sure to put peace in the air.

Sometimes too much stuff of negative vibrations isn't good. Let go of old energy patterns. Write songs of love, especially for this [concert] series. Rappers can write of triumphant times and help children see [the] harm [in] guns and [that] violence isn't needed.

The Macombers: The Guides said the following about the concert series: "We want it to be an ongoing telethon."

This seems to mean that the Guides would like to see each concert that is staged televised, with people calling in donations (and making them via the Internet) similar to what happened with the original Live Aid. Is this correct?

The Guides: Just a small series of concerts may not be enough. We said we want some little ones going on, but big ones will bring in more money. You see, telethons reach many people. Let us set it straight: Small shows will bring in cash to some extent, and even though telethons exist largely in big venues, even PBS has captured their audience.

So, yes, telethon style is good for a lot of venues. But make no mistake, it must be different kinds of music. We must appeal to all people. So, although music of rock-and-roll faith has appealed to many over the years, we need to see more classical music.

Jazz musicians can help a great deal as they see themselves as innovators of new music. Jazz scenes around the world can bring in lots of money from the people who love that music. We say this because jazz enthusiasts are, well, enthusiastic about their music, the music they love and sing and dance to.

The televised shows must be helped by television industries, too. There are lots of venues that can take place on small television stations. Some may want to donate not only their airtime, but money as well.

Telethon is the way to go for some. But keep in mind, concertgoers are aware of their impact, too. So paying customers who are having a good time will add to the shows. Let's not forget them.

At this point let's start small and get bigger. Make it start off slow, but not too slow.

The Macombers: The Guides said in a recent transmission that eventually billions would be raised through the concert series. It would seem that donations and sales of recordings of these events will contribute to this, but what about the issue of tickets? Should admission be free like for the recent LIVE 8 concerts or should tickets be sold?

The Guides: Yes, of course, live recordings can be made and sold. But remember, the fans are the ones who make music make money, so give away some tickets.

Take donations at the doors and sell some tickets. Big-ticket shows would do well to give away tickets to poor kids.

You see, children hold a lot of power in their love for music. Give a portion of tickets to kids, and their reactions will help sell the records. A good audience is only as good as the show, but to poor, underprivileged kids, an excitement gets the show started with free tickets.

Get kids involved in the organization. Some poor kids may make the show better with their own expertise. There may be lighting and technology kids who will blow the stage away with their know-how.

Children today, teenagers in particular, are dying to show themselves. This is a great way for kids to learn and shine in a way they never have before.

Children are the future.

We are all the present; and look not to the failure of the past, but dream what can be made of that.

So, put aside tickets for poor youth.

Donations play a big part too. A certain number of tickets should be donations on a pay as much as you can basis; and thirdly, some pay for the full price because they can.

You see this is multifold.

It will bring together people who normally would not be together; every piece fits. We make suggestions on planes that affect everything we see. Everything affecting everything: the interconnectedness of it all. All things.

Again, stay alert to this idea of interconnectedness. Poor, middle, rich—all together again.

Jane's Reaction

After Jane had received the above transmission from the Guides in which they answered our question about the ticket aspect of the concert series, she sent an e-mail to Cuac containing the following description of how she felt during that particular automatic writing session with our cosmic co-authors:

It made so much sense to me. I really got a very clear sense that what they are saying is so true. Bringing different walks of life together. It sounds so simple a way to do that. Of course, you haven't read it yet, but you'll know what I mean when you read it. It was a really clear reading. Again, the importance of children was overwhelming in this reading. It made so much sense. And also incorporated a new way for children to help.

Yet the Q and A session with the Guides wasn't over:

The Macombers: The Guides said that, right from the start, one-third of the proceeds [from The World Aid Concerts] should go to Third World nations. How should this money be distributed? Should it be given to actual governments? Or should it be given to existing organizations that solicit donations for such countries? There are also micro-loan programs that loan small amounts like $100 to individuals who end up repaying the money after they get on their feet, thus making the money available again to help more people. Should the money go toward something like this? Or is there another method by which we should try to get the funds directly into the hands of actual individuals?

The Guides: You should try it both ways.

One thing DATA incorporates is people helping themselves, so small loans that are repaid are good for some people, interest free of course.

But a large part of the money should go directly to getting people everyday toiletries, toilets too, medication, basic foundations–food, clothing, shelters, and medicines.

Children should be well-dressed in mind and body. Schools should be built.

Education about everything–from AIDS to their own poverty–should be taught.

Lessons *from* the children should be taught.

Let the builders of the schools be builders of knowledge, too.

Get them clean drinking water, buildings, medicine, and education.

True educators and organizations can help the most.

It should go straight to the people, not governments.

Rally on, my friends. Rally on!

The Macombers: If the ongoing concert series is eventually going to generate billions, should such funds be used to leverage much bigger commitments from the richest nations' governments?

The Guides: Absolutely. Get the rich to start giving.

Look at that movie *Rat Race* [which shows how great giving can feel]. Give people something to feel good about themselves.

Give twenty to thirty percent of what is raised–that's what we want, twenty or thirty percent of what is raised. So, twenty million is raised; give five or six million.

Let the numbers go up as is seen with success. That is, let every dollar count. Start low and then generate more. So, start low and when progress is made, then more countries will give.

The U.S. should give one million for every Iraqi killed, every American. Just an idea, but we hold Americans responsible for much, as they see themselves as so important. Let them put their money where their mouth is.

We hold you accountable because you say you are the richest and greatest country. Let's see some action on these statements. Hogwash no more.

So, for now, goodbye and good luck.

Jane sent the following e-mail to Cuac after completing this last question about the concerts series:

I got a clear message that the U.S. needs to own up to the greatness it says it holds. Time to stop talking and take action. Take what is great and share it.

From the Macombers to Bono

Bono, because the Spirit Guides have repeatedly stressed the critical leadership role they hope you will play in helping organize your colleagues in the entertainment industry to make The World

Aid Concert Series a reality, we are writing to you directly to under-score just how important a part of Heaven's Action Plan for Planet Earth they say you are.

We realize you already have a schedule that is jam-packed full. We understand you are already doing all you can to help our world. And we definitely know full well that we are asking you to associate your sterling reputation with a concept that many might scoff at and even more will say can't be done.

In spite of all of this, however, we believe with all of our hearts that the type of unprecedented change for the better envisioned for humanity by the spirit realm can and *will* happen. You see, we truly feel that Heaven is trying to help us help ourselves.

The spirit world is reaching out to all of us to lend a hand so that we can help one another. The residents of Heaven know that you are already running yourself ragged trying to do just that. Yet the net effect of the implementation of their ideas would be to leverage and multiply the positive results emanating from all of the work you are already doing to help others.

Anyway, Bono, we know that we're asking for a lot. We're ordi-nary everyday people saying that we've been contacted by spirits in Heaven with a message to help all of humanity. And now we're asking you to help get the project off the ground and to implement these spirits' ideas.

But that's the truth of the matter. All we can do is to tell you what's happened to us, convey to you the spirit realm's request for your aid, and ask you on a human-to-human level to help make Heaven's dream for our world come true.

A Final Message for Bono

We realize that you are *extremely* busy. So do the Spirit Guides. In fact, at one point, they said to us:

Bono's own obligations may make it hard for him to take time out, so incorporating the concert series into his already busy schedule will be the one thing that goes a long way.

But the Guides believe you will help and already are on board:

Bono has run away with the idea even before we presented it. Look what the ONE Campaign has accomplished.

And Bono will make great strides with his ONE Campaign. His mission is on the right path that lights the way for others.

What a great way to put it: *Lighting the way for others.* Certainly you've brought light to the lives of many who've known far too much darkness. And in so doing, you set an inspiring example for the rest of us to follow.

Part of what you have demonstrated in your approach to tackling our planet's biggest problems is the importance of belief: belief in others *and* belief that we as a race are capable of curing the chief ills of our planet. Such belief is not only exactly in line with what the spirit realm has been advocating since it first started sending messages to us to share with the world, but, according to these communications from Heaven, *belief* is the very substance from which the solutions to our problems will be molded.

As we explained early on in this book, the importance of "belief" was brought to our attention by the Spirit Guides in the first few days of this project's existence when they said:

The very essence to peace is the belief it can happen.

Right now, you may be trying to decide whether or not you believe what has been written in this book. And even if part of you might be inclined to think there is something to it, you could well be wondering to yourself what, if any, involvement should you have with this bunch of Macomber people? What are you to think about all that has been said about spirits in Heaven apparently asking for your help with The World Aid Concert Series, a cornerstone of the Action Plan for Planet Earth?

To all of this—and to probably many more skeptical ruminations that are likely rumbling around your brain—all we can do is to say we understand how implausible the contents of this book may seem. On the other hand, however, you made a statement to your friend Michka Assayas in the book *Bono* that might contain a useful litmus test with which to gauge the validity of what has been presented here: "A feeling is much stronger than a thought."[17]

As you will see in a subsequent chapter, the Spirit Guides, as well as the three of us, are big believers that the truth is to be found in our feelings. And so, as you decide what to do with the information contained in this book, we will share with you two quotations that have been of great help to us as we have sought guidance about what direction to go in our own lives:

> *"Feeling is the language of the soul."*[18]
> —Neale Donald Walsch, *Conversations with God*

> *"There is a very interesting mechanism that the universe has to help you make spontaneous choices. The mechanism has to do with sensations in your body. Your body experiences two kinds of sensations: one is a sensation of comfort, the other is a sensation of discomfort. At the moment you consciously make a choice, pay attention to your body and ask your body, 'If I make this choice what happens?' If your body sends a message of comfort, that's the right choice. If your body sends a message of discomfort, then it's not the appropriate choice. Consciously put your attention in the heart and ask your heart what to do. Then wait for the response—a physical response in the form of a sensation. It may be the faintest level of feeling—but it's there, in your body. Only the heart knows the correct answer."*[19]
> —Deepak Chopra, *The Seven Spiritual Laws of Success*

CHAPTER 49

Elton John:
An Old Soul

"Elton John is an old soul, as Earthlings say....He is pure of heart."

−The Spirit Guides

The first person the Spirit Guides said they hoped would work with Bono on The World Aid Concert Series was Elton John. Just three days into this project, the spirit realm gave us their first glimpse of how Heaven views Sir Elton John:

> **Europeans are good, and they are spiritual by nature. To get help from them will be easy as pie.**
>
> **Elton John is an old soul, as Earthlings say. His wisdom through the ages has taught him much about the kindness and goodness in the world. He can be a tremendous amount of help.**

This came during the same transmission in which the Guides had begun their writings about Bono. We were not only stunned, but also touched by what our new friends from the spirit world had to say about Elton John. And it wasn't too long before these residents of Heaven weighed in at more length on both musicians.

"These truly great men should be listened to."

A little more than a month after their initial messages about Elton John and Bono, the Spirit Guides returned to their discussion of the pair:

> To get back to well known people, we have already named Bono and Elton John as leaders in the concerts we hope will take place. It is their love of the human race that will see many, many millions of dying young children freed from their plight.
>
> We do not throw these names around lightly, and their place in this world is no great coincidence. Their names hold meaning here on this side, as their celebrity is not in the names or money or influence because of it, but for their greatness of heart and love for the entire planet and its people. Their bright, shining stars and unified manner are what they are famous for here in Heaven.
>
> To do what they do and have their entire lives spread out in the tabloids and papers is not easy. We recognize what they have given up by being who they are. Privacy is a great sacrifice in the eyes of the Lord, and we appreciate their efforts now more than ever.
>
> The music world has a great impact on the world, and the voices of these truly great men should be listened to. We are not just flattering you here, boys; we are sincere in our words about the depths of your souls.

When these words about Elton John and Bono came forth from one of Jane's automatic writing sessions with the Guides, we were deeply moved. Not so much because the transmission dealt with such famous individuals, but because of what Heaven was saying about "their greatness of heart and love for the entire planet and its people." And so, just as with Bono, we made it a point to learn more about a certain English piano player and the man behind the music. And, once we did, it didn't take long to understand why the spirits in Heaven were speaking so fervently about Elton John.

Elton John: "Do-Gooder Extraordinaire"

As we began to delve into the life and career of Elton John, it quickly became apparent that he had been a true pioneer in the field of charity work. No wonder the Guides viewed him as a human being with the capability of doing a great deal for the people of the world: He had already proven that time and time again. We just hadn't been aware it.

Once we started learning a little bit about Elton John's journey through life, we found out that he had begun doing benefit performances back in the 1970s and has been a leading voice for those in need ever since. Here's just a smattering of some of what we came across about Elton's extensive work on behalf of others:

- In the mid-70s Elton was involved in a fundraiser to benefit Britain's "Sports Aid Foundation, a government backed body set up to provide financial support for British athletes in every field....Rock music and government had never consorted so openly before."[1]

  "He is one of the first pop stars to have performed for charity; early in his career he supported the National Youth Theatre and Goaldiggers, a charity to provide football facilities for deprived children. He has also supported...the Invalid AID foundation, Live Aid, the Princess of Wales Memorial Fund, and many others. In 1992, he established his own charity, the Elton John AIDS Foundation, to help fund the fight against the disease....He is also a patron of many AIDS-related organizations, including UNAIDS and Amnesty International."[2]

- During 1985's Live Aid concerts, "Elton was allotted an unprecedented thirty-minute spot at the end of the day's marathon from Wembley"[3] and was one of the leading figures in the event.

Since Elton established the Elton John AIDS Foundation (EJAF) in 1992, the nonprofit organization has raised tens of millions of dollars for its work on many fronts in the war against AIDS. As Elton himself states on the foundation's Web site, EJAF has helped provide funds for "the most basic needs in the areas hardest hit by the epidemic and to counter ignorance about HIV/ AIDS with information."[4]

NOTE: To learn more about the work of Elton's foundation, you can visit its Web site at: www.ejaf.org.

- Many famous figures initially maintained a low profile on the subject of AIDS when it first surfaced as a major health problem, but Elton "was among the most visible supporters both of research into finding a cure and of the charities set up to shelter and counsel AIDS victims. It was in large part his doing that rock music's new conscience…embraced the problem, drawing millions into awareness of it via multi-star fundraising concerts and charity records like his pioneering ["That's What Friends Are For" with Gladys Knight], Dione Warwick and Stevie Wonder."[5]
- He was knighted in 1998 by Queen Elizabeth II for his distinguished music career and tireless work on AIDS, becoming "Sir Elton John."

"Elton John we could write a book about."

After having done a little bit of research into Elton's long history of using his talent, fame, and resources to come to the aid of numerous causes, it was easy to understand why the Spirit Guides had been so generous in their praise of him. And as this project progressed, the Guides elaborated on why they felt he possesses the ability to help effect even greater change for the good in our world:

Elton John we could write a book about. Elton John should remember words of wisdom from his mother's family and take to the skies.

He is unforeseen in his mission of the heart. He takes whatever life throws at him and turns words of sorrow and hurt, love and joy, into motion with his music.

That is why music is so important; it speaks to hearts, minds, and souls alike. Stories as old as the ocean are told through music.

And Elton John should keep the music of his heart up. His relationship with David [David Furnish, whom Elton married in 2005] is a stellar example of this. He went through so much in his own soul to finally find peace with David. And the world will find the same peace if it partners with each other and everyone to bring about peace.

Elton's main message is one of the heart. His heart's felt around the world because he is pure of heart.

The celebrities have a lot more on the mind than making money. Love makes the world go round, not money. Love is what they have to give.

Love. Over and over and over again, the spirit world kept coming back to that one basic emotion as holding the key to unlocking the solutions to our planet's greatest troubles.

A Personal Plea to Elton John

Elton, we fervently believe that the love you have in your heart for your fellow sisters and brothers around the world can have a major impact on making Heaven's dreams for humanity a reality. Yet, as we were concluding this book, we learned of two things that may affect how you view the Spirit Guides' request to the entertainment world to establish the ongoing World Aid Concert Series:

1. Some supposed friction may have developed between you and Bono as a result of U2's declining your request to use one of its songs on a benefit album you were putting together to further the work of your foundation.

2. Your feeling that, although you had been "very pleased" to be one of the headliners of 2005's LIVE 8 concerts and strongly supported the project's goals, the performances didn't, from a musical perspective, live up to the standard set by the original Live Aid concerts.[6]

Elton, we do not pretend to know the specifics associated with either of these issues or what your true feelings about them are. What we do know is that you were a major player in both the Live Aid and LIVE 8 concerts, not only as a musician, but also in an organizational and promotional capacity...and that a tremendous amount of good has resulted from these events.

Given, first, this history of successfully helping others and, second, the many millions of lives that are at stake, we would respectfully request that you attempt to see past whatever differences may have arisen with your friend and colleague Bono, consider doing all that you can to make The World Aid Concert Series the best set of musical performances that they can possibly be, and help the spirits in Heaven help all of us.

If, however, you decide that you are not interested in participating in The World Aid Concert Series, then please know how grateful we are for all that you have already done and all that you continue to do to help those in need all over the planet. Furthermore, the Guides also wish to let you know that, regardless of whether you choose to join in with the concert series envisioned for Earth, they recognize the wonderful work that will result from your ongoing efforts to do good in our world:

> **When we first suggested he go along with Bono, we saw the potential good that the two could do; but things do get in the way.**
>
> **It actually might be a way for them to mend fences, so to speak. They are huge celebrities, and they could show the world a thing or two about patching things up.**

In time they may see eye-to-eye, but his [Elton's] musical interests may not make him available to do more. Elton can do a lot of good on his own. He should still be outspoken about AIDS and awareness.

What Do You Think "Evil" Wants to Happen?

As the spirits in Heaven have explained it, there truly is a war between "good" and "evil" of epic proportions happening here on Earth. Although the spirit realm has said it's really better described as a showdown between the human emotions of "love" and "fear," it all still boils down to, as the spirit realm has put it, "spiritual warfare"—a battle in which the positive is pitted against the negative. The power of light versus the forces of darkness slugging it out on a scale grander than any imagined in the wildest of fantasy movies.

So it is against this backdrop that we pose the following question: *Do you think that the negative elements of existence would prefer to see you and Bono united or separated?*

The two of you have been identified by Heaven as some of Earth's heaviest hitters in terms of the abilities you possess to help pull this planet out of the mess we're all in. Whereas we're just bit players serving as messengers bringing this information forward, individuals such as you and Bono are the ones who are in a position to take leadership roles and run with the solutions being offered by Heaven to help fix our broken world.

Yet Heaven can only tell us what's possible. What actually happens to humanity is up to us.

And so, as you contemplate the contents of this chapter, it is in the interests of *love* prevailing on this beautiful planet that we ask you to keep in mind two statements from Heaven about you and Bono:

1. "It is their love of the human race that will see many, many millions of dying young children freed from their plight."

2. "Their bright shining stars and unified manner are what they are famous for here in Heaven."

CHAPTER 50

A Final Few
Words to the
World's Musicians

If the concert series envisioned by Heaven is going to bring about the tremendous amount of good envisioned for the people of Earth, it goes without saying that it will take many, many musicians to make it happen. Like other musical benefit performances that have come before it, including The Concert for Bangladesh, Band Aid, We Are the World, Live Aid, Farm Aid, the Rainforest Foundation Concerts, the Human Rights Now! Concerts, We Are the Future, LIVE 8, and countless others, an endeavor such as this is going to need the participation, commitment, and support of numerous performers from all around the globe.

So, if you are a musician from any genre, we hope you will consider making Heaven's vision for The World Aid Concert Series become a reality. In so doing, please keep in mind a couple of messages the spirit realm has sent specifically for you:

1. **"You are all ready to do your part. And it has all started, so we speak now. We are all really in this together. All the world's a stage, even this world [Heaven], and we will all**

play our parts. From Heaven and afar we will all play our parts. Each and every one of us."

2. "[We're] getting excited about the concerts we have planned. Oh, and we have been helping plan them for years now. There are energies from all over the galaxy and the entire universe that are rooting for this project, and we see it coming along just fine."

So, musicians and entertainers of the world, there you have it. The spirits in Heaven are asking for you to perform on the biggest stage there is. They said it, not us. It's the ultimate venue. We're talking "the entire universe" here.

As difficult as it may be to believe, there's a galactic audience out there just waiting for you to play and put on a performance for the ages. The eyes of the universe will be upon you as this ongoing festival unfolds and you play a major, major role in helping shape the future destiny of the entire human race.

Strong words to be sure. But, ladies and gentleman, these spirits in Heaven are very sincere in their message that this really is The Big Gig and that all of your previous performances have been just warm-up acts in preparation for taking center stage in the grandest musical event the cosmos has ever known.

These spirits very much wish for your love of humanity to overcome any fear you may have about what it's "going to look like" for you to get involved in something that has its beginnings supposedly rooted in messages from Heaven. Yes, it's going to take great courage and commitment for you to sign onto The World Aid Concert Series, but we believe you will ultimately come to understand that the greatness of your mission dwarfs any concerns you may have about this project's origins.

And although you may not believe in all of this "spirit stuff," we know you do believe in the power of music. And so do these spirits in Heaven. But even more significantly, they believe in *you*.

Bob, Quincy, and Willie

As the Spirit Guides have fashioned a general framework for The World Aid Concert Series, their automatic writing transmissions have included communications about individual entertainers and celebrities. As described earlier, our invisible co-authors have identified Coldplay's Chris Martin as a person they hope will help them execute their plan to turn our world around. Three other luminaries in the music field whom the Guides have talked about as being potential candidates to work on The Big Gig are Bob Geldof, Quincy Jones, and Willie Nelson.

Bob Geldof

Since Bob Geldof has served as a primary organizer of both the Live Aid and LIVE 8 concerts and possesses immense experience and expertise in this sort of endeavor, we asked the Spirit Guides if we should ask him to take a leading role in The World Aid Concert Series. They replied with the following:

> Let's say about Mr. Geldof that he may be skeptical at first. Consulting may be his way of helping.
>
> Bob Geldof may not want to say you are crazy, but a little bit of him may think you are ripping him off at first.
>
> This is an enormous task we face, no two ways about it. But it does exist in the minds of people like Bono and Geldof. They just may not know it yet (we mean all this guidance from angels stuff).
>
> Bob Geldof is overwhelmed [by all of his various responsibilities], so consulting may be Bob's thing. Get as many people involved as possible.

Bob, Please Keep an Open Mind

Bob, this is the Macombers speaking now, not the spirits who have asked us to bring these messages about The World Aid Concert Series to you and the rest of the entertainment community.

We understand that you may be more than just a little bit skeptical about all of this. Understandably so. This stuff is pretty unusual, to say the least.

All we can say is that the idea of launching such a massive project was *definitely* not our idea. We certainly don't know anything about such matters, nor, to be quite candid, did we have any prior interest in becoming involved in such an undertaking. But then we started getting all of these messages from the spirit world and felt like we had a responsibility to follow through on what they were saying was the best way to go about repairing our world.

That is why we're talking to you. You *do know* how to pull off what these invisible Guides are saying needs to be done. We don't.

You have dedicated much of your life to doing the type of things the Spirit Guides are talking about. You've not only been a source of inspiration to Bono in his early years of tackling the problems besetting the Third World, but the two of you have since worked side by side on many fronts to help make our world a better place. In short, there's no one on the planet better qualified than you to make The Big Gig happen.

So, Bob Geldof, we could easily go on at great length about how your life's work to date closely mirrors the type of approach the spirit realm says holds great promise for our future as a race. Instead, we will keep our request to you relatively short and simply ask you not to dismiss out of hand what is being said in this book. We hope that you will keep an open mind about helping Heaven implement this plan. The spirits in residence there say that it will give the best possible chance of survival for those here on Earth whom you have already been helping for decades.

From the bottom of our hearts, thanks for listening.

Quincy Jones

Another major player in the field of benefit concerts about whom the spirit realm weighed in on was the inestimably talented Quincy Jones. A key figure in numerous charitable events, one of Quincy's projects caught Cuac's attention as he was reading *USA Today* during the spring of 2004.

A March 22, 2004, article authored by Edna Gundersen, titled, "Quincy Jones reaches out to help kids: All-star charity concert will be televised worldwide," jumped out at Cuac as he leafed through the paper. Gundersen explained that the concert was called We Are the Future and that it included Evander Holyfield, Alicia Keys, Angelina Jolie, Carlos Santana, Chris Tucker, Oprah Winfrey, and numerous other celebrities and high-profile individuals from many different fields.[1] The We Are the Future concert was held in Rome later that spring and sought to help children who live in war zones.

The article explained that the intention of the We Are the Future concert was not only to raise funds for such children and bring increased awareness around the world about their plight, but also to develop a sense of empowerment in such youth through "local participation."[2] What stood out above all else in Ms. Gundersen's piece were some heartfelt words from Quincy Jones about children in general and those living in war-torn areas in particular:

> *It's their future, and it's ridiculous that all these old people are deciding it for them. The elders should provide experience and expertise, but let the kids tell you what they want....*
>
> *There's no greater paradox than to bring children into this world and have their survival endangered.*[3]

As Cuac read the words of Quincy Jones, he was struck by the extent to which they paralleled statements the Spirit Guides had made in some of Jane's 2002 automatic writing transmissions. Take a look for yourself, and see if you don't agree:

> Children are dear to God because they listen to the good-
> ness in their hearts and so much want love to take the shape
> of things to come. There are many things children want to say
> just because they know what's right and what's wrong.
>
> What we want to tell you now is the importance of children's
> lives, as they are going to be the ones to lead this world in the
> near future. They have much wisdom and knowledge, some of
> it far beyond their elders. It is their future as much as it is
> anyone's, and they have a right to have a voice in their own lives
> and in the affairs of the world.

"It is their future." Pretty tough to argue with that logic, wouldn't
you say?

When we subsequently did a little digging on the Internet to
learn more about We Are the Future, we located a site called
www.TakingITGlobal.org. A collaboration between Quincy's Listen Up Foundation, "a charity which connects youths with
technology, education, culture, and music," the Global Forum, the
World Bank, and MIT, the site explained that We Are the Future's
aim is "to set up child centers for children living in conflict areas and
across the developing world, while building global city-to-city networks to support these centers."[4]

Emphasis in such centers would include education, health, the
arts, sports, and a wide array of other areas of focus. A pilot program was being started with six initial We Are the Future centers
being established in Afghanistan, Ethiopia, Eritrea, Palestine,
Rwanda, and Sierra Leone. Each center would be administered by
the local municipality, including representation of local children
through delegates from the Global Youth Parliament, as well as the
Youth Peace Corps.[5]

Not only did the specifics provided by the TakingITGlobal Web
site seem to have a lot of similarities with the Spirit Guides' specific
suggestions for helping the youth of the world (which will be described in detail in the second book in this series), but there were

two quotations that perfectly captured the absolute core of the spirit realm's message about the pivotal role that the children of the world can play:

> *"Peace is possible around the world and children are the answer."*[6]
> –Quincy Jones

> *"The smallest hands hold the key to the world's future."*[7]
> –Uri Savir

We learned just who Uri Savir was on another Web site (www.allAfrica.com), which explains that he is an "Israeli peace negotiator" and the founder of Global Forum. An article by Tamela Hultman on the site called "Africa: Rome Concert Launches a Movement, Says Quincy Jones," explains that Global Forum is "a Rome-based NGO...which encourages city-to-city collaborations for development."[8]

The article went on to state that the May 16, 2004, concert had been a tremendous success, drawing 500,000 people "to Rome's historic Circus Maximus."[9] Hoping that the six pilot cities would begin a movement that would "spread to cities across the developing world," Quincy Jones declared that "the effort is the most important cause he's ever been involved in...."[10]

Given Quincy's long history of participation in so many charitable events, including his central role in the We Are the World project, this was quite a statement. So much so that we felt compelled to ask our colleagues in the spirit realm to comment on the We Are the Future project. This is what they said:

Let us say that Sir Quincy Jones has the biggest heart of anyone on Earth. He takes things to his heart and that is why he is successful.

He sees a future for children in war-torn countries. Not everybody does that.

To turn a blind eye is to actually be blind. To blind your heart is treacherous. But the We Are the Future organization is un-blinding people. Its very core is to shed light on the light in children.

So many times, people want children to shut up and listen. What Quincy Jones's organization is saying [is], "Shut up, adults, and listen to the kids."

How can you empower children when you silence them? How can you share your wisdom if you don't allow the kids to hear it and share theirs with you?

Quincy Jones is at the heart of the music industry because he is heart. Pure heart.

And he hears the children's hearts beating. He wants to free them. He knows all too well from times past how children can be put under the rug. How they can be shrugged off as menial labor or some such thing.

Let's say we continue to support this work with this organization because music can bring so much to the world. And children understand better than [adults] how music can change the world. Lullabies are but one form of music children relate to. You open your heart to music and children and you have a winning combination.

We would like to see more children perform at these concerts. Get them involved not only by playing for them, but let them be a part of the program.

We said this about our own concerts. "The Big Gig," as Cuac calls it. Get them involved in their own futures.

Quincy Jones, to you we bid good graces. You are a bigger man than many, and your humble attitude is much appreciated. "Hats off" to you and your organization.

Bonus Information

To learn more about Quincy's Listen Up Foundation, visit its Web site at: www.qjluf.org.

The two Web sites we reviewed in searching for additional information about Quincy Jones and the We Are the Future project are both wonderful resources. Here's how they describe themselves:

> *www.TakingITGlobal.org is an online community that connects youth to find inspiration, access information, get involved, and take action in their local and global communities. It is now the world's most popular online community for young people interested in making a difference, with hundreds of thousands of unique visitors each month. TIG's highly interactive Web site provides a platform for expression, connection to opportunities, and support for action. Join now and connect with thousands of other young people around the world!*[11]

NOTE: If you are even just the least bit interested in the plight of children around the world, please take just a few minutes and check out this site. It's truly inspiring.

> *allAfrica.com is among the Internet's largest content sites, posting over one thousand stories daily in English and French and offering a diversity of multi-lingual streaming programming as well as over 900,000 articles in our searchable archive.*[12]

NOTE: allAfrica.com is a really incredible repository of information about all things Africa.

Willie Nelson

After we completed a first draft of the manuscript for this book, Cuac kept looking at one remaining item on his list of things to consider including in this book: Willie Nelson and his potential role in the concert series.

Willie, along with Neil Young and John Mellencamp, was a founder of the Farm Aid concerts. But, beyond that, a CD by Mark Victor Hansen (co-author of the *Chicken Soup for the Soul* book series) that Cuac had heard had explained that Willie had started a "BioWillie" fuel project to help employ farmers by growing crops such as soybeans to produce a more environmentally friendly form of fuel called "biodiesel."

Yet Cuac felt that he didn't know whether we should talk about Willie in the book because none of us really knew much about him or his music. Then Cuac saw an update on TV of a *60 Minutes* piece that had been done on Willie by the late Ed Bradley. It showed Willie talking to farmers and displaying the type of compassion, sincerity, and concern that can only come from one place: *the heart.* Cuac thought to himself, *"This guy's just filled with goodness. He's the type of person the Guides are talking about that the world needs more of."*

Still, Cuac felt like there was so much to do on the project that he shouldn't add one more thing on his "to do" list. Already feeling guilty that it had taken so long to get a manuscript completed for this book, he thought to himself, "This has got to stop somewhere."

Then, on Monday, September 4, 2006, Cuac woke up at 3:45 in the morning. Unable to sleep any longer, he decided to go to work and get an early start on the day. As he was going down the stairs, somewhat bleary-eyed, "Willie Nelson" popped into his head. Once again, Cuac wondered if we should consider mentioning Willie in the book. Very much uncertain about the matter, he decided to first check his e-mail before doing anything related to the book.

As Cuac got online and started scrolling down through the list of new e-mails, one jumped out at him and hit him like a ton of bricks

with its subject line. It said, "WILLIE NELSON AND MARK VIC-
TOR HANSEN" and had come in during the night at 12:52 A.M.
while he was asleep.

Cuac was stunned.

The e-mail was from Mark Victor Hansen's organization and
was an invitation to a free teleseminar the next night in which Mark
would interview Willie and talk about his life's work. In the e-mail,
Mark wrote:

> *I interview Willie Nelson, live, by teleconference on Tuesday,
> September 5....I will co-host* **Healthy Wealthy n Wise** *magazine's
> Passion series....*
>
> *There is one thing which makes all the difference, one thing
> which has been the basis of both my success and Willie's
> success...which can transform your entire life...passion....*[13]

Listening to the teleseminar, Cuac realized it was as plain as day
that Willie Nelson was *exactly* the type of human being Ruth and the
Spirit Guides' project needed:

- Willie knows how to organize big benefit concerts.
- Willie wants to help people...especially "the little guy."
- Willie knows what it's like to have tough times and has not for-
  gotten how difficult it can be just to survive day-to-day.

In view of the sequence of events involving Willie Nelson, Cuac
made a special trip to Amherst later that week to visit with Jane and
to see what the spirit world might have to say about the matter.
Here's what the Guides said about Willie:

> **First off, we say "hats off" to you, Cuac, for keeping Willie
> on your list of things to do for our book.**
>
> **He is an old soul, to say the least. He has led many life-
> times to get to where he is today.**
>
> **His purpose in life is very clear. Music is, of course, what
> most know him for, but his heart is big. Way big.**

His purposeful intent has led him to where he is through years of lifetimes. He finally realizes that being purposeful is what makes him happy, whether it's reaching out to the world with his music, biodiesel [fuel], or farming. His life has great purpose.

So, to any of you who think he's just a pot-smoking hippie: *Think again.* This man has been successful for two reasons: his heart and his purpose.

He sees all men as created equal. And although he holds farmers and the underdog in high esteem, he sees the importance of all mankind. He is trying to get the rest of the world to see this, too.

Like John Mellencamp, he is a champion of the underdog, as we like to say on Earth; but really, they are top dogs in our book.

Bono has taken on African causes. Willie and his group, American farmers. These big names take on causes dear to their hearts.

[Put the] concerts on Willie's list of big projects. He would make a fine consultant when it comes to our world concerts.

It may lead him to help farmers all over the world. You see, there are some very good ideas that farmers from around the world can share, and he might be a good person to get American farmers involved in helping other nations.

You see, if you put minds together rather than tear them apart, you will see results, far more workable solutions to problems that may have seemed insurmountable. It all boils down to "Love your neighbor"–even your African [or] Honduran neighbor–as you would yourself.

In a way, the American farmer can relate to people in developing nations. They may not be starving themselves, but they understand the idea that a bad year in crops can be very grim. They know hardship, but they can take that knowledge far.

And in their recognition, they will see the world in an even more open way. There may be prejudices that are stifled or gone.

If you take farmers' passion and spread that passion, then the world will heal more quickly.

So, while Willie may be a great consultant for the concerts, his ability to reach farmers, and the help they bring to the rest of the world, will be a match made in Heaven. He is one of them and he's popular. So, if he can be brought on board, so to speak, then many hands will be raised high in the sky for his good works.

He is a working man, and, as *Healthy Wealthy n Wise* knows, passion doing something you love and earning a living can be miraculous. We have said this so many times: If people work at what they love, the world will be a happier place.

So, while Willie Nelson has reached out to farmers here in America, we ask him to ask them to reach out to the world with their knowledge of ground, soil, and crops. We see everything being brought into this.

The fact that stars today are unselfish and helping is really a sight to see. So many of us were not successful in helping others when in physical form. It is a relief to see that not only can you be successful, [but also] help others.

It is our sincere hope [that] the farmers of America will share their know-how and be open to the knowing of other nations. They can help each other. There is a two-way street there, and we hope all singers, farmers, and farmers' daughters will join hands to help the plight of the world.

So, Willie, there you have it. This stuff may sound pretty far-out, no question about it. Yet, as improbable as it all may seem, we would like to ask you, on behalf of these spirits from Heaven that can't be seen, to help them help the many people around the world who can be seen and who are in such dire need of assistance. In short, as the Spirit Guides have said, if you can put this project on your own "to do" list, it will send a powerful message of hope to millions of our sisters and brothers around the globe and greatly advance the cause for goodness in our world.

Bonus Information

1. If you are interested in learning more about Willie's biodiesel project, which is good for both the economy and the environment, its Internet address is: www.wnbiodiesel.com.

2. Also, if you'd like to find out about the free online magazine, *Healthy Wealthy nWise,* take a look at: www.healthywealthynwise.com.

A Plea from the Heart to a Most Unlikely Pairing: The Dixie Chicks and Toby Keith

There are some professional musicians whom we would respectfully consider being a part of The World Aid Concert Series...*together.* Toby Keith and The Dixie Chicks. Although differing perspectives on politics have caused these folks to have their differences in the past, we believe that a joint performance on the same stage by these talented entertainers would send a mighty message about healing old wounds to millions of people not only in the United States, but around the world.

Now, Emily, Martie, Natalie, and Toby, your first reaction to such an outlandish idea is probably something like, "Yeah, right. Next joke. Who do these Macomber people think they are even to suggest such a thing?"

The answer to such a question is that we're just ordinary people who think that the union of your two musical acts would constitute a tremendous force for good in our world. We truly believe that, united together for just one song, the four of you possess the ability to effect, in just a few minutes, more positive change in the hearts and minds of people in America and around the world than with any other single act that any of you could possibly do apart—and we know that all of you have already done much on your own for your fellow human beings.

And we would like to suggest a song for the four of you to sing together in front of the entire world. It's one that you're likely familiar with; it was made popular by Tina Turner, was written by Steve DuBerry and Lulu, and is called "I Don't Wanna Fight." Contained in the chorus to that song are a few simple words about the importance of ceasing to prove who's right or wrong that succinctly sum up what we all need to do if our world is to have any chance of healing itself and surviving: *"This is time for letting go."*[14]

Given what we all see when we read, watch, or listen to the news about the state of affairs both at home and abroad, if it isn't time yet, when will it be?

Entertainers of the World, as You Contemplate Your Potential Participation in The Big Gig, Consider This:

When Cuac met Mark Victor Hansen at a 2004 publishing industry trade show in Chicago, the *Chicken Soup for the Soul* co-author graciously sat down with him for breakfast and offered some very instructive suggestions about how to make this project a reality. Although time did not permit Cuac to go into the automatic writing component of this endeavor, he did provide Mark with a basic overview of its goals. When the conversation reached a description of the concert series that is being proposed, Mark suggested that we look into what Ken Kragen had done as a principal architect of the We Are the World recording project.

When Cuac returned back to Vermont and subsequently followed up on Mark's kind advice, he learned the extent to which Ken Kragen was a major figure in the entertainment industry and that he had managed many noted musicians including Kenny Rogers and Harry Chapin. On a Web site dedicated to Harry Chapin–www. rememberingharrychapin.com–Cuac found the following statement Kragen had made about the We Are the World project:

> *[Harry frequently said] "When in doubt–do something!" [He taught me that] it is much easier to accomplish the impossible than to do the ordinary....*[15]

The Web site article went on to tell of an incident that happened to Ken Kragen a few weeks after the We Are the World recording session. In New York at the time and elated upon reviewing an upcoming eight-page *LIFE* magazine spread on the We Are the World project, Kragen had a remarkable experience after he departed from the publication's office. While in his car, all of a sudden the entertainment industry giant was overcome with a wave of deep emotion and later described what happened next in these words:

> *I'm not...overly religious, but [right then] I felt Harry Chapin had crawled up inside of me....I really physically felt it happen [and said to myself]... "You son of a gun, you're directing the whole thing."*
> [16]

Soon after, the We Are the World recording was released all over the globe. And on Good Friday of that year, virtually all radio stations around the world played the landmark benefit song at exactly the same time.

Ken Kragen's description of his participation in the We Are the World project really helped strengthen our belief that The World Aid Concert Series will become a reality. As we prepared to go public with the information contained in this book, there have been plenty of moments when doubt has crept into our minds and fear has entered our hearts about the enormous scope of what the Spirit Guides have outlined in their Action Plan for Planet Earth. It was truly inspirational, however, to read Kragen's words about taking on such a massive undertaking as the We Are the World endeavor and then, with the help of many, many other talented and committed individuals, pulling off the feat.

When we read Ken Kragen's narrative about feeling Harry Chapin's spirit crawl up inside of him, it heightened our sense of confidence in the viability of the music community putting together the ongoing series of global concerts envisioned for our planet by the spirit realm. If such a prominent mainstream figure as Ken Kragen wasn't afraid to ascribe to a dead person the role of serving as a critical catalyst in an unprecedented worldwide happening such as the We Are the World project, then we needed to dispel our own doubts, quell our personal fears about being ridiculed for being involved in putting forth such seemingly implausible goals, and, as Harry Chapin would say, *"Do something!"*

So, with profound thanks to Mark Victor Hansen for pointing us in the direction of some information that has made us believe more than ever before in the viability of The Big Gig, and on behalf of all of our fellow sisters and brothers around the world, we ask members of the entertainment industry to put your own doubts and fears about such an undertaking aside, join together, and, as Mr. Kragen and Harry Chapin would say, "Accomplish the impossible."

CHAPTER 51

The Israeli-Palestinian Conflict: "...and kiss one another on the cheek..."

The importance of not allowing fear to dominate our lives was a topic to which the Spirit Guides repeatedly returned. And according to them, fear is at the heart of the Israeli-Palestinian conflict.

Jane, here with you, back at the keyboard. Although this chapter is quite short and touches on a topic we will be returning to as this project progresses, the issue is too critical not to address at least in brief. That being said, let's take a look at what the Guides said about fear being the root cause of one of our world's greatest problems:

> **There is much discussion about the ways in which humans turn trouble into fear and we want to stress that it is unneces-**

sary to take these measures. Every good life has had some good times and bad times and every person has his own trials and tribulations.

It is when we get caught up in fear that we lack the heart to discover a way to resolve our problems. Our fear turns to anxiety, our anxiety to depression, and our depression to neurosis.

And once you let go of fear and anxiety, you will fare better than before. To be scared is only human, but to let it wreak havoc on your life is a waste of time. In such troubling times the Palestinians and Israelites need to put down their prejudices and weapons and kiss one another on the cheek and say enough is enough. The main thing that they hold onto is their fear of change and fear of separation from one another (within their separate groups). But if they put their fears aside and let their real God speak and let their real humanitarian natures surface, then and only then will there be peace in the Middle East.

I have never studied Palestine or Israel. I don't know many specifics about the war they have been waging against each other for all these years. But I agree with Lily and friends. Their statement that "Palestinians and Israelis need to put down their prejudices and weapons and kiss one another on the cheek and say enough is enough" is simply beautiful.

CHAPTER 52

Can All of This Psychic Stuff Truly Be for Real?

You have probably asked yourself this question countless times as you have read through this book. We often felt the exact same way as we were writing it, saying to ourselves (and each other), "*Can this really be happening?*" Indeed, it is something that Ruth and the Guides had to reassure us about constantly as we worked our way through this project.

What would you think if all sorts of spirits from Heaven started getting in touch with you? Wouldn't you question your own sanity? How could you not wonder whether what was happening was real? We sure did.

Jane's Doubting Came Early On

On the third day that this project began, July 13, 2002, Jane was in the midst of a transmission from the Guides and was mentally questioning the whole notion of automatic writing in general. Sensing her doubt, the Guides provided a rapid response to her question:

This is for real Jane. This is for real, not a joke. We are real.

Jane's disbelief kept creeping back into her mind during the next few days, prompting the Guides to reiterate that what seemed to be going on really was happening:

This is not really a joke. We are serious about everything. We need to get information out to as many people as possible. There is much work to be done, and we will get it done. We have faith in you, Jane. We need your faith to make this work.

Ruth Weighs In

Ruth and the Guides were aware of the questions we were asking ourselves about whether the automatic writing transmissions were real and how the world would view the book we were writing. Time and time again, our co-authors sought to allay our fears about what was happening, saying on one occasion to Jane:

We put Ruth in the running when we did because she was a well-respected political writer, and we knew that some people would think this business totally unbelievable. We must remind everyone that she was credible in her field for a very special reason; and that was so, one, people would not think she was crazy and, two, so she could pave the way for you, [so] people wouldn't think you are crazy.

Jane, we can tell you now that people are far more interested and believing than when Ruth started. She says to tell you, Jane, not to worry as she sees your open mind and personality being a gateway to people's believing. She says

you are to go to the press, the news shows, anywhere that will spread the word. And she knows that you will be fine and believed, because you already have credibility with anyone who knows you. And you will be a good and interesting guest in many areas.

Ruth repeatedly let Jane know that she understood what it was like to wonder about the validity of something so seemingly far-out as receiving messages from "dead" spirits. One of these instances came after Jane had been talking on the phone to different friends and was then attempting to reconcile her conflicting feelings in a computer journal entry about what everyone would think once this book was published:

> *I have been looking forward to writing today and have not been letting my own doubts get in the way. After I let the whole doubt thing get to me, I began to think I must be crazy to put myself on the line like this. The whole world will be laughing at me, I thought. But those moments don't last too long. I am glad there are other people–like John Edward–out there already doing this sort of thing. Anyway, I'll let the Guides do their thing:*

Jane, it is Ruth Montgomery here. I'm glad you are not letting your own skepticism get in the way too much. Imagine how I felt when I was doing it. It was little known back then, and it was terrifying, but exciting, all at the same time. When we first started out, I wanted to check everything out; prove to myself that I wasn't nuts! But my reputation of [being] a good journalist preceded me, and so not everyone thought I was a kook. My husband did tell me to be careful, but he had faith in me, and we did good–I think. As will you.

So, Jane, part of our mission is to convince the world that you are a worthy person and are not some nutcase. Remember, it is your very worthiness that people find so appealing.

It is not every day that people take another for just being human.

One time Ruth even went so far as to come to Jane in a dream in order to bolster her confidence in moving ahead with this book, resulting in the following entry in Jane's computer journal:

> *Ruth Montgomery came through to me in a dream, just like she said she would early on. The only thing is, I don't remember what she said to me. Some psychic I am! She was younger than she was at the time of her death, but I knew that it was her. Trying to jog my memory, I vaguely recall her telling me that I was doing the right thing and to keep up the good work. Maybe she will come back again. I do remember thinking it was neat to be able to actually see her. Here we go again with not wanting to see ghosts. Dreams are safe because you can say it was just a dream. Isn't it funny how the mind rationalizes things?*

Wanted: Believers *and* Non-Believers

Although we Macombers sometimes questioned whether we were really in touch with spirits from Heaven, among our family members, it was our brother Joe who doubted most—and still does to a very large degree—the reality of the whole notion of "automatic writing." As someone not at all persuaded that there is even any form of afterlife, never mind the ability to communicate with spirits there, Joe wondered more than just a little—not in a critical way, just in plain disbelief—whether his siblings had flat out gone off their rockers. At one point as we were working on this book, Jane said to Rob, "Joey thinks that we're all nuts." Yet that didn't seem to faze the Guides in the least bit:

It is your job, Jane and Rob and Phyl and Paul and Laura and Sarah—and even Joey, to get as much information out as you can. It may be Jane and Rob that are putting forth the

most effort in getting this book done, but it is the collaboration of all of you that will make it happen. You were not
randomly put here together; you chose to do this together.
Even Joseph's disbelief will play a huge part. He is the non-
believer—and we need non-believers for this to happen. We
need people to challenge this.

Picking up on Jane's surprise that the success of the Guides' recommended Action Plan for Planet Earth depends on people
challenging what is written in this book, Lily and company continued their explanation of the central role played by non-believers:

> Yes, you heard correctly, Jane. We need people to chal-
> lenge this. At first. Because we need people to trust their own
> instincts, which really are good if you let them question these
> very instincts at first. People need to believe that they are
> knowing, too.
>
> And once the [people of the] world have questioned their
> own instincts, they will see that they are correct. That is to
> say, that the world does need to be turned around—and the
> only way to do that is to question where it is we need to go
> and how to get there. By putting out these ideas and these
> questions, the world will answer them for themselves.
>
> Once we really get rolling, people will see that it is the
> right thing. That is, what we were just talking about. When
> people really ask themselves, "Is what these people, these
> Macombers, say real and true, or is it just a bunch of bolo-
> gna?"
>
> These questions need to be asked: Do we need world peace?
> Do we need world order? Do we need the human race to stop
> fighting amongst each other and settle into a state of believ-
> ing in each other and most importantly our*selves*? Let's pull
> together and enjoy ourselves!

Some of you may scoff at this notion at first, but when you listen to your inner self, your real self, you will know that the mysteries of life are not mysteries at all. Just a language of sorts forgotten.

Don't forget what we said: Non-believers can play just as big a part as any, maybe even more so. For it is those who are transformed the most that will bring this to light even seven and seven thousand fold. It is the non-believers, turned believers, who will shine the light on the world, along and beside the believers. You see, it is up to everyone—and everyone is up to it.

Take this wisdom and pass it on to your brothers now, Jane. Peace be to you and all the world.

These words of the Guides about the respective roles of "believers" and "non-believers" really made us reexamine how we were looking at this whole project. We had initially envisioned the intent of this book to be to help mobilize those among the "believers" into action to help implement the Action Plan for Planet Earth outlined herein. Never had we imagined that "non-believers" would be so essential to its success.

Yet the more we thought about it, the more sense it made. It's sort of like the person who's smoked cigarettes for many, many years and then is finally able to quit: These people are often the most zealous anti-smoking advocates of all. Because they've experienced firsthand how harmful to their own personal health such a senseless addiction has been and are profoundly grateful for having been able to free themselves from the vice-like grip of nicotine, former smokers often bring an almost religious fervor to any discussion about smoking.

So, how would you characterize yourself? Are you a "believer" or a "non-believer"? And when we use that term, we don't mean, *Do you believe in everything that is written in this book?* No, definitely not, for even if you concur with much of the information it contains, there are sure to be some points with which you would take issue. And many of you may disagree with a great deal of what you are reading in this book. Nor does our understanding of what constitutes a "believer" require that you believe that there exists some sort of God or Higher Power. No, it's much more basic than that. We would suggest that, as the Guides have stated, being a "believer" boils down simply to believing:

> **[T]hat the world does need to be turned around–and the only way to do that is to question where it is we need to go and how to get there...[that] we need world peace...[that] we need world order...[that] we need the human race to stop fighting...and settle into a state of believing in each other and most importantly ourselves.**

So, what's the whisper of your *heart* saying to you *right now*? Believer or non-believer? Do you *feel* that the world needs to be turned around, and do you *believe* that it can be done? Or does your *mind* tell you something different? Does it *think* that the planet's problems are too overwhelming to be solved and that we as a race are simply incapable of all getting along together and sharing what we have with each other?

So what did you decide? Do you know that you're definitely a believer and feel that, as formidable as the obstacles may be, the tremendous challenges facing us can–and will–be overcome? If so, then please know that we're *so* glad that you're already on board. It's true that there is strength in numbers. Strength of commitment, strength of will, strength of spirit...strength of belief.

Or does the situation on Earth appear just too bleak and big ever to work itself out? Do you watch the news and think to yourself that the world's just a monumental mess and always will be? When you read newspapers or magazines, do you just skim over–or completely ignore–the articles about world affairs, figuring that things for lots of people on the planet are just plain hopeless and that you're glad you're not one of them? Do you rapidly scroll by the sad stories on the computer screen because they're just too depressing to click on and read? When you're driving in the car and listening to the radio, do you sometimes switch to a different station when the news comes on so you don't have to listen to more downer stories about what tragic thing has just happened?

If you answered "yes" to any of the questions in the preceding paragraph, then join the crowd. Haven't we all done these things? Who among us hasn't looked at what's going on around the globe—unprecedented terrorism, devastating poverty, millions of people starving to death, the spread of numerous incurable diseases, environmental destruction, one war after another, etc.—and thought that things will just never change?

Yet, at the same time, haven't you had at least a fleeting thought along the lines of, *Wouldn't it be nice if things could be different?* Don't many of us actually *believe* that it would be great if the problems of the world could be solved? But, on the other hand, aren't we afraid that if we started to give serious consideration to how these issues might best be solved, that the prospect of almost certain failure makes such thoughts a bad investment of even the slightest bit of time, energy, or emotion? Doesn't the issue really boil down to the fact that most of us just don't believe it's possible to solve the world's pressing problems? Until this book project unfolded in our own lives, we certainly didn't.

So, it seems that most everyone is a believer to a certain extent. In fact, how many people could you really find who would say they didn't believe that it would be good if the planet's problems could be resolved? Where the disbelief comes in is with the question of whether it is possible for the various things that are "broken" on the Earth to be "fixed." Ah, there's the rub. That's where things get sticky. "*Get real,*" you think. Well, we would respectfully like to request that right now you stop "thinking" for the next couple of minutes and just focus on your "feelings" as you read the rest of this chapter.

Tune Down Your Mind and Crank Up Your Heart

So, have you turned down the "thinking" volume in your head? Not off, just down to a level where the subtleties of the tug of your heart can be felt and reconciled with what your mind is thinking. We hope so, for your experience in reading the end of this chapter will likely be enhanced if you have.

Ready? Here's what the Guides would like you to consider:

> **What we need to do right now is get the world in order. Get the people back on track. The ideas will come together as the people of the world come together.**
>
> **It is really quite simple; and we see that a lot of you are reading and understanding, even as you may tell yourselves that you do not. It is this little inclination, that little tug, that little notion inside your head and heart and soul that tells you the truth. That maybe, just maybe, there is a little—or a lot—more to this than meets the eye. Maybe.**
>
> **Think on this and you will be sweetly surprised when you remember. You know that feeling when someone reminds you of something you did together, some time you shared? And you say, "Oh, my God, I forgot about that!!!" And you are flooded with feelings of joy and elation when you remember? It will be the same feeling, only a billion times stronger, when you remember the things we are talking about.**
>
> **And you are even correct when you say, "Oh, *my* God." He is your God. He is you. She is you. You are her. Him or it. Whatever you want to call whatever it is *We* are.**
>
> **So we ask those of you who are reading this book, this collection of ideas, let your imaginations run away with you, even if just for a moment. Let your *true self* be. Just *let it be*, as that great Beatle Paul McCartney sang once upon a time.**

We Would Like to Ask You to Do the World a Favor

There is one small thing that we would respectfully like to request that you do: The next time you're reading a newspaper or magazine, watching the news on television, listening to it on the radio, or motoring along on the computer screen, please stop and take just a few minutes to focus your feelings intently on whatever "bad" story is being told by the media.

It doesn't matter whether the story's about people in another country, your own nation, your home state, or the very city or town in which you live. The point is to really attempt to feel whatever it is that your heart may be telling you about the information you are taking in. For starters, try to feel what the person or people in the story are going through or have gone through. A lot of us did this after the 9/11 tragedy at the World Trade Center in New York, but there are stories in the news every day that are also deserving of our compassion.

Next, try to feel what your heart is telling you should be done about the situation. Put aside any "logical" considerations about what may or may not seem practical or possible to do. Rather, let your heart tell you what you feel *should* be done if anything were possible. And whatever response you get is what *needs* to be done. It doesn't matter how improbable the answer may seem or how impossible to achieve you may think it is. What is important is to identify what your heart tells you.

Finally, after you've learned what your heart has indicated is the truth, search through both your heart and mind to see whether you can find just a glimmer of hope that maybe, just maybe, things can be changed. Don't you already believe that they *should* be? Doesn't it really just boil down to whether you believe they *can* be?

But Where's the Proof?

The bottom line is that we can't "scientifically" prove that any of the information contained in this book came from Heaven. All we can tell you is that we *know* deep in our hearts and souls that it didn't come from us.

But what about you? How are you to evaluate what you are reading? Here's what the Guides suggested in one of their transmissions through Jane:

> For people who want proof of the authenticity of our writings, tell them we know their heart of hearts and we are all in this together. It is nay-sayers and laymen that will really bite into this book, as its message of positive reaffirmation is so strong.
>
> When we talk of people that are on this side, we see many skeptical things in the eyes of many, but they should not fear that there is another side. There is a lesson to be learned in each lifetime, and we see that it is time for a break for many here on Earth.
>
> We interchange our talk of here and there, as we are both on that side and this. It is much easier to get things done on different levels when you have many people controlling the thought lines of communication. That is to say, we can open many channels to people if they will open their own minds as you have done; and we see many people doing that as we reach out in many different directions. Now we know a lot of you reading this are going to say that we are crazy, or that Jane is crazy, but we are not and neither is she.

So, ultimately, only you can decide what you believe and what you do not. Accept whatever your heart tells you has the feel of truth and discount the rest to whatever extent makes sense to you.

You may decide that everything in this book is pure hogwash and that it's just too fanciful to be at all possible. If so, then please know that we sincerely respect how you feel and are grateful that, in spite of your doubts, you are taking your time to read this book. On the other hand, if parts of what you have been reading ring true in your gut, then that's great. But either way, don't kid yourself. Be honest with the person in the mirror about how you are really *thinking* and *feeling*. Only then will you be able to decide for yourself what's real and what's not.

One thing is for certain, though: You have picked up this book for a reason—and make no mistake about it, there is a reason for *everything* that happens in life. Perhaps you have always been interested in the spiritual aspects of existence and wished to learn more. Maybe you are someone who has never read anything like this, but are curious about life's big questions and wonder whether there is anything to this psychic mumbo-jumbo. Or it could be that you are a staunch skeptic who simply wanted to see what a book such as this had to say.

Whatever the reason behind this book coming across your path, we would humbly suggest that you look within your heart of hearts and ask yourself one critical question: *Why did I pick up this book?* Before turning the page, please reflect on this for a moment and then answer yourself honestly.

Right now, at this very instant, you probably know why you were interested enough to delve into this book. And as you prepare to turn the page, we'll close this chapter by saying, *Isn't it possible that we would all—both believers and non-believers—like to, as the Rod Stewart song goes, "Find a reason to believe"?*

The Final Chapter
...of *This* Book

A s you begin the last pages of this book, we would like to thank you for taking the time out of your life to read it. Because time is, in many ways, the ultimately finite commodity in our earthly lives, we do not at all take for granted the hours you have invested with us—or you spending your hard-earned dollars on this book. To the contrary, we greatly appreciate your interest in our collaboration with Ruth Montgomery and the Spirit Guides in their ongoing work to help our world.

But although this may be the final chapter of the book you are now just concluding, it is really just the start of our efforts to bring to you words of wisdom from Heaven. We cannot say where this continuing adventure will lead us, but we are certain that *Ruth Montgomery Writes Again!* marks only the first step in a journey that will continue until we join Ruth and the Guides on The Other Side. In fact, the Guides themselves described the scope of our assignment in a transmission Jane received from them following a hiatus in her automatic writing sessions:

Anyway, Jane, we have been with you right all along since the last time we sat down at the computer together. You have learned much in many ways.

And the break you seemed to have taken was not a break at all, as everything you've experienced has brought much insight to you. Not a break at all really, but a re-attachment of sorts. Insight that will help with this project and book.

We differentiate between the two, because the book is only part of the project. The project is a lifelong, ongoing project that won't end.

Simply put, we are in this "project" for the duration and are playing for keeps. We take our responsibilities as messengers for the spirit realm very seriously and are honored to have been asked to work with them. But that's all we are...and nothing more.

We've simply been given some messages that need to be delivered. Some information that needs to be shared. And we intend to do our best to deliver it to you. So we hope that you will stay with us as we continue our exploration of all that Heaven says humanity can be.

What's Ahead in the Next Book

As we move forward toward a future that the spirit realm says can be a wonderful one for the human race, the spirits in Heaven have more to say about how we can make that possibility a reality.

In fact, you might say things are just getting warmed up in this first book. And in the second book, things are really going to shift into overdrive as Heaven puts the pedal to the metal and unleashes some truly eye-popping material. And the interesting thing about the spirit world's message is that we, the people of the Earth, have only to make a few fundamental changes in how we approach life in order to improve the planet drastically for everyone's benefit.

Heaven's attempt to provide the residents of Planet Earth with a roadmap that shows how to reach a bright and glorious future is described in more detail in our next book. In the second volume of this series, the spirits on The Other Side cover a broad range of subjects, including the following:

1. A lot more specifics on the Guides' three-part Action Plan for Planet Earth. Whereas *Ruth Montgomery Writes Again!* provides a general framework for the strategy that the spirit world says holds the key to humanity solving its biggest problems, the second book explains how to set up a series of initiatives that will literally change the world.

2. Individual chapters on many of modern society's most pressing issues, including money, power, terrorism, women's rights, education, and the world's rain forests.

3. An in-depth look at the war in Iraq and a description of how Jane was paid a visit by the Secret Service when we, at the Guides' request, stopped work on this book for several weeks in the winter of 2003 and mounted a small letter-writing campaign to warn the U.S. government against starting the war.

4. A chapter titled "Earth Changes: Mother Nature's 'Shock and Awe' Campaign." The Spirit Guides discuss the climate changes that are happening on our planet and update their forecast for the cataclysmic Earth Changes that they originally predicted in the books Ruth Montgomery wrote prior to joining Lily and the Guides on The Other Side.

   As part of this chapter, we will examine an important statement from Deepak Chopra's *Peace Is the Way* and to what extent the issue of awareness of the potential catastrophic effects of environmental destruction must be balanced against the possibility of people unintentionally energizing such a scenario by focusing on it too much. In this insightful book, Chopra says:

It's disturbing that so much of New Age thought is centered on catastrophic earth changes, such as earthquakes and the depleted ozone layer. It encourages the prophecy to come true when what we want to do is exactly the opposite....Nature will factor those thoughts as your vote for the future.[1]

5. The animals of the earth. When the Spirit Guides spoke of making the Earth "a safe place for everyone," they weren't just referring to human beings. Just look at a small sample of what they had to say about animals:

    The animals of the Earth need to be saved. Dolphins are smart because they hold the knowledge of the Earth, as do all animals. Killing and extinctions [are] killing the very essence of the planet. We are meant to share the earth, not destroy it. The animals will help us if we help them.

    This is a subject to which we'll be devoting an entire chapter in the second book of this series. But for now, let's simply say that the spirit realm has made it abundantly clear that our fate as a race is inextricably entwined with that of The Animal Kingdom.

    Although there will be a wide variety of other topics examined in the next book, it will have one connecting theme. We've come to call it "The Eternal Equation."

Good Against Evil = Love Versus Fear

This is not only the main theme of the next book, but is also intended to be its title. Moreover, it is our sense that "Good Against Evil = Love Versus Fear" will be the thematic thread that connects the entire body of work that we end up doing over the years through our communications with the spirit realm.

In the series' second title, we'll explain how the examination of good, evil, love, and fear that we began in this book evolved into the equation "Good Against Evil = Love Versus Fear."

Good or evil. Love or fear. Since the very beginning of this project, we have been reviewing material about these topics. A lot of it originated from Ruth and the Guides. Some of it came from reading other authors' books. And sometimes our exploration of these polar opposites involved simply reading the newspaper.

After digesting various types of information from numerous sources and concluding that "Good Against Evil = Love Versus Fear" captures the essence of the human experience, we wondered if it could really be that straightforward. You may well be asking yourself the same question this very moment.

Could everything in life really boil down to something so simple? After asking ourselves some very specific and revealing questions about our own personal experiences, we ultimately concluded that it truly could.

So that you can decide for yourself whether the negative aspects of earthly existence are really ultimately rooted in fear, here are the three most important questions we have asked ourselves about the subject that we would now pose to you:

1. Take a minute and think about the biggest mistakes you have made in your life and the most profound regrets you have in your heart.

   As you contemplate the things you either did or didn't do that led to these difficult memories, did fear play a primary role in these experiences?

2. Next, make a mental list of the things that often keep you awake at night.

   How big a part of what causes you literally to lose sleep has to do with fear?

3. Finally, think about the aspirations you have for your future. The things you want to do; the ideal visions you have pictured in your mind; the goals you wish to achieve; the experiences you hope to have.

To what extent does fear play a part in whatever doubts you have about your ability to realize your dreams for the future?

Only you truly know just how much of a common denominator fear is when evaluating the past, present, and future aspects of your life. For us, it was incredibly liberating when we realized that fear was the root cause of the negativity that exists in our lives. And we all have plenty of negativity that confronts us on a daily basis.

So, just imagine what Life would be like if you could conquer your fears, see past them, and take the action you know is necessary to lead the life you really want. Toward that end, we hope you will continue along the journey with us in *Good Against Evil = Love Versus Fear* and discover how The Eternal Equation spelled itself out for us as a universal truth to share with you.

Some Last Words

"The thousand years of peace that has been talked about—and has been waiting—is here for the taking.... We can see from our perspective that God wants nothing more than peace on Earth and in the Heavens....And even if man is unwilling to listen, we will keep talking until he does."

–The Spirit Guides

We hope you have enjoyed taking this first leg of the journey with us and will sign off for now with a few words from each of the principal participants in this book's creation. These concluding messages are offered straight from the souls of their authors to yours and are sent your way with the most possible sincerity and the deepest of heartfelt appreciation for joining us in this adventure.

The Spirit Guides Sign Off

We will reiterate that we are not being judgmental in these observations, but we are simply telling the truth. The truth that many are willing to step up to now.

As we have told you many times before, once the ball gets rolling, it will snowball with fire-like fury. The world is getting ready for this even as we speak.

We are ready now to show you the real world. The world of what was meant to be. The thousand years of peace that has been talked about—and has been waiting—is here for the taking.

This is why we want to write this book, so that the world will be spiritually awakened. As we told Ruth Montgomery in her sessions, to be spiritually awakened, people need to first look inside themselves, which people worldwide are doing. And then they need to look to each other to share experiences such as this book.

To give oneself a chance to realize that it is goodness that we all want, we all have to work at this. Even the angels in Heaven and we Guides need to help too.

We can see from our perspective that God wants nothing more than peace on Earth and in the Heavens. But what price will men have to pay to figure this out when it's been right in front of them for so long?

We say this, Jane Macomber, as you know how much we all want this to be so. And even if man is unwilling to listen, we will keep talking until he does.

God has great faith in the men of the Earth. He wants them to recognize this and seek faith not only in Him, but in themselves.

What we are trying to do is help man and woman to realize their potential for greatness, true greatness. Whether you are Democrat, Republican, or from Zimbabwe, we want the men and women of the world to realize that they can do great things if they will allow themselves to.

We are here on this planet to learn and to grow, but first we must listen to the self within the self that knows what is right and good. We need to stop, sit, and listen to our inner voice–our real inner voice. Not the ones that say, "We'll buy this and that and make so much money from this," but the voice of reason that will lead us to right, not wrong.

Jane

Because the Guides have helped me so much with understanding the world in which we all live, I am going to use my final pages to share with you a few especially important excerpts from my dialogue with them. The material selected for this sign-off is central to the teachings of Lily and the Spirit Guides. It is intended to allow you to get one final glimpse of who I am, and, most importantly, will, I hope, be instructive to you in assessing your own role in helping turn our world around.

Let's begin by taking a look at a journal entry I made prior to beginning one of my automatic writing sessions with my spirit friends:

> *I am making tea for myself now. I will put in a few words of my own and then go to the Guides.*
>
> *Rob came by last night and copied yesterday's transmission. I was at Annette's having dinner, so I wasn't here to talk about it. He did leave me a message on the answering machine about how eloquent he thought it was.*
>
> *I am always pleasantly surprised after reading the transmissions at how good they sound. I didn't read yesterday's, as I had had several young boys over for Caleb's birthday celebration.*

When I am doing the transmissions, the words don't always sound like great bits of insight. I am taking down the information and not really processing what the words are saying. Sometimes I feel like I am writing the same things over and over. Usually I will write what the Guides impart to me and go back over it later. Once my mind is clear and I am refreshed, it sounds the way it was intended.

I remember on this particular night I was bummed out that I couldn't talk to Cuac about the transmission. My brothers and I feed off of each other's energies. But I did have a great dinner and a nice evening with my neighbors! So, on to what was said in the Guides' transmission that day:

Today we will start the transmissions with a lesson about the benefits of joy in a person's life. There is one thing that joy does for humans and that is to lift up the spirit.

Isn't it true? When you are happy, you are lifted up. You have more energy, good energy. It makes us feel like we want to do good things, for ourselves and other people.

The Guides continued:

That is the main purpose of this book. It is not to bring people down with horrible thoughts of destruction and disaster. It is not meant as an avenue of criticism.

This is a very important subject. You may think some of this is "doom and gloom"; it is not meant to be. Yet certain things do need to be brought to our attention. They are observations about the possibilities that exist for all of us. It is about the joy we will experience as a race if we follow these suggestions. Joy for everyone, not just a select few. The spirits are saying we should take the half-full cup and fill it up. That's all. And Ruth and her friends acknowledge that other people have said this before:

We realize there are people the world over who have been saying these exact same things for many years. Global warming is nothing new. And neither is anything else in this book. These are ideas that man has had himself.

We are just reaffirming what so many of you already know. It is not our intention to justify this to the people who are already listening and doing everything they can to save them-

selves and the lives of others and the planet itself. They already know this.

This is an idea that hit me early on. I thought, "We aren't saying anything that hasn't already been said." Fear began to creep in as I thought people might think we are just trying to leverage ourselves by using Ruth's good name.

Nothing could be further from the truth. I like my privacy. Before this project began, I didn't even really know that much about Ruth. I had read only her last book, and that was all. It wasn't until I was well into this endeavor that I realized the magnitude of who she had been. To be very specific, it was only in the fourth year of this project, when I read the summary of Ruth's books that Cuac had drafted, that I recognized what a major figure she had been.

If I wanted notoriety, I would not be where I am today. If that had been my primary desire, then I sure as heck would have chosen a different path in life.

It's very true that what Ruth, the Guides, and we are saying is not new. It's just being said in a different way, coming from another source—an unconventional source, but a source nonetheless. And according to the Guides, that's because humankind's attention needs to be grabbed every so often:

Every now and then man needs a reminder that he did not create life. That he did not create this universe or this world. He is a part of it indeed, but he is not all of it.

I have said that I believe we are all a part of Life. I believe that. And I think we all had something to do with Creation. So what I think the Guides are saying here is that it is all of us, not just the Earth or humans, but everything in the universe that matters.

In this vein of inclusion, the Guides went on:

Where would man be today if he did not share in his good works? We want only to extend that in all directions of the planet.

This is true if you really think about it. Where would we be if we were selfish all the time? Where would hurricane victims be if we didn't reach out?

Look at how the world pulled together when the tsunami in Indonesia hit. That was a catastrophic occurrence, and the entire world community stepped up to the plate and hit one out of the park. I believe the same type of togetherness is possible for the various issues the Guides have spoken about.

All you really have to do is ask yourself two questions:

1. *Do these problems exist?*

2. *Is there anything I can do to help?*

I think most of us can honestly answer "yes" to both.

As the Guides have so aptly stated, these ideas are nothing new. A lot of people have been plugging away at these causes for a long time.

I can remember seeing ads on TV to help impoverished countries when I was young. Save the Children, UNICEF, The United Way. These organizations and many, many others have been digging deep at such problems for years. I think the difference now is that the recognition for the need to take action is much more widespread today.

Of course, with technology seeming to advance quicker than the speed of light, it is now much easier to spread the word. I get my e-mails from the ONE campaign, and all I have to do is spend a few minutes asking Congress to support this or that or sign a bill. It takes just a little bit of time, but with everyone doing it, it gets results.

I don't think it's a coincidence that all of this technology is taking hold in today's world. We need it, and we are ready for it. The Guides sure think so:

When the world is ready for something, it will happen. And we know that the world is ready for this. There is a glorious time awaiting us all, here on Earth and in Heaven.

Our state of mind has everything to do with all of us. Bring forth all those thoughts that bring love in the world and it shall be so.

Let's go back again to the saying "When the student is ready, the teacher will appear." I think our teachers have appeared. And I think they are all over the place. Not just Ruth Montgomery and her convoy of spirits, but thousands of other teachers as well.

After all, some people learn in different ways than others. So whereas some may benefit from our collaboration with Ruth and the Guides, others may find enlightenment in another way.

Everyone has a part to play. It's the balance of life. If we were all the same, life would be boring.

So, teachers and students are pairing up. And sometimes the roles are reversed. I can't tell you how many times I have felt like my children have taught me more than I have taught them. It's a two-way street. Each one of us is both a student and a teacher. So let's all eagerly further one another's knowledge and do our sincere best to help each other out.

Paul

It's July 23, 2006, and I'm sitting in the Mill Valley Library, the place where, almost ten years earlier, I found and read my first Ruth Montgomery book. I haven't been here for almost five years and for some reason, without forethought, had decided to come here today to finish my part of this book.

I didn't recognize the synchronicity of this myself, but when I mentioned to Rob that I was coming here this morning, he pointed out that this is where the whole project had started a decade before. I read my first Ruth book here, and then found a copy to send to him. We both eventually read all of her books, and, well, you know the rest of the story.

How ironic and very meaningful it is now that I'm here writing the finishing paragraphs to my last entry to the book. The initial chapter of this project has come full circle since I read my first Ruth book here ten years ago. It should be interesting to see how the next ten years unfold.

I think most of us would agree that the state of the world today is not good in many respects.

The way we have been treating the Earth, our only place to live, is shameful. The amount of toxic pollutants we produce and inject into our society in the name of progress needs to be rethought. We are becoming a more technologically advanced society, but at what cost? The number of diseases that are caused from the by-products of these advances is staggering. There has been an irresponsible disregard for the ultimate ramifications of all of this that we can no longer overlook.

Global warming is a perfect example. For years, many people– persuaded, in my opinion, primarily by big business–tried to deny the validity of global warming. Now, however, it is more widely accepted as an obvious truth that we must face. We can no longer bury our heads in the sand.

The way we treat our planet is second only to the way we treat ourselves. If you stop and think about the way humans have been treating one another down through the ages, it is sad.

We have been killing one another over such things as money, oil, different religious and ideological beliefs, the color of one's skin, etc. Fighting isn't necessary. There are more than enough resources here for all of us to have comfortable lives.

We need to learn how to communicate better and get along with one another before it is too late. We need to realize that we're all in this together. We can start to unite to help one another to solve these monumental issues we're all facing, such as world starvation, poverty, global warming, and war, or we can continue on the path of fragmentation and self-destruction. We won't have to look far to see where this will lead us.

My belief is that the solution to these rather daunting worldly issues needs to start not only with our governments, but also with each and every one of us. We need to start, in whatever little ways we can, to make this world a better place.

It can start with treating the people around you with respect and dignity, no matter their class, color, or income level. It's about being forgiving instead of resentful, understanding instead of getting angry, generous instead of greedy—going out of one's way to help someone for no reason other than the person needs help. It's about smiling at people when you walk down the street, instead of frowning or just looking down. It's about thinking positive thoughts instead of negative ones.

It's these little things that can have a ripple effect and help to make the world a happier, more pleasant place to be. One person in a room who's in a good mood can infect all the others with his or her positive energy, just as someone who's in a bad mood can spread his or her negative energy around equally as fast.

Let's choose to be positive people and think and do the good things that we're all capable of doing.

We need not only to start treating one another better, but our planet as well. We can't continue on this path of planetary destruction. The damage we've done in the last hundred years is frightening: global warming, high levels of toxicity in the air we breathe, the destruction of coral reefs and rain forests that cleanse our air, chemicals polluting the ground where we grow our food and raise our children. I think these are things we hear about so often that we've become callous to the truth of what this all really means to our environment, health, and future.

Certainly, governments need to play a big role in this awakening, to right the wrongs that have been taking place, but we, as individuals, also need to take responsibility ourselves and do our part. We need to be conscious of the actions that we take and how they affect the planet.

I know there are a lot of people who take the attitude that their single actions, for better or worse, aren't going to affect the overall outcome one way or another. That simply isn't true. If we all take this attitude, then we surely will never turn the tide to start saving our planet. Our individual actions do matter.

It starts with things such as recycling, not buying products that are harmful to the earth, supporting and buying products from companies that are ecologically conscious, conserving energy whenever possible—even if it's only turning out the light when you leave a room. It's all of us doing these types of little things that not only help to begin to turn things around, but also spread awareness to those who may be less conscious of such matters.

I love the saying that "saving our world isn't a spectator sport." We all must be participants. And we can, if we just believe we can, and then take action from those beliefs.

I encourage you to try to be more aware of your world and how you impact it. Build upon the positive ways you know are already adding to it and, also, rethink the things you do that may not be for the good of our planet.

I, personally, have been trying to raise my awareness of the world around me and how my actions affect it. I'm certainly no saint, and the Green Party definitely hasn't been knocking on my door asking for my candidacy, but knowing that I've been changing my ways, at least to a modest degree, in a manner that's good for our world and the people I share it with, truly makes me feel good inside. In fact, I think we all have that inner barometer that tells us whether what we're doing is the right thing or not. We just need to listen to it more often.

Ruth and the Guides seem to have a pretty clear perspective from where they now exist on The Other Side, Upstairs, in Heaven, or whatever or wherever you want to call it. They can see where we're headed if we don't change our ways. Yet they can also see the possibility of a peaceful, beautiful world where we're all living joyfully together without all the wars, poverty, greed, and disease that we currently have.

I honestly feel that changing our world is a matter of belief. We must all believe we can change our individual ways and, by doing that, we can change collectively. It is from this place of working together that we'll start to make our world a better place.

We've given all the other past negative and destructive ways a try—and look where it has gotten us. So why not try something a little different and see what happens?

Cuac

As I contemplated what I wished to say to you as my siblings, our invisible co-authors, and I part from your company, I kept coming back to my favorite sign of all time. No, not a sign from The Other Side of any sort, but a simple road sign I saw on a hot summer day back in the 1980s in front of a waterslide park in Trenton, Maine. It was one of those signs with changeable letters that many businesses use. Written on it was: *"Scream until Daddy stops the car!"*

As soon as I saw the sign, I broke into a wide grin. Not only was it just plain funny, but its message was also a marvelous call to action.

The operators of the waterslide park knew they had an experience to offer that children would love. But before the kids could enjoy the sensation of shooting down one of the cool, wet rides, the person driving the family car would first have to make the decision to stop the car and let them join the fun.

I feel like that's what Ruth and the Guides want my family and me to do—to add our "scream" to the chorus of those "yelling" the message that we all have to wake up and admit we need to pull together if we're going to survive as a race.

And let me tell you, I intend to "scream" *loudly and often!* I know that it will take some time for this project to build momentum and for our family to become familiar with how to bring worldwide attention to it, but I can tell you that I plan to do my absolute best to carry out my assignment from the spirit realm.

And if you're now wondering whether my siblings and I have a specific political agenda, let me share with you something the Spirit Guides wrote about my siblings and me on this subject:

> **Know** **that they are not left-wingers or right-wingers or wingers of any sort. They are of the mind that all humans can live peacefully on this Earth and share its contents and beauty, simply because they have opened their minds to it.**
>
> **They are on this path because they chose to be, not because anybody else put them up to it. They are people who understand the human heart, and they understand the concept of love. Not just for one group or for the sake of one idea, but for the sake of all humanity.**

Although these words of the Guides humbled us and gave us high ideals to live up to, it seems clear that it is imperative for each and every one of us to realize the job can't be done alone; no one person, no one party, no one organization, no one nation can get the job done alone. Only if we decide that it's better to go it together instead of alone can we bring about the bright future that the spirits in Heaven say awaits us. But we must listen to what they're saying to us and to what each of our own hearts is telling us, if we'll only be honest enough with ourselves to listen.

Before this happens, we have to *want* to start working together and helping one another, not just talking about it. You may have heard the saying that people don't do what they need to do, but what they *want* to do. And I need look no further than my own bathroom mirror to see that I'm an example of that.

Although I instinctively knew that I *needed* to make some serious changes in my one-dimensional, materialistic approach to my daily existence, it wasn't until my path in life began pummeling me over and over again that I decided I wanted to make those changes. The essence of why I finally–albeit gradually and inconsistently–began to alter the way I was living is contained in a quotation from a book I received as a gift from our sister Sarah:

> *"There is no desire that anyone holds for any other reason than that they believe they will feel better in the achievement of it. Whether it is a material object, a physical state of being, a relationship, a condition, or a circumstance–at the heart of every desire is the desire **to feel good**."*[2]
>
> –Esther and Jerry Hicks, *Ask and It Is Given* (emphasis added)

I only began to adopt a more balanced approach to life because I had reached such a low point that I wanted to change my existence. I was feeling such extreme pain and anguish inside myself that I grasped onto the spiritual side of life because I needed some answers to help me understand why my life was crashing down all around me. I *wanted* to feel better.

The spirits in Heaven want *all* of us to feel better. They know that if we humans will heed their advice, open our eyes a little bit, and listen to what our hearts are telling us, then what we *need* to do and what we *want* to do will become the same thing.

And you know what? I believe when we do that, it will produce the most fun any of us has ever had. Just as when adults sometimes stop being "grown up" for a brief time and start being festive by joining the kids for a rollicking ride down a waterslide, we will remember how great it is to put our individual egos aside, see past our personal problems, and do stuff together in life.

Now, you may be thinking, *"How can you compare taking a small, frivolous thing like a brief ride down a waterslide to the monumental task of turning around the entire world?"* Fair enough question. But I would suggest that you only have to look at your own experience in Life to know how much joy can be created by people helping one another.

Can you recall how good it felt when someone helped you when you were in your own hour of need?

- Maybe it was someone loaning or giving you money when you were really down and out. You had nowhere else to turn, and that one person came through for you when no one else would. Do you remember how good it felt to experience the relief someone else's good deed produced deep inside of you?

- Or perhaps you received a second chance from someone who had no reason to give it to you. I doubt there's a person among us who doesn't know what it's like to want a second chance at something. And although "getting a second bite at the apple" doesn't happen very often, when it does, doesn't it produce feelings of incredible gratitude?

- And then again, it could be that you've needed someone to care enough just to listen at a critical time in life. Haven't we all "been there?" And isn't it nice when someone reaches out and is sincerely interested in hearing about what's troubling you? Tough to beat, isn't it?

But let's now look at things from the flip side. If there's anything that can possibly trump the feeling of being helped because another person cares enough about you to do so, it's being on "the giving end": the gratifying sense of being the one who offers the helping hand; the liberating feeling of being the one who is granting the forgiveness; or the warm feeling you get in your heart when you're the person who's there to listen when someone really needs to talk.

There's simply no experience like being on the "giving end" of things in life. It just plain feels good. And who doesn't want to feel good?

And just how good can it get if we start deciding that we want to pitch in and help solve the world's most pressing problems? Well, Ruth Montgomery has an answer for that question.

"It is the true goodness in people's hearts that we want to come out. Because it is there."

–Ruth Montgomery

Ruth Montgomery Writes One More Time

It is time not to point fingers about the past, but recognize the mistakes and clean things up for the present and future. There is a grand future and a happy now, just waiting to be discovered.

It's like the ruins of so many civilizations that archeologists dig up beneath the earth. Only it is buried deep within our souls. Only it's not really that deep at all. As a matter of fact, it really lies just beneath the surface.

Some people have more layers of betrayal on them. But I tell you this: It is just as easy to lift a hundred layers as it is to lift one. Just let it go and it's done with. It is really all so simple.

It is the true goodness in people's hearts that we want to come out. Because *it is there.*

But Wait...the Most Important Participant in This Book Has Yet to Be Heard from: *You!*

"Humans are powerful spiritual beings meant to create good on the earth. This good isn't usually accomplished in bold actions, but in singular acts of kindness between people. It's the little things that count, because they are more spontaneous and show who you truly are."[3]

–Dannion Brinkley, *Saved by the Light*

That's right. You are the most important participant in this book. By far.

Yes, Ruth Montgomery and the Spirit Guides have shared a lot of wonderful wisdom with the world in this book. And we have given our best efforts to be their messengers and to communicate this information to you. But it is you who will determine how much good will be done as a result of this project. Remember, Heaven has said that *if* humanity follows the Action Plan for Planet Earth, *then* we will usher in the long-awaited Thousand Years of Peace.

Now, you may still be skeptical about your ability as one human being to help bring about the good times around the globe that Ruth and the Guides say is possible. But have no fear! As the saying goes, "Many hands make light work."

The spirits in Heaven believe in you. They believe in us. And when we say "us," we're talking about the entire human race. Why? *Because,* just as Ruth Montgomery said, *"the true goodness in people's hearts...**is there**."*

Now it's up to us to decide whether we believe in ourselves. In each other. Do you?

Since you are the most important participant in this book, we would like to hear from you about how you *feel* about the ideas that have been presented to you in *Ruth Montgomery Writes Again!* Because we are interested in what you have to say, we have four questions for your consideration:

1. Do you believe that the ideas contained in this book will make our world a better place?

2. If so, why?

3. If not, why not?

4. Regardless of your answers to the first three questions, what ideas do you have about how to make our world a better place?

You can e-mail your answers to: ideas@goodagainstevil.com

Or, if you prefer to send us your response by mail, our address is:
Distinctive Publications for the World
P.O. Box 888
Hanover, New Hampshire 03755

Thanks again for joining us on the journey, not just by reading this book, but most significantly, for being one of our fellow adventurers down here on Planet Earth.

In closing, if you could ask Ruth and the Guides one question, what would it be? We will be posing more questions to them in the future and intend to base some of them on the feedback we get from you and other readers. Please let us know by sending your questions to:

questions@askRuthMontgomery.com

or

mailing them to:

Distinctive Publications for the World

P.O. Box 888

Hanover, New Hampshire 03755

SPECIAL OFFER

To receive a *free sample excerpt* from our next book with Ruth and the Guides, *Good Against Evil = Love Versus Fear*, send an email to freesample@goodagainstevil.com, and we will be happy to provide you with a glimpse of what lies ahead in this series.

MEMO

TO: You
FROM: Us
DATE: The day you help Heaven help humanity
SUBJECT: **Sharing copies of *Ruth Montgomery Writes Again!* with others**

Dear Fellow Resident of Planet Earth,

Do you feel in your heart that reading *Ruth Montgomery Writes Again!* has been a good use of your time and money? If your answer is "Yes," then <u>we would like to ask you a favor: Please buy some additional copies of this book and give them as gifts</u> to your family, friends, work colleagues, or anyone else you think might benefit from reading it.

Why should you buy additional copies of this book for people you care about?

Because Heaven's call to action is to *all* of us. The "Action Plan for Planet Earth" is a "we" project. And, as the Spirit Guides have said, <u>we all have a meaningful part to play</u>:

> **We want to see every person available involved in some way, even if it is a small contribution. Small contributions add up to big love. This is the whole reason we are doing this book.**

What difference in our world can you make by giving a few books to others?

Do you remember how the path that led us to write *Ruth Montgomery Writes Again!* all started with one of us sending to another an unexpected gift of two books written by Ruth Montgomery? That's right. The book you now hold in your hands all began because one person decided to do exactly what we're asking you to do.

Who knows what good in our world may be automatically triggered when you take action and share Ruth Montgomery Writes Again! *with others?*

With deep thanks for your consideration... from our hearts to yours,

Jane Macomber

Paul A. Macomber   *Rob "Cur" Totaro Macomber*

P.S. Have you ever asked Heaven for help in an hour of need? Well, now Heaven is asking for yours and wishes to reiterate their message of appreciation to you:

> **We want everyone who joins in to know that we are grateful for your efforts in advance.**

411

Imagine how good you will feel in your heart when you give your family, friends, and colleagues the meaningful gift of *Ruth Montgomery Writes Again!*... And how touched they will be in theirs by your kindness.

You clearly care about our world or you probably wouldn't be reading this book. Indeed, the urgency of all of us working together to solve our planet's problems is underscored in Chapter 43 by the following declaration from Heaven that:

"The state of the world is such a mess today that *we* need to clean it up as soon as possible."

—Ruth Montgomery

Would you like to receive free e-mail updates on this project?

We have an e-mail newsletter that will keep you posted on:

1. Upcoming books in the GoodAgainstEvil.com series.

2. CD sets containing additional information from Ruth Montgomery and the Spirit Guides about a diverse range of topics.

3. Free excerpts from upcoming books and articles.

4. Details about our annual fall teleseminars.

NOTE: If you would like to submit questions for these teleseminars, please send them in an email to:

teleseminars@askRuthMontgomery.com

5. A look ahead at some of the questions that we intend to pose to Ruth and the Spirit Guides as we work on asking the people of the world to help implement the Action Plan for Planet Earth.

6. Summaries of questions that readers such as yourself have for Ruth and the Guides.

7. Comments about this project that we have received from people all over the world

We invite you to keep in touch with Ruth Montgomery and the Spirit Guides' ongoing efforts to help humanity and learn more about their Heaven-sent messages to us all.

To begin receiving these e-mail newsletter updates, simply send a blank email to:

updates@goodagainstevil.com

ENJOY!

Would you like to receive free e-mail updates on this project?

DEDICATIONS

The first two people to whom we dedicate this book are our parents, Marge and Bob Macomber. Although there is an entire chapter that details their tremendous influence on our lives and critical roles in our collaboration with the spirit realm, we feel that some words written well before the completion of this book capture the essence of Margaret Elizabeth Allen Macomber and Robert William Macomber, Sr.

Our Mother, Margaret Elizabeth Allen Macomber

Note: The following is an entry Rob wrote about our mother for the wedding program when he got married in 1998. So, although written by one of us, it reflects how all three authors of this book most definitely feel about her.

When God created Mum Marge, he decided to bless the world with a living angel. Her life personifies the word "love" and has served as an ideal that Robbie will forever strive to learn from and to which he will always aspire. Mum's ceaseless dedication to doing things for others, unwavering commitment toward her family members, and countless personal sacrifices for their well-being have made Marge an inspiration to all those who know her, and an idol to her son Robbie.

Robbie is not alone among his siblings in how he views Mum Marge. To the contrary, she gave all of her children an endless supply of love, served for the six of them as a model of how best to live one's life, and, to this very day, continues to do everything in her power to make all of their lives easier and happier. Robbie knows that his sisters and brothers revere their mother just as he does and that they share his deep sense of appreciation for all of her lessons about "love" and "togetherness." He can still remember Mum Marge taking her children to the movies to see *The Sound of Music* and telling them how it was a good example of the importance of families sticking together—no matter what. Indeed, it is a tribute to what Mum Marge has taught her children that they all truly love spending time together and frequently structure their vacation plans around visiting one another. In this vein, Phyl has long noted that Cuac has said to her more than once, "You could take any two of us six kids, put us by ourselves for an entire month, and we'd have a gas together."

Mum Marge instilled not only a sense of love of family in her son, Robbie, but also a love of "being little." For instance, he can remember coming downstairs in the morning as a child and finding that she had prepared a breakfast of cake and ice cream for her children, saying, "I thought of how much I'd love it if I were a kid, so why not?" Whenever a Walt Disney movie would be showing at the theater when he was a child, his mother would always manage to find a way to get her children to see it. She felt that it was very important for them to have the opportunity to see these films of fantasy, magic, and fairy tales.

While Robbie has irreplaceable memories of going with her to see *Pinocchio, Snow White, Bambi,* and a host of other enchanting classics, the thing that made the most lasting impression on him is that his mother was every bit as excited to see these movies as he and his sisters and brothers were. Her sense of enthusiasm for these timeless flights of fancy, the irrepressible youth of her soul, and her unshakable belief in happy endings are all part of Mum Marge's legacy to her son Robbie. To this day, his two favorite movies of all-time in the entire world remain *The Wizard of Oz* and *Peter Pan.*

In sum, Marge Macomber is one of those rare individuals who truly lives each day according to the Golden Rule. It is not at all hyperbole or the distorted perspective of a biased son to say that the world would be a better place if there were more people in it like Mum Marge. In Robbie's eyes, she is a symbol for all that is best about the human race and will forever sit atop the highest possible pedestal.

Our Father, Robert William Macomber, Sr.

Note: The following is a tribute to our father that appeared in 2003 in our hometown newspaper, the "Castine Patriot." It was written by Stanley Levine, a dear friend of our dad who wrote a weekly column called "Stan's Stanza's." A journalist, musician, and English professor, Stan has worked in television for ABC, CBS, NBC, and public broadcasting and has written for the jazz magazine, "Downbeat." But the most impressive part of his multifaceted resume is the fact that, in 2006 at age eighty-one, Stan returned to Castine after having spent almost two years in Africa as a member of the Peace Corps. Having taught English in Cameroon, Stan is the oldest person ever to serve in the Peace Corps. He is a sterling example of one person doing his part to address what the spirit realm says is our world's most pressing problem: the plight of the Third World.

"Uncle Bob" by Stan Levine

Uncle Bob is from away because he was 1½ years old when he opted to come to Castine from Portland. Except for a hitch in the Air Force, he has already spent more than three score and ten in this town. He raised a family that still adores him. His various jobs here include grocery store manager, golf club greens-keeper, house painter, fishing boat captain, carpenter, shipyard worker, cook, and more.

He reads everything he can gets his hands on and remembers everything he reads. He is a brilliant man with a gentle soul, and, although he is my junior, he is (whether he likes it or not) my adopted father.

Talk with Uncle Bob
to hear America singing
to taste fresh corn on the cob
to feel local love beginnings.

But the senses are deceptions.
Nostalgia's not his bag.
Very today are his perceptions
(50 not 13 stars adorn his flag).

He knows how it was and is
and how it got like this.
Knows how all the players play,
whether native or from far away.

U.B. doesn't make this claim,
I do, against his wishes.
He has a story for every name,
positive, never malicious.

Castine is his launching pad
into a universe of interests:
planes, boats, poetry, Baghdad,
jazz, little more, he insists.

Well, what about baseball,
booze, family, architecture?
Yes, he's into it all,
and add heavy literature.

The most loveable part
of this most loveable elf
with the big brain, big heart:
he hasn't a clue about himself. [1]

Our Agent, Bill Gladstone

Another person who has played an absolutely vital role in the birth of this book is our agent, Bill Gladstone. Not only did he arrange distribution for it through Perseus Distribution Services, but he also provided us with invaluable guidance in the editorial process. A senior editor at publisher Harcourt Brace Jovanovich prior to starting his own literary agency, Bill's considerable experience and expertise were essential in distilling down an original manuscript that was nearly twice the length of the book you now hold in your hands.

Right from the beginning, Bill's credentials signaled to us that we were fortunate to be working with someone of his caliber. Here is how his firm's Web site (www.waterside.com) explains his professional qualifications:

> Bill Gladstone founded Waterside Productions, Inc. in 1982 and has personally placed more than 5,000 titles with dozens of publishers. He has represented stars of the technical world ranging from Peter Norton to Linus Torvalds and was responsible for selling the first "For Dummies" book, *Dos for Dummies* by Dan Gookin, which led to the phenomenal series which now has sold over 100 million copies.
>
> Mr. Gladstone advises publishing and training companies on mergers and acquisitions and has been involved with transactions ranging from six-figure to mid eight-figure deals. In addition Mr. Gladstone represents award-winning photographers such as Doug Menuez and continues to represent individual authors such as Dick Wolf, creator of the *Law & Order* Television series, Eckhart Tolle, the author of *The Power of Now*, Tom Hartmann, author of *What Would Jefferson Do?*, Marilyn Tam, author of *How to Use What You've Got to Get What You Want*, international peace advocate Dr. Ervin Laszlo, the Club of Budapest USA, acclaimed futurist Barbara Marx

Hubbard, infomercial mavens Kevin Trudeau, Dean Graziosi, and Barbara Carey, and many other outstanding authors and professionals dedicated to creating books which will inspire and improve the world.

"Improve the world." That's what Bill Gladstone truly wishes to do. As accomplished as he has been in his career, what is most telling about Bill to us is how he uses his success in the business world as a platform from which to assist his fellow human beings through a variety of organizations, endeavors, and projects.

In sum, we feel most fortunate to be working with Bill, not just because of his professional expertise, but, even more significantly, because of his genuine desire to help others. Bill is, as a close colleague and friend of his once remarked, "a really great man." But it is Bill's own words that reveal the most about one William Gladstone. Written in response to an expression of appreciation from us for his having gone above and beyond the call of duty in his efforts on this project's behalf, Bill replied by saying the following:

"My pleasure really. I do feel I am just doing what I came here to do and really is a pleasure to be helping. Glad my life allows me to be of service...."

"To be of service." That is what Heaven would have us all do.

Jane's Individual Dedication: To my sons, Justin and Caleb Satterfield

I would like to dedicate this book to my children, Justin and Caleb. You are wonderful individuals who were not afraid to believe in this book when the idea first came about. As time went on and you grew more into yourselves, you were also not afraid to question it and challenge me with your inquisitive natures. You have given up a lot of time and activities so I could get this book done, and I love you both more than you know. At times, I feel you have taught me more than I have taught you. I dedicate this book to you both.

Paul's Individual Dedication:
To my wife, Sasha Meador

I dedicate this book to my wife Sasha, who enriches my life in so many ways, makes me happier than I've ever been, and is my best friend, lover, life partner, and so much more. Thank you for loving me for who I am and making me feel so loved. Being with you makes me a better person. I feel blessed to have you as my beautiful wife and am thankful for each day we spend together. I look forward to all the years of magical times still to come and cherish the memories we already have. Thank you for sharing your life with me and doing it in such a loving and wonderful way!

Rob's Individual Dedication:
To my wife, Phyl Totaro Macomber

Before our family's communications with the spirit realm ever began, Phyl had already demonstrated the type of love, commitment, and sacrifice that one often reads about in fairy tales, but seldom finds in real life. Indeed, as I went through the many years of gut-wrenching, horrific business litigation that is described in this book, Phyl never wavered and responded at every turn with complete empathy, selfless dedication, and a willingness to do whatever was required for us to survive the financial and emotional turmoil of those times. But perhaps the best description of Phyl's devotion is found in the title of a moving Martina McBride song that describes the indestructible love of one life partner for another, "I Ain't Goin' Nowhere."

So, while you've seen how Phyl brought that same sense of determined love to the creation of this book, I can think of no better way to conclude this tribute to my eternal soulmate than by sharing with you the words from my August 16, 1997 marriage proposal to my real-life fairy-tale princess:

Once upon a time;
Eleven years ago to be exact.
Not at all far away;
At this very intersection in fact.
I found you, my Princess—Again.
And now I`would like to ask you,
My Princess,
If you would do me the honor of marrying me,
Of spending eternity together,
And living happily ever after?

ACKNOWLEDGMENTS

Because we are firm believers in the saying that "spirituality begins with gratitude," we have a lot of "thank-yous" to express.

First and foremost, we would like to thank God: for our lives, for our family, for the opportunity to collaborate with the spirit realm to help our sisters and brothers here on Earth...for all of our blessings.

We would also like to express our profound thanks to Ruth, Lily, Art, Bob, and the rest of the Spirit Guides, the invisible co-authors of this book. The three of us deeply appreciate being given the privilege of assisting them with their ongoing mission to help humanity and are moved beyond words to have been allowed such an honor.

But there really have not been three of us who have co-authored this book with the spirit realm; there have been four. That is because Cuac's wife, Phyl Totaro Macomber, has been one of this project's "Four Musketeers" from the very beginning. In fact, this book simply would not exist had Phyl not made a total commitment toward its creation. Beyond her having authored two of its chapters, she also provided ongoing financial support that allowed *Ruth Montgomery Writes Again!* to become a reality. But, by far, the most important contribution Phyl has made to this project—and for which we will never cease being thankful—was perfectly described by the Spirit Guides: *"Her heart is in it for real."*

We next would like to say thank you to our three siblings—Laura, Sarah, and Joe—for making the journey down to this beautiful planet so that we could all be Macombers. This book would simply not be had they not done so, for our perspective on Life has everything to do with our shared experience as family members together. And our experience as a family was greatly shaped by all of the love we received from our extended family members. These beloved individuals to whom we are so indebted for their loving influence include: our maternal grandparents, Verna (Graves) and Paul Allen; our paternal grandparents, Ida (Orino) and Austin Macomber; our aunts Lara Allen, Constance Allen Juvkam-Wold, Gail Macomber, Nona Thompson, and Mary Macomber Weissblum; and our uncles, Hans Juvkam-Wold, William Macomber, Russell Thompson, and Walter Weissblum.

Our Book Team
About Books, Inc.

About Books is the company that assisted us with the production of *Ruth Montgomery Writes Again!* Throughout the process of this book's creation, the following folks at About Books have provided us with *immense* help every step of the way:

Debi and Scott Flora: The owners of About Books, Debi and Scott have been a true joy to work with. A model of professionalism and integrity, the Floras are the type of people with whom anyone would enjoy doing business: bright, personable, honest, and...just plain nice. As is their son Brad, who, while doing some part-time work at About Books, displayed the same type of client-centered, people-oriented approach to business as that of his folks.

Cathy Bowman: In charge of typesetting and interior design, Cathy went out of her way to show us previews of what this book would look like in print—and did so in a most gracious manner. Indeed, her willingness to *repeatedly* go through this process was immensely helpful to this project.

Mark Bremmer: Highly skilled at his craft, Mark is the artist who designed the initial renditions of the cover for the book. He paid great attention to detail, was a true professional in every sense of the word, and demonstrated a commitment to this project that will not soon be forgotten.

Allan Burns: Senior Editor at About Books, Allan spent many, many hours editing and reediting the manuscript as it evolved into its final form. Besides having a superb command of the language, Allan's breathtaking breadth of knowledge about a multitude of topics provided us with extremely insightful feedback about the contents of this book.

Cindy Crosby and Del Greywolf: Although we may not have worked as closely with these two About Books staff members as we did with some others, that does not at all mean we have not appreciated their behind-the-scenes role in the evolution of this project.

Kate Deubert: As the person handling many of the details of taking this book from concept to reality, Kate deftly steered us through what were, for us, uncharted waters. Being able to rely on her experience was both comforting and reassuring.

Deb Ellis: A Vice President at About Books, Deb was our original contact person with the firm. From the moment she first explained how the company's services worked, Deb has exhibited an extremely methodical and easy-to-work-with manner that makes us very much look forward to doing more projects with her.

Melanie Ethridge: The proofreader for this project, Melanie's trained eye corrected things in the manuscript that we had missed, overlooked, or just simply got wrong. Indeed, her careful review of this book's contents was essential in creating the final result you now hold in your hands.

Marilyn and Tom Ross: The founders of About Books who sold the company to Debi and Scott Flora subsequent to the start of our relationship with the firm, Marilyn and Tom authored the book that has served as a roadmap for us in this project: *The Complete Guide to Self-Publishing.* So, although their presence in our family's collaboration with the spirit realm may have been short-lived, their influence has not.

The Rest of the Team

Brita Bergland: Brita has served as our in-house editor for this project. Although her keen intellect provided many significant contributions to the project, none were more instructive than when she said, "I understand that your family is excited to share the information from the spirit realm with the world, but you need to do a better job of explaining how you came to be in contact with dead spirits. It may now be a part of your family's everyday life, but it most assuredly is not for most of us."

Perseus Distribution Services: It is important to us that the staff at Perseus, the distributor for this book, know how grateful we are for their help. We appreciate their patience with the time it took to complete *Ruth Montgomery Writes Again!* and look forward to working together for a long time to come.

Ming Russell and Tiffany Bartram: An agent in her own right at Waterside Productions, Ming has served as Bill Gladstone's right-hand person in guiding us on this project. We are very grateful for her making this book a priority in her exceedingly busy schedule, including repeatedly reading through the manuscript in its various incarnations. And during Ming's time away from the office, Tiffany graciously stepped in to lend much-appreciated help as this book neared its completion.

Marion Gropen: A seasoned veteran of the publishing industry, Marion served as a consultant for the project and helped us make sense of how things work in this new field our family is entering. With an impressive background in finance, Marion explained how all of the numbers fit together on the business side of the equation, as we sought to understand how to proceed along the often scary path of self-publishing.

Donna Hill: Among other things, Donna entered into the computer hundreds of quotations we had highlighted in numerous books and clipped from various magazines. Although we ultimately only used a small fraction of these quotes, being able to have all of these excerpts at our immediate disposal made us very thankful for all of Donna's work.

Phil Huff: Phil was to be the Web master and Internet marketing specialist for this project, but died in a tragic accident prior to this book's publication. Although we were just starting to get to know him, it was obvious that he was not only an expert in his field, but, even more significantly, a wonderful soul.

Publishing Industry Professionals: Fred Ferguson, Mark Victor Hansen, John Kremer, and Bella Stander. Although contact with each of these individuals was very limited (so much so that it is doubtful they even recall the name "Macomber"), their impact on this project has been significant. Indeed, although the interactions with these seasoned veterans of the business were fleeting, we came away from each of them with knowledge that has been crucial in figuring out how to proceed in this enterprise—and for which we are extremely thankful.

Sally Rice: Sally performed multiple tasks at different stages of this project. These included transcribing ideas for the book that had been put on a microcassette recorder, as well as doing typed transcriptions of some of the handwritten messages we had received from the spirit world. For these and the many other things she did to help out, we express our gratitude.

Lloyd Rich: A leading publishing law attorney, Lloyd has provided legal advice to the project and done so in a most affable manner. Blessed not only with a sharp mind, but also an engaging personality, he has been a true pleasure to work with. And because Lloyd used to be a high-level executive on the business end of the publishing industry for both Simon & Schuster and Prentice-Hall, he has brought an exceptionally pragmatic perspective to our work together.

David Rippe: After Phil Huff's untimely passing, Bill Gladstone introduced us to David, who is founder and president of Celestia

International, a strategic marketing communications and creative services firm. That he has agreed to help us with the Web-based aspects of this project is something for which we are most grateful. Indeed, with a historical client roster that includes IBM, Wendy's, Microsoft, Sony, Navigant, Xerox, Kendle International, Ingram, 3Com, and Cisco, we consider ourselves fortunate to have the fledgling Distinctive Publications for the World join that list.

Pam Ryan: We are so glad that we came in contact with Pam just prior to this book's completion. She is a multitalented woman, not only a psychic and writer herself, but also passionate about making others aware of Ruth Montgomery's work. (Pam has an upcoming book about Ruth Montgomery that we are excited to see in print.) We are *very* thankful that she will be helping us publicize this project and getting the word out about the spirit realm's Action Plan for Planet Earth.

Linda Shelton: The best way to describe Linda's role in this enterprise is to say "Special Friend to the Project." From providing unsolicited financial support at the outset of this adventure with the spirit realm, to being an ongoing source of emotional support and an ardent believer in its merits, Linda has left her imprint on this project in a most memorable way...and on our hearts—which say, "Thank You!"

Maryrose Snopkowski: Sister to Phyl Totaro Macomber and experienced graphic designer, "Rosie" has made contributions to this project literally too numerous to mention. Besides lending her professional expertise to this endeavor and being willing to drop everything repeatedly to help in whatever way needed, she has generously donated computer equipment and also surprised us with a gift from her firm, Revelations Advertising, to ours, by having company jackets made up for Distinctive Publications for the World. Beloved family member, cherished friend, respected professional colleague: Rosie is all of these to us—and more.

David Wilk: Like David Rippe, David is another first-class professional with an enlightened worldview, to whom Bill Gladstone referred us. Formerly a Vice President at our distributor, Perseus, David serves as Marketing Director for this project. An individual with an extensive resume that includes executive positions held in publishing, wholesaling, and distribution, David has worked in the book industry for more than thirty years. We are blessed to be the recipient of his vast expertise.

INDIVIDUAL ACKNOWLEDGMENTS

Jane

Besides my two sons, Justin and Caleb, there have been many other children who have believed in this book and the automatic writing process. Two in particular stand out whom I would like to thank for their encouragement and belief.

First, Alex Echeverri. Your sincere and continuing question, "When's your book coming out, Jane?" gave me more drive and dedication to finish it than you know. Thank you for allowing me to be a part of your life and believing in me.

Second, I would like to thank Isaac Hightower, a person who has a strong spirit and unmatched sense of humor, especially when imitating a certain late night television psychic! Your immediate belief in this project and support of me, as well as your fiery spirit and sense of humor, have left their marks on me for life. Thanks for being you, Isaac!

Although we have collectively thanked our family, I would like to thank the first two people who knew about my automatic writing: my sisters, Laura and Sarah. You are my best friends, and I love you both very much.

I would also like to thank our mother, Margaret Macomber. I couldn't imagine life without you and cannot believe I am so blessed to have you for my mother. I love you more than you know.

The same goes for our father, Robert Macomber. Your passion for life is a sight to behold. I love you, Dad.

The first person outside of the family to know about the writing (even before Rob and Paul) was my fellow parent and friend, Jackie Pinn. Jackie, thank you for listening to me with interest and without judgment. You are a great lady, and I am blessed to know you.

When first starting this book and trying to get the information about it out, we wrote to several individuals we thought would be interested. Two of these people responded immediately with phone calls and gave this project a huge confidence boost with their knowledge and faith in our cause.

The first is Scott Jones. To a man who is doing so much himself to bring peace to the world, thank you for your wisdom and belief. I have enjoyed our few, yet inspirational talks and hope we can work together in the future.

Next, I would like to thank Jan Tober for her quick response and instant belief in what we are doing. Although we only spoke once, I took a lot away from our conversation and am honored that you called. Your own life's work with the *Kryon* book series is a great example to follow.

Two of my biggest supporters are my friends Marcie Crago and Julie Jones. This book would literally not have been possible without your support and faith. Words cannot express the gratitude I feel toward both of you. You have shown me so much support, in so many ways, and I am truly blessed to have you as my close friends.

Although I haven't known Phil Hardwick as long as some of my other friends, he has been on the front lines in being a champion for our cause from day one. Thanks for being so open and accepting of this project and of me from literally the very first time I met you.

Another person who helped in more than one way was Linda Shelton. Your generosity and faith are greatly appreciated. Thank you.

This list of "thank yous" would not be complete without my wonderful group of friends from the James Van Praagh weekend I attended at The Omega Institute, those who belong to the *Mediums*

R Us group, as well as everyone else I met there. Your openness, support, and belief have helped me more than you could ever know. The warmth and generosity of spirit I feel from you all is a treasured gift I carry with me every day. Thank you from the bottom of my heart.

Another lady who shares her spirit just as freely and lovingly is Linda Keen. Thank you so much for listening to me and being a part of what I am doing.

There are some people who, although not directly involved with this book, have been by my side over the years and have been pillars of strength for me when I needed it most.

The first is my wonderful second mother and grandmother to my boys, Georgia Satterfield. I never could have made it this far without your love. You have given me a rare gift that some only dream of. I love you more than you know.

The next person who has always been there for me over the last eleven-and-a-half years is Carolyn Toomey. You are a wonderful, wonderful woman, and I hope we have many more garden parties throughout the years!

Words cannot describe how lucky I am to know my lifelong friend, Ronnie Bakeman. I love that you are always there for me but that you also challenge me, question me, and keep me on my toes. We have shared so much over the years, and I know that no matter what I am—into "voodoo writing" as you call it, or anything else—that you are there for me. From Maco to Bake-o, thanks for being you and being my friend.

Another person who has had a profound effect on my life is my friend Tony Burkhart, my counselor from years ago—but even more than that, a truly great human being. Tony, even though we haven't been in touch in years, you are at the top of my list and one of my favorite people in the whole world.

Another great friend from years past is Henry Canby. I will be forever grateful for your wisdom and insight. I think of you often and am so glad we met you. You're another one of my favorites.

And how could I forget the three people who made this whole project possible, my brothers, Rob and Paul Macomber, and Rob's wife, Phyl. Without their drive, belief, energy, and support, this project would not have been possible. They are the pillars that have held me up, especially in times of doubt.

Phyl's sister, Rosie, also needs to be mentioned here. The computers, expertise, and most of all, love, that you provided to this project do not go unnoticed. You're the greatest, Rosie!

And last, but certainly not least, the biggest thank you to Ruth Montgomery, Arthur Ford, Lily, Bob Montgomery, and all the other "Guides" who write through me! I am honored to carry on your work.

Paul

I would like to thank all the people, friends, and family in my life whom I have ever known who have been a part of my life and helped me to be who I am today. There are far too many of you to name all individually, but it is our relationships, our experiences together, and all that we've shared that makes me the person I am today. I thank you all from the bottom of my heart and the depths of my soul for all the wonderful times we've had—and, also, for the not-so-great ones that we've gotten through, as it is all of life's experiences that make us who we are today.

There are a few people to whom I'd like to pay special thanks:

Our mom for teaching me that love is absolutely the best and most important thing there is in this life. For her selfless way of always putting her family first and showing me that giving is better than receiving. I couldn't imagine having a mother who is more thoughtful, loving, caring, and kind. Thank you, Mom, for being you!

And profound thanks to our dad, for the love he's shown me and the sacrifices he's made to make me a better person. Not only for being my father, but also a confidant and best friend. Our daily phone calls are the highlight of my day!

To our Grammy Al, Grammy Ida, and Grampa Austin, for all their love and support throughout my years growing up in Castine. To our Uncle Bill, for his love and care throughout the years and shared discussions on the spiritual aspects of life. To our Aunt Lara for introducing me to that first book that started my exploration of the spiritual side of life. To our Aunt Mary, for her love and friendship, whose generosity made Dad's new house a possibility. To my Uncle Russ and Aunt Connie, who have since passed, who made me realize as a child that aunts and uncles are truly people who love you dearly.

Cuac

Although there are many people whom I wish to thank, I will start with a collection of individuals whose presence in my life either influenced me in a direction that ultimately led to my participation in this book, reflected the ideals it attempts to embody, or both. And although I list almost all of them alphabetically, there are two who will be taken out of order: my siblings and co-authors, Jane and Paul.

Jane and Paul Macomber

Because the word "together" has defined my collaboration on this project with Jane and Paul since its very inception, that is the only appropriate way for me to go about expressing my feelings of gratitude to the two of them.

There are many things that make me grateful to Jane and Paul: for taking on this project at a time when both of their lives were already seemingly filled to capacity; for voicing their intuitive feelings early on to me that they each had a sense that 50% of the project's profits were supposed to be given away; for their continued belief in this endeavor, even when it seemed like it was taking forever to get this first book completed; and, most of all, for making this collaboration with the spirit realm *just plain fun!*

For the past five years, I have gone to sleep most nights so excited about this project that I literally haven't been able to wait to wake up to get back at it. And although part of the reason that I've frequently headed downstairs in the wee hours of the morning to my office to get back to work on this book has been because of the excitement of the adventure and the thrill of working with Ruth and the Spirit Guides, just as significant has been the sense of incredible enthusiasm I've felt as the result of sharing the most amazing experience of my life with people I love. Yes, indeed, it's tough to beat doing something you love, with people you love…"together."

Lara Allen

Although I could easily write much about all of my other aunts and uncles, both here and on The Other Side, who have been so *incredibly* good to me (and will, in a future book that includes "family" as one of its focuses), there are two to whom I owe a special debt of gratitude with respect to my involvement with this book: our Aunt Lara, our mother's sister, and Uncle Bill, our father's brother.

If you're reading this section of the book, then it probably means you've read it in its entirety and are already familiar with the absolutely essential role Lara played in the evolution of my perspective on spiritual matters by introducing me to Kyriacos Markides's books about the spiritual healer from Cyprus, Daskalos. There are not enough words in the English language for me to thank her adequately for having shared that material with me. Had she not done so, I almost certainly would not be involved in the writing of this book.

Yet Lara's positive influence on my life started long before she gave me my first Daskalos book. Throughout the years of my childhood, she gave me books she thought I might enjoy, went on walks with me along the beach in Castine and taught me to appreciate the beauty of the driftwood and pieces of glass worn smooth by the sea, and took me to concerts to hear classical music at the University of Maine–just to name a few. And during my adult years, Lara has done everything possible to assist me in the longstanding litigation in which I became embroiled. Whether it has been providing financial help, preparing welcome meals that served as a respite from the pitched legal battles, or simply offering a caring ear during particularly trying times, she has gone out of her way at each and every turn to help. Thus, it is most important to me that Lara Allen knows how very grateful her nephew Robbie is for everything.

Verna Graves Allen

I will express my thankfulness for all that my three deceased grandparents, Ida Orino Macomber, Austin Macomber, and Paul Thomas Allen, did for me in a subsequent book. I wish at this time, however, to acknowledge the many things Verna Grave Allen, our Grammy Al, has done for me during the course of my lifetime.

Grammy Al literally watched me come into this world, as the delivering physician, Dr. Harold Babcock, thoughtfully asked her if she would like to come into the delivery room as I was being born...and she has looked out for me ever since. When I was five years old, she gave me my first book, a copy of *Black Beauty*. Throughout my youth, Grammy constantly emphasized the importance of education and how books were "friends" to be treasured. As I became an adult and entered the business world, she often offered me wise counsel. I listened closely, for, since becoming a real estate broker, insurance salesperson, and notary public all on the same day that she became legally eligible to do so at age twenty-one, she had been a lifelong businesswoman herself. And when she and I both became enmeshed in the business litigation that is chronicled in this book, she, over and over again, provided me with financial assistance to help me survive.

Indeed, as I sit here writing these words at age forty-eight, it just struck me that I am now exactly half my grandmother's current age of ninety-six; I only hope I can end up being just half the human being she has been.

But of all of the countless things Grammy Al has done for me and fond memories I have of her, the most special of all came in the form of a two-sentence statement she uttered to me in 1990. She and I were beginning the drive back to Maine from a trip to Massachusetts (that included seeing her deceased husband's namesake, my brother and co-author, Paul Allen Macomber, graduate from college) and were crossing over the Mystic River Bridge heading out of Boston when Grammy said, "Paul grew up somewhere down there in Charlestown. I've never visited his childhood home, but I remember the address." And so the two of us got off at the next exit. Not only did we find Grampa Paul's home at 9 Prospect Street, but also the very Charlestown Five Cents Savings Bank building where the two of them had met so many decades before. Afterward, as we got back on the Mystic River Bridge, with the sky fading into a beautiful sunset, Grammy Al said to me, "Thank you. I didn't think I'd ever see Paul's home before I died." A true highlight in life that was almost mystical.

Leslie C. Brewer

I have known Mr. Brewer since I originally went to Bar Harbor in 1978. When Charlie Sawyer first introduced my dad and me to him at that time so long ago, however, little did I know how important a role this man would play in my life. At various times, he has worn many differing hats in assisting me: business partner, adviser, financier, problem solver, and throughout—loyal friend. He often co-taught many of the Courses In Life that Professor Charlie Sawyer held for me and has always been incredibly giving in terms of his time, formidable talents, and God-given ability as a thinker.

Mr. Brewer is the type of person who has always been actively involved in the business community, Bar Harbor's municipal government, numerous local institutions, and charitable organizations too numerous to count. I do not take lightly having had the opportunity to get to know Mr. Brewer well enough to understand his generous nature and to witness firsthand the personal commitment he makes to the causes in which he believes. To the contrary, I will always possess a deep appreciation for Mr. Brewer's making me one of those causes.

Lorraine DeSimone

The mother of Rob and his brother Jamie DeSimone, Lorraine DeSimone has played a huge part in my life from the time I was nineteen. As a person who had recently retired from the restaurant business prior to Rob and me getting into the moped business in 1978, Mrs. DeSimone came up to Maine to help them get the enterprise off the ground. As it turned out, she would be an integral part of my life, as she has "been there" ever since.

There are numerous things for which I must thank Mrs. DeSimone: for devoting years of her life to helping Rob and me in business; for the great meals she used to cook for us (her fried chicken is the best I have ever eaten); the multiple times that she was there for us with financial assistance; the set of golf clubs she so generously gave to Phyl; and even a car she gave to me…the list could go on and on. But what I wish most to express my appreciation for is not one specific thing, but rather the sense of genuine kindness and goodness behind all of these acts of caring. For that I am especially grateful.

Elizabeth Hardwick

When I was in grade school, the white fence on Elizabeth's lawn formed the right-field fence for our schoolyard softball games on Castine's Town Common. But it was my high school years that provided my mind's most vivid memories and my heart's everlasting gratitude with respect to Elizabeth Hardwick.

A wonderful friend to the entire Macomber family, Elizabeth provided summer employment for me with odd jobs such as lawn mowing and painting; she sent very generous checks to me during the winter months during my time at Milton; and, in my final year of high school, she wrote a letter of reference for me during the college admissions process. But the most lasting thing that this woman of letters did for me during these formative years was to engage me in stimulating conversations about books, thus forever reaffirming to a young boy their extreme importance in Life.

William F. Macomber, Sr.

Our "Uncle Bill" is my godfather and our father Bob's brother. From the time I was born, Uncle Bill has been nothing but good to me. Ever since I was a little boy, I have felt a relationship with Uncle Bill that is difficult to put into words and has encompassed many things: giving me a generous check when I was heading off to Milton; helping with the start-up of the moped business; and forgiving a long-standing debt when my litigation troubles wreaked financial havoc in my life.

Although there are many other things that Uncle Bill has done for me and are special to me, it is in recent years that we have added an element to our relationship that has been most meaningful: we have both delved into the spiritual side of life and attempted to grapple with the mysteries of being. The conversations about this subject with Uncle Bill while indulging in his famed spaghetti dinners (which, being Italian, Phyl loves) are ones that I have treasured and are an ongoing source of enjoyment to me.

As Uncle Bill and I have read books and listened to tapes about spiritual topics, the central theme that we have—not surprisingly—gleaned from our inquiries is that LOVE is the single most important component of existence. As I can well attest, that is something that comes quite naturally to our Uncle Bill. Indeed, the love and support I have felt from him as this book project has unfolded has been a *great* source of strength for me as I have sought to follow through on my assignment from the spirit realm.

Frank D. Millet

As Milton Academy's Director of Admissions and Financial Aid at the time of my application for entrance to that school, Mr. Millet was the person singly most responsible for my being able to attend Milton. Simply put, he made it possible for this son of a fisherman and carpenter to enjoy the privilege of spending four glorious years inside the white-fenced boundaries of that special campus located in zip code 02186, a place that truly changed my life, helped mold my mind, and forever touched my heart. For myself and generations of other Milton students of the past sixty-five years, Mr. Millet was—and is—Milton Academy.

As Mr. Millet well knows, when I think of him, I am reminded of the wisdom found in two quotations about a term that he defines—"character"—as shown below:

> *"Education has for its object the formation of character."*[1]
> —Herbert Spencer

> *"Life in spirit is governed in a truly democratic manner. You arrive into the realm that you have earned through your actions. The amount of money and connections you have in the physical world hold no power in this land. Your character is your position."*[2]
> —Mary T. Brown, *Life After Death*

In short, the same type of wisdom that Frank D. Millet has been teaching young people for decades.

Charles W. Sawyer, Jr. (1921–2002)

I first met Charlie Sawyer during a trip our dad and I made to Charlie's office in the winter of 1978 when I was nineteen. Charlie was a very successful businessman who took me under his wing and helped make the moped rental business idea of Rob DeSimone and mine become a reality. As the years unfolded, Charlie became many things to me in business: partner, financier, and mentor. More significantly, however, Charlie was also many things to me personally: friend, sounding board, and second father. But perhaps the word that best describes what Charlie was to me is "teacher."

Charlie made a conscious effort to glean the salient lessons learned from his own experiences in life and pass the nuggets of wisdom contained therein on to me. While I sometimes succeeded at properly applying the teachings that Charlie offered and at other times severely tried the patience of my Professor In Life as I stumbled on different parts of the curriculum, I always found wisdom in the words of "The Olde Master." As a person who quietly did a great deal for numerous individuals and institutions, Charlie will forever serve as a sterling example to me of the importance of each person doing whatever they can to help others. For all that Charles W. Sawyer, Jr., did for me, for all that he taught me, for all of the memorable meals and conversations, and, especially, for all of the caring in his heart behind his efforts, I am eternally grateful.

As much as I miss Charlie, however, there is someone who feels his absence even more keenly than myself: his widow, Mrs. Barbara Sawyer. Since Charlie's passing, I have gotten to know why he said that she was "a true lady who has real class." And in keeping with Mrs. Sawyer's beloved husband's sharing of life lessons with me, she has provided me with a kernel of wisdom about the pain of losing one's life partner that can only come from personal experience: "You don't know until you get there." That one sentence has been more instructive than she probably knows, as it has forever enhanced my sense of appreciation of life in general and reinforced for me the importance of thinking of others.

Gerald "Chick" Scaccia

Because Phyl's "Uncle Chick" helped raise her, she once said, "Most people don't think of three people when they think of their parents, but I do." During the nearly two decades that Phyl and I have been together, I have grown to understand why, for I have come to love him dearly myself (and not just because he's a truly great Red Sox fan). So much so, that when we got married, Uncle Chick served as one of my best men.

Since, at its essence, this book is about the power of love, I will share with you why few people I have ever met have "walked the walk" of love like Gerald P. Scaccia. When Chick's father Caesar was called home by God at a time way too early for us mere mortals to understand, his son Gerald stepped up to the plate in the batter's box of Life and hit one out of the park. Out of love for his mother because she needed him to provide for her and look after her, Chick made significant personal sacrifices in his own life so that he could be there for her...*love*, the most powerful force in the universe. Gerald "Chick" Scaccia is one of God's children who get what it's really all about.

Bertha and Leonard Totaro

Bertha and Leonard are Phyl's parents. They are "Mom Totaro" and "Dad Totaro" to me.

Although there are many qualities of Mom Totaro's that mean a great deal to me, the one that stands out most in my mind in the context of this book is her incredible faith in God. A very devout Catholic all of her life, Bertha Totaro truly *believes*. Most impressive has been her dedication to prayer and confidence in it. Time and time again, I have seen Mom Totaro's faith allow her to derive tremendous strength. This has been a true inspiration to me.

Mom Totaro, however, is not alone in her belief in prayer, as her husband Leonard also believes mightily in its ability to help those of us here on Earth. In fact, he has shared with me that, for years now, he has prayed daily for this book project and its future. That is Leonard F. Totaro through and through: asking for others and not himself. A true giant of a man, Dad Totaro is a person I thought about before I ever met him. I say that because prior to meeting Phyl, I never thought that I would find anyone with whom I would want to spend my entire life...but I knew, if she did exist, just the kind of human being her daddy would have to be in order for her to have turned out to be who she was.

I will conclude this tribute to Mom and Dad Totaro by sharing with you words of thanks I wrote to them years ago. Although sent at the time to express my appreciation for the magnificent wedding that they gave Phyl and me, they accurately reflect how I feel about my Totaro parents in general:

> *I can only say that I am truly humbled by the extent of your goodness, awestruck by the depth of your love, and blessed by God for allowing me to be your son. I will be just as grateful on the day that I draw my last breath as I am now and will love you forever!*

As special a role as the aforementioned individuals have played in the direction of my life leading up to this book, there are many others to whom I would also like to express appreciation. They are:

Beloved Aunts and Uncles from Phyl's Side of the Family: Although Jane, Paul, and I have paid tribute to our aunts and uncles on our parents' side of the family, I also wish to recognize how loved I have been made to feel by Phyl's aunts and uncles...who are now mine. They are: Nellie (who is now on The Other Side) and Samuel Polizzi, Evelyn and Lou Totaro, Parma and Anthony Totaro, and Patty and Dominic Totaro.

Chief Cheerleader–Jamie DeSimone: It is impossible to imagine any-one being more enthusiastic about this project than Jamie DeSimone has been. Already blessed with three decades of unwavering friend-ship with Jamie, I guess I shouldn't have been surprised by his wholehearted support of this book. Yet the degree to which he rooted for this endeavor truly touched me in the most wonderful way. But then again, that's what Jamie DeSimone does best…touch people's hearts.

Comrades in Life: Terry Bonus, Andrew Bowden, David Bowden, Alan Brewer, John Brushwein, Michael Donahue, David Einhorn, Rip Kinkel, Paul Levinson, Bill Macomber, Jr., Michael Macomber, Ken Oberg, John Prasch, Dave Prouty, Wendell Reilly, Paul Steeves, Mark Van Allen, David Weiler, Harris Weiner, and Steve Winthrop. As they well know, although most of us may not see each other as often as we used to earlier in life, time will *never* diminish how spe-cial our shared experiences along the way are to me.

Rob DeSimone and Jeff Butterfield: As with my tribute to Jane and Paul, I group these two dear friends of mine together because "*to-gether*" is perhaps the best word to reflect what our shared experience symbolizes to me. With Rob, I have traveled the Road of Life for more than three decades and, with Jeff, nearly a quarter of a century. The three of us have seen our fair share of ups and downs as we encountered turbulent waters in the business world but rode out the storm arm in arm…*together*.

The depth of Rob's and Jeff's friendship was never in evidence more than when I explained to them more than a decade ago that I had read some books by a woman named Ruth Montgomery and would be splitting my time between Maine and Vermont. Although it was obvious that my unusual decision would impact their own lives with respect to our mutual business endeavors, the two of them were as gracious and understanding as can be imagined. And now that Ruth's work has become a part of my own, I am happy to report that both Rob and Jeff are quite aware that I hope this project progresses to the point where they can join me in it if they wish so that we might work helping others... *together.*

Michael Dunton: Mike once shared with me a book that had had a profound impact on his view of Life, *The Peace Pilgrim*. Reading it turned out to be one of the important steps for me along the path in my own journey. Though this may have been many years ago, my gratitude for having been exposed to that wisdom-filled book has only increased since then.

Kim Foley: Although Kim is someone whom I've never met or even spoken with on the phone, she has turned out to be someone who has been a source of unexpected support for me on this project. Since this good-hearted soul who busies herself with her own work to help others reached out to me by e-mail after learning about this book, we have had an e-mail dialogue about matters spiritual that has been truly uplifting. I hope that Phyl and I someday get to meet Kim and her husband.

The Hanover Inn: During the several years that it has taken us to complete the manuscript for this book, much of my writing time was spent working on a laptop computer in the dining facilities of this lovely establishment in Hanover, New Hampshire. Often arriving there early in the morning to begin my workday with breakfast, I came to view the Inn as a "home away from home" and a place where the entire staff made me feel exceedingly welcome. So, in recognition of their many kindnesses over the years, I would like to thank Gary Bomhower, Alan Chow, Dick DuMez, Rick Folt, Christina Gorman, Matt Guaraldi, Ellen Harp, Alex Herrera, Barbara Merrill, Jim Miller, Tom Rice, Jaspal Sappal, and Shirley St. Peter. And then there are Betsy, Carlene, Donna, James, JoLyn, Judy, Julia, Julie, Misty, Steve, Tim, and many others whose names I am not familiar with, but whose friendly faces have brightened many of my days spent in Hanover. Indeed, when I was in the hospitality business myself, I once read in a book about the industry that what was being offered to the public wasn't simply a meal to eat or a room in which to sleep, but rather "an experience that hopefully would be memorable." Well, I can well attest to the fact that the folks at The Hanover Inn do just that and live up to that ideal on a daily basis.

John Hynes: A high school classmate of mine, John is also the person who, at a Halloween Dance at Chatham High School in October of 1973, introduced me to Rob DeSimone. During that school year, John and I began a dialogue about the spiritual side of life that was resumed in the two years prior to this book's publication. As we have exchanged various quotations that we've found moving and offered each other feedback about our respective paths toward attempting to understand "The Big Picture," it has been most meaningful to see how the early ruminations of two young boys have evolved into an ongoing investigation of Life for each as adults.

Sasha Meador: That Paul's wife has been so understanding of Paul's commitment to this project is something for which I will be ever grateful. Not only has she been supportive of Paul's desire to help others through this book, but she has also demonstrated how very generous a person she is by the degree to which she and Paul do things for our parents and other family members. In short, I could not ask for a better sister-in-law and am most appreciative of who she is as a person.

Meditation Group–Maine: To the meditation group in Orono led by Professor Kyriacos Markides, I owe an eternal debt of gratitude. "Group," as Phyl and I came to call it, was comprised of a wide cross-section of individuals. Besides Kyriacos and his wonderful wife, Emily, and faculty colleague Susan Greenwood (who organized the sessions), Group included folks from all walks of life and soon became a cherished event on the calendar. Group was a place where all of us could, as Professor Markides once noted, "talk about things that, a few hundred years ago, would have gotten us all burned at the stake."

Meditation Group–Vermont: Introduced to a different "Group" by Emma Bragdon, Phyl and I were fortunate to find a new collection of people in Vermont with whom to meditate, discuss metaphysical matters, and just simply enjoy ourselves. In addition to Emma, Marty Cain, Anne Dean, and Eugenie and John Smallman constituted the circle of individuals who soon became our friends...friends who gave helpful feedback on parts of the manuscript and whose interest in this project in general has meant a great deal to me.

Justin and Caleb Satterfield: Jane's two sons have had their mother devote large blocks of time to this project. Because this has required significant interruptions in their family life, it is important to me that my nephews know that I am deeply grateful for their recognition of the importance of their mother's work on this endeavor...and that I love the two of them *very* much.

Paul Smith: A writer himself, Paul is someone who has authored a screenplay about Ruth Montgomery's life–which I hope gets made into a film as soon as possible so that the world can learn more about this remarkable woman. Although we have never met each other and have gotten to know each other solely by e-mail, Paul's interest in this project and encouragement have been very meaningful to me.

Supporters: Although there have been many, many people who have been supportive of this project, there are some whose encouragement to Phyl and me has provided an extra boost: David Anthony, Bev Bilsky, Terry Bonus, Kathy Boudreau, Debbie Boyce, Deb Butterfield, Joan Campbell, Ellen and Ralph Cameron, Tracy Churchill, Jan Crow, Belinda Decker, Jamie DeSimone, Olga DeSimone, David Einhorn, Kim Foley, Rose Golini and husband Steve, Johann Grobler, Frannie and Geoff Guzy, Eilenn Haddon,

Jenn Harper, Deb and Tim Hartt, Peter Haubrich, Bernie Hils, Ron King, Kathryn Livermore, Donna and Nibs Loughney and their daughter, Collen, Bah Macomber (my brother Joe's wife, whose requests for status reports on this project were much appreciated), Bill and Leah Macomber (whose encouraging e-mails along the way helped keep me going), Danielle Macomber (my beloved niece, who is my sister Laura's daughter and who still sometimes refers to me as "Robbie-Dog" in reference to putting her on my back and crawling around the floor when she was a toddler), Terry Ballentine Martin, Chris Mattern, Don Meyers, Heather Murray, Kwame Nyarko (my brother-in-law who is married to my sister Sarah and whose daughters, Samantha and Serena, are bright lights in their Uncle Robbie and Aunt Phyl's life), Linda Orr, Darlene Petke, Pam-Pam Polizzi, Roseanne Polizzi, John Prasch and Janice Wightman, Jean Rock, Max Rottersman, Tammy Stanwood, Linda Darlene Stern, Fran Stevens, Warren Strout, Alison from Hilde's Salon, and, last, but most certainly not least, the members of Phyl's spinning class at the Dartmouth gym and their partners, Art and Rosemary, Jane, Jodi and Wally, Karen and Tom, Kathryn, Kit, and Nora and Tom.

Although there are many other family members (including lots of cherished cousins, who will be recognized as this project progresses), friends, and business colleagues who have been an important part of the road that led to my involvement, I will "put a period" on things—but only for now—and wrap up this enjoyable exercise in gratitude. But I do so most reluctantly, for I firmly believe that, when it's all said and done, people are what Life is all about.

NOTES

Chapter 1: "The Most Amazing Experience of Our Lives"

1. Ruth Montgomery with Joanne Garland, *Ruth Montgomery: Herald of the New Age* (New York: Doubleday/Dolphin, 1986) 1.
2. Ruth Montgomery, *The World to Come* (New York: Three Rivers Press, 1999) 153. First published 1999 in hardcover by Harmony Books.

Chapter 2: So Just Who Was Ruth Montgomery Anyway?

1. Montgomery with Garland, 13–14.
2. Ibid., 27–36.
3. Ibid., 37–38.
4. Ruth Montgomery, *Hail to the Chiefs: My Life and Times with Six Presidents* (New York: Coward-McCann, Inc., 1970) 14–22.
5. Bart Barnes, "Ruth Montgomery Dies; Wrote Account of Seer Jeane Dixon," *The Washington Post*, 19 June 2001, sec. B, p. 7.
6. Ibid.
7. *Naples Daily News*, 11 June 2001, sec. DN, p. 2.

Chapter 3: Ruth, the Conventional Author

1. Montgomery with Garland, 104–105.
2. Ibid., 108–109.
3. Ibid., 115–116.
4. Montgomery, *Hail to the Chiefs*, inside front and back flaps.

Chapter 4: Ruth, the Automatic Writer

1. James Van Praagh, *Heaven and Earth: Making the Psychic Connection* (New York: Pocket Books, 2002) 85. First published in hardcover 2001 by Free Press.
2. Montgomery, *The World to Come*, 11–12.

3. Montgomery with Garland, 103.

4. Ruth Montgomery, *A Search for the Truth* (New York: William Morrow & Company, Inc., 1966) 94; and Montgomery and Garland, 100–103.

5. Montgomery, *A Search for the Truth*, 94–100.

Chapter 5: Ruth Montgomery's Spirit Guides

1. Montgomery, *A Search for the Truth*, 54, 109.

2. Ibid., 109–113.

3. Ruth Montgomery, *Companions Along the Way* (New York: Coward, McCann & Geoghegan, Inc., 1974) 215–216.

4. Montgomery, *The World to Come*, 23–24.

5. Ibid.

6. Montgomery, *Companions Along the Way*, 216–217.

7. Ibid., 218–219.

8. Ibid., 219.

9. Frank C. Tribbe, *The Arthur Ford Anthology: Writings by and about America's Sensitive of the Century* (Nevada City, CA: Blue Dolphin, 1999) 7–13.

10. Ibid., 7–11.

11. Ibid., 8.

12. Montgomery with Garland, 92–98.

13. Ruth Montgomery, *A World Beyond: A Startling Message from the Eminent Psychic Arthur Ford from Beyond the Grave* (New York: Coward, McCann & Geoghegan, Inc., 1971) 17.

14. Tribbe, 13.

15. Ibid., 147–148.

16. Ibid., 165.

17. Montgomery, *A World Beyond*, 4–6.

18. Ibid., 180.

19. Montgomery with Garland, 201.

20. Tatiana Elmanovich, *Ruth Montgomery: A Conversation in Naples, Florida on April 2, 2000*, http://www.tanika.com/ruth.htm.

Chapter 6: Ruth Montgomery: Psychic Author Extraordinaire

1. Barnes, sec. B, p. 7; and Montgomery with Garland, 109.

2. Montgomery with Garland, 109–113.

3. Montgomery, *A Search for the Truth*, inside front and back flaps; and Montgomery with Garland, 109–113.

4. Montgomery, *A Search for the Truth*, 11.

5. Montgomery, *Hail to the Chiefs*, 305–306.

6. Ruth Montgomery, *Here and Hereafter* (New York: Coward-McCann, Inc., 1968), inside front and back flaps and 13–14; and Montgomery with Garland, 114–133.

7. Montgomery with Garland, 134.

8. Ibid., 135.

9. Ibid., 162–164.

10. Ibid., 145–164.

11. Montgomery, *A World Beyond*, inside front and back flaps and 3–7.

12. Ibid.

13. Ibid.

14. Montgomery with Garland, 166–170; Ruth Montgomery, *Born to Heal* (New York: Coward, McCann & Geoghegan, 1973) inside front and back flaps and 9–16; Montgomery, *Born to Heal*, "Book Description" [online advertising], www.Amazon.com; and Montgomery, *A Search for the Truth*, 212–230.

15. Montgomery with Garland, 171–177.

16. Ruth Montgomery, *Companions Along the Way* (New York: Coward, McCann & Geoghegan, Inc., 1974) inside front and back flaps.

17. Ibid.

18. Montgomery with Garland, 178–179.

19. Montgomery with Garland, 184–192; and Ruth Montgomery, *The World Before* (New York: Coward, McCann & Geogegan, Inc., 1976) inside front and back flaps.

20. Montgomery with Garland, 184–192.

21. Ruth Montgomery, *Strangers Among Us* (New York: Coward, McCann & Geogegan, Inc., 1979) inside front and back flaps; and Montgomery with Garland, 193–210.

22. Ibid.

23. Ibid.

24. Ibid.

25. Ibid.

26. Ibid.

27. Ibid.

28. Ruth Montgomery, *Threshold to Tomorrow* (New York: G.P. Putnam's Sons, 1982) 22.

29. Ibid., 23–42.

30. Ibid.

31. Ibid., 10–11.

32. Ruth Montgomery, *Aliens Among Us* (New York: G.P. Putnam's Sons, 1985) inside front and back flaps; Montgomery with Garland, 218–232; and Montgomery, *The World to Come*, 39–40, 88–96.

33. Montgomery, *Aliens Among Us*, inside front and back flaps; and Montgomery with Garland, 218–232.

34. Montgomery, *Aliens Among Us*, 9, 88–96.

35. Montgomery with Garland, viii and ix.

36. Montgomery, *The World to Come*, 19, 66–77.

37. Ibid., 26–30.

38. Ibid., 30–38.

39. Ibid., 26–38.

40. Montgomery, *A Search for the Truth*, 60.

Chapter 10: Some Details about Rob "Cuac" Totaro Macomber

1. Friendly's Web site, "Menu: Desserts—Sundaes," http://www.friendlys.com.

2. Ted Williams as told to John Underwood, *My Turn at Bat: The Story of My Life* (New York: Simon & Schuster, 1969) 20.

Chapter 13: Paul's Spiritual Background

1. Mary T. Browne, *Life After Death: A Renowned Psychic Reveals What Happens to Us When We Die* (New York: Ivy Books, 1994) unnumbered page opposite inside front cover.

Chapter 14: 1992–1996: An Inferno of Litigation, Non-Stop Fear, and a Search for Answers

1. Kyriacos C. Markides, *Homage to the Sun: The Wisdom of the Magus of Strovolos* (London, England: Penguin Books, Ltd.) 7.

2. Betty J. Eadie, *Embraced by the Light* (Placerville, CA: Gold Leaf Press, 1992) 51.

3. Ibid., 42–49, 69.

4. Ibid., 41–42, 53.

5. Ibid., 61.

6. Ibid.

Chapter 17: And While Phyl Was in Italy

1. Montgomery, *Strangers Among Us*, 225–233.

Chapter 27: The July 14, 2002, Transmissions: Some Commentary on Their Importance

1. Eadie, 61.

Chapter 28: Arthur, Bob, and a Protector Named Jesus

1. "The Atheist and the Materialist," *Ladies Home Journal* (October 1991): 215; Celebrity Atheist List, http://www.celebatheists.com/index.php?title=Katharine_Hepburn.

Chapter 40: Heaven's "Action Plan for Planet Earth"

1. Bono, "Bono at TED: Bono's Address as inaugural winner of the TED Prize, February 24, 2005," *TED——Technology Entertainment Design*, 24 February 2005, http://www.ted.com/ted2005/moments/bono_transcript.cfm. "About TED," *TED——Technology Entertainment Design*, http://www.ted.com/about/introduction/flash_page.cfm.

Chapter 42: Guatemala: A Sacred Place with a Special Role

1. "The World Factbook: Guatemala," *CIA*, http://www.cia.gov/cia/publications/factbook/geos/gt.html1#Intro.

2. "Eucalyptus," *herbs200.com*, http://www.herbs2000.com/herbs/herbs_eucalyptus.htm.

3. Ibid.

4. "The Petén, Guatemala," *Archeological Research in the Petén—NASA*, http://www.weather.mfsc.nasa.gov/archeology/peten.html.

5. Janet Kornblum, "Conjoined twins separated at last," *USA Today*, 7 August 2002, sec. A, p. 1.

6. Emma Bragdon, *Spiritual Alliances* (Woodstock, VT: Lightening Up Press, 2002) 103.

Chapter 43: The Special Power of Celebrities to Help Save the World

1. Joseph Kahn, "Why We Feel Cheated When Celebrities Cheat," *The Boston Globe*, 7 June 2003, sec. D, p. 6.

2. Carol Brooks, "What Celebrity Worship Says About Us," *USA Today*, 14 September 2003, sec. A, p. 21.

3. Ibid.

4. Bob Tomas, "Hollywood Iconic Rebel Dies at 80," *The Dailypulse*, http://aolsvc.news.aol.com/entertainment/article.adp?id=200407021.

5. Sean Smith and David Ansen, "Jamie Foxx—Picture Perfect," *Newsweek*, 31 January 2005, p. 53.

Chapter 44: AIDS! "Where There's a Will There's a Way"

1. Sumana Chatterjee, "House OKs increase spending on AIDS," *The Miami Herald—— Herald Link*, 1 May 2003, http://www.aegis.org/news/mh/2003/MH030501.html.

2. Greg Behrman, *The Invisible People: How the U.S. Has Slept Through the Global AIDS Pandemic, the Greatest Humanitarian Catastrophe of Our Time* (New York: Free Press, 2004) inside front flap.

3. Michka Assayas, *Bono: In Conversation with Michka Assayas* (New York: Riverhead Books, 2005) 265.

4. Jane Wardwell, "Global AIDS Epidemic Hits New Levels," *AOL News*, 25 November 2003, http://aolsvc.news.aol.com/news/article.adp?id=2003112509090999.

5. Assayas, 264.

6. Steve Sternberg, "AIDS Neglected, Report Warns," *USA Today*, 14 May 2003, sec. D, p. 9.

7. Rosemary Althea, *The Eagle and the Rose: A Remarkable True Story* (New York: Warner Books, Inc., 1995) 126.

8. Rick Weiss, "Advances Inject Hope Into Quest for Vaccine," *washingtonpost.com*, 3 September 1997, sec. A, p. 1, http://www.washingtonpost.com/wp-srv/national/longterm/aids/aids4.htm.

9. John Solomon, "Doc Makes Candid Comments on HIV Vaccine," *The Associated Press*, 26 December 2005, http://www.aegis.org/news/ap/2005/AP051240.html.

10. Dr. Seth Berkley, "We're Running Out of Time," *Newsweek International*, 30 January 2006, http://www.msnbc.msn.com/id/10965125/site/newsweek/.

11. Associated Press, "Ray of Hope," *St. Petersburg Times Online*, 2 December 2003, http://www.sptimes.com/2003/12/02/Worldandnation/Ray_of_hope.shtml.

12. Matt Steinglass, "Killing him softly," *The Boston Globe*, 8 December 2002, sec. D, p. 4.

13. World Entertainment News Network, "Sharon Stone Blasts US for Ignoring AIDS Victims," *Starpulse News Blog: Celebrity News*, 26 January 2006, http://www.starpulse.com/news/index.php/2006/01/26/sharone_stone_blasts_us_for_ignoring_aid.

14. Sogyal Rinpoche, *The Tibetan Book of Living and Dying: A New Spiritual Classic from One of the Foremost Interpreters of Tibetan Buddhism to the West* (New York: Harper San Francisco, 1992) 332.

15. "Beyonce and Bono Lead AIDS Show," *BBC News——Entertainment*, 29 November 2003, http://news.bbc.co.uk/2/low/entertainment/3249442.stm.

16. Shannon Baker, "Kay Warren: The Church must be 'seriously disturbed' about HIV/AIDS," *Purpose Driven*, http://www.purposedriven.com/enUS/AboutUs/PDintheNews/Kay_Warren_The_Church_must_be_seriously_disturbed_about_HIV_AIDS.htm.

17. Steve Sternberg, "Evangelist Joins Global Fund chief in battle against AIDS," *USAToday.com*, 16 August 2006, http://www.usatoday.com/news/religion/2006-08-16-warren-aids_x.htm.

Chapter 45: Bill and Melinda Gates: The Couple That "Made Global Health Cool"

1. Amanda Ripley and Amanda Bower, "From Riches to Rags," *Time*, 26 December 2005, 78.

2. "Gates, Bono, unveil 'DATA agenda' for Africa," *CNN.com:Sci-Tech*, 3 February 2003, http://archives.cnn.com/2002/TECH/industry/02/02/gates.bono.africa/index.html.

3. Melinda Gates, "Global Health Conference, 28th Anniversary—Remarks," *Bill and Melinda Gates Foundation—Newsroom*, 31 May 2001, http://www.gatesfoundation.org/MediaCenter/Speeches/MelindaSpeeches/MFGSpeechGatesAward2001-010531.htm.

4. Melinda Gates, "XVI International AIDS Conference Keynote Speech," *Bill and Melinda Gates Foundation—Newsroom*, 13 August 2006, http://www.gatesfoundation.org/MediaCenter/Speeches/MelindaSpeeches/MFGSpeech2006AIDS-060813.htm.

5. "Medicinal Treasures of the Rainforest," *Rainforest Action Network*, http://www.ran.org.

6. Patty Stonesifer, "Statement on Bill Gates' Transition Plan," *Announcements—Bill and Melinda Gates Foundation*, 15 June 2006, http://www.gatesfoundation.org/AboutUs/Announcements/Anounce-060615.htm.

Chapter 46: A Shout-Out from Heaven to Warren Buffett

1. Carol J. Loomis, "A Conversation With Warren Buffett," *Fortune Magazine* 25 June 2006, http://money.cnn.com/2006/06/25/magazines/fortune/charity2.fortune/index.htm.

2. Ibid.

Chapter 47: The World Aid Concerts (a.k.a. "The Big Gig")

1. "Music of my mind," *The Boston Globe*, 29 December 2002.

2. Christopher Phillips, "Vision Quest: A Conversation with Clarence Clemons," *Backstreets: The Boss Magazine*, 76 (Winter/Spring 2003): 25.

3. Ibid., 25.

4. http://www.bobgeldof.info.

5. Ibid.

6. http://www.live8live.com.

7. Brian Hiatt, "Live 8's Global Uprising," *Rolling Stone*, 28 July 2005, 32.

8. "Music of my mind."

9. http://www.live8live.com.

10. Edna Gundersen, "A bid to save the Gulf Coast's music," *USA Today*, 27 March 2006, sec. D, p. 1.

Chapter 48: Bono!

1. CBS/AP, "Bono Seeing 'Red' Over AIDS," *The Early Show*, 26 January 2006, http://www.cbsnews.com/stories/2006/01/26/earlyshow/main1241892_page2.shtml.

2. Madeleine Bunting, "A Day with Bono: 'We Have to Make Africa an Adventure,'" *The Guardian*, 16 June 2005, http://www.atu2.com/news/article.src?ID=3941&Key=&Year=&Cat=14.

3. "What is DATA?" http://www.data.org.

4. Ibid.

5. Ibid.

6. Ibid.

7. Ibid.

8. Josh Tyrangiel, "Bono," *TIME in Partnership with CNN*, 24 February 2002, http://www.time.com/time/magazine/article/0,9171,212636-2,00.html.

9. Ibid.

10. Assayas, 81, 189.

11. "About One: What Is One?," *ONE: The Campaign to Make Poverty History*, http://web1.one.org/about#What%20is%20ONE?.

12. Ibid.

13. James Traub, "The Statesman," *The New York Times Magazine*, 18 September 2005, 82.

14. Ibid., 187.

15. "The ONE Declaration," *ONE: The Campaign to Make Poverty History*, http://action.one.org/ActionSignup.html.

16. Bono, "Bono at TED: Bono's Address as inaugural winner of the TED Prize, February 24, 2005," *TED—Technology Entertainment Design*, 24 February 2005, http://www.ted.com/ted2005/moments/bono_transcript.cfm.
"About TED," *TED—Technology Entertainment Design*, http://www.ted.com/about/introduction/flash_page.cfm.

17. Assayas, 74.

18. Neale Donald Walsch, *Conversations with God: An Uncommon Dialogue* (New York: G.P. Putnam's Sons, 1996) 3. First published 1995 by Hampton Roads Publishing Company, Inc.

19. Deepak Chopra, *The Seven Spiritual Laws of Success* (San Rafael, CA: Amber Allen Publishing and New World Library, 1994) 43.

Chapter 49: Elton John: An Old Soul

1. Philip Norman, *Sir Elton: The Definitive Biography* (New York: Carroll & Graf Publishers, Inc., 2001) 317. First published 1991 as *Elton*.

2. Judy Parkinson, *Elton: Made in England* (London: Michael O'Mara Books, Ltd., 2003) 11.

3. Norman, 427.

4. Elton John, *Elton John AIDS Foundation*, http://www.ejaf.org.

5. Norman, 492.

6. "Elton calls Live 8 'anti-climax'," 4 August 2005, http://news.bbc.co.uk/1/hi/entertainment/tv_and_radio/4745375.stm.

Chapter 50: A Final Few Words to the World's Musicians

1. Edna Gundersen, "Quincy Jones reaches out to help kids: All-star charity concert to be televised worldwide," *USA Today*, 22 March 2004, sec. D, p. 1.

2. Ibid.

3. Ibid.

4. "We Are the Future," *www.TakingITGlobal.org*, http://projects.takingitglobal.org/waf/ about/.

5. Ibid.

6. Ibid.

7. Ibid.

8. Tamela Hultman, "Africa: Rome Concert Launches a Movement, Says Quincy Jones," *allAfrica.com*, 19 May 2004, http://allafrica.com/stories/200405190001.html.

9. Ibid.

10. Ibid.

11. *TakingITGlobal*, http://www.TakingITGlobal.org.

12. *allAfrica.com*, http://www.allAfrica.com/whoweare.html.

13. Mark Victor Hansen, email message to Rob Macomber, September 4, 2006.

14. Tina Turner, *What's Love Got to Do with It?*, © 1993 Virgin Records, CD. Originally written by Lulu, Billy Laurie, and Steve DuBerry.

15. Mike Grayeb, "Behind the Song: '*We Are the World*,'" *Circle!*, Winter 2005, http://www.rememberingharrychapin.com.

16. Ibid.

The Final Chapter...of *This* Book

1. Deepak Chopra, *Peace Is the Way* (New York: Harmony Books, 2005) 22.

2. Esther and Jerry Hicks (The Teachings of Abraham), *Ask and It Is Given: Learning to Manifest Your Desires* (Carlsbad, CA: Hay House, Inc., 2004) 103.

3. Dannion Brinkley with Paul Perry, *Saved by the Light: The True Story of a Man Who Died Twice and the Profound Revelations He Received* (New York: Harper Paperbacks, 1995) 25. First published 1994 in hardcover by Villard Books.

Dedications

1. Stanley Levine, "Stan's Stanzas," *Castine Patriot*, 18 September 2003, 4.

Individual Acknowledgments

1. Herbert Spencer, *Social Skeptics: Or, the Conditions Essential to Human Happiness Specified, and the First of Them Developed*, (London, John Chapman, 1851).

2. Mary T. Brown, *Life After Death*, (New York: Ballantine Books, 1994) 6. s

INDEX

Free Special Mini-Report!

"How the Mafia is Viewed in Heaven"

We would like to express our thanks for your interest in this book and say that if you would like to receive this <u>free special mini-report</u>, just send a blank e-mail to:

<u>mafia@goodagainstevil.com</u>

This special report contains thought-provoking messages from Ruth Montgomery and the Spirit Guides about how the Mafia is viewed in Heaven and will immediately be sent to you via e-mail upon receipt of your blank e-mail message.